P9-CRX-018

Pamela Salzman's

QUICKER THAN QUICK

Pamela Salzman's
QUICKER THAN QUICK

140 CRAVE-WORTHY RECIPES
for HEALTHY COMFORT FOODS
in 30 MINUTES OR LESS

PAMELA SALZMAN

Photography by **Amy Neunsinger**

Go
hachette
BOOKS
NEW YORK

Hachette Go
Hachette Book Group
1290 Avenue of the Americas, New York, NY 10104
www.HachetteGo.com
www.Facebook.com/HachetteGo
www.Instagram.com/HachetteGo

Printed in Korea

First Edition: April 2020

Hachette Books is a division of Hachette Book Group,
Inc. The Hachette Go and Hachette Books name and
logos are trademarks of Hachette Book Group, Inc.

The publisher is not responsible for websites (or their
content) that are not owned by the publisher.

Print book interior design by Toni Tajima.

Library of Congress Cataloging-in-Publication Data
has been applied for.

Library of Congress Control
Number: 2019956186

ISBNs: 978-0-7382-8567-2 (hardcover);
978-0-7382-8566-5 (ebook)

4CG

10 9 8 7 6 5 4 3 2 1

***

In memory of my remarkable

father, Mario Mignone,

who taught me so many things:

to put family first,

to work hard at something I love,

and that without health,

nothing else matters.

***

You don't have to cook fancy or complicated masterpieces—just good food from fresh ingredients.

—JULIA CHILD

Contents

109 Appetizers and Light Bites

137 Vegetable Sides

167 Starchy Sides

191 Instant Pot

211 Mains

287 Desserts

317 Basics

Introduction

A few years ago, I had finished teaching a cooking class with recipes that were a little quicker to prepare than usual. I typically don't teach ultrasimple or fast recipes in my classes since I prefer to demonstrate more complicated recipes that really benefit from live instruction. Two of my students came up to me after class and said, "Pamela, we need more recipes that are quick." I responded, "Like the ones I just taught? Those were pretty quick." To which one of them replied, "Then, we need quicker than quick." I started to hear the same pleas class after class. "Pamela, we love the really quick recipes! Give us more of those!" I took note.

As I wrote in my first book, *Kitchen Matters*, my students help me be a better teacher. They come to my classes from different stages of life, with different priorities, at different skill levels, in different comfort zones. They tell me about their fears, obstacles, weaknesses, and needs. Then, I develop class content accordingly. When I first started teaching, my goal was to help people be the healthiest versions of themselves by starting with food. (I also had children in mind, which is why my first classes were with mothers of school-aged children.) The way I knew I could impact people's health was to teach them how to incorporate whole, unrefined foods in their cooking. The more we cook from scratch with a wide variety of nutrient-dense foods, the less processed food we eat. I started with simple, whole food recipes—and while food trends come and go, ultimately with respect to my approach to cooking, not much has changed since then. My goal continues to be to empower my students—and you—to really feel comfortable in your own kitchen and understand the value of cooking from scratch.

There has been an undeniable grassroots movement to eat more "real" food, buy local, and cook more. More people than ever understand the connection between what we eat and how we feel, and the resulting implications of those choices on both short- and long-term health. So, why isn't everyone, including me, cooking three meals a day, seven days a week? The most common reason I hear is time. Life, especially for people with children at home, whether one works outside the home or not, is really, really busy. In a perfect world, we would write out our meal plans for the week, shop accordingly, do a little meal prep on Sunday, and cook those nutritious meals every day with ease. Some days, that happens, but life does not always proceed according to plan. Some days, the orthodontist visit runs late, or there's more traffic than usual, or the chicken was never defrosted, or a million other reasons. And some days, we just don't have the energy to cook for an hour even if we have the time.

Enter this book. Granted, I cannot teach you how to cook in *no* time. But if you give me thirty minutes, you can make almost everything in *Quicker Than Quick*. It is the book you will reach for when you need to make something quick but nutritious. You will not need to marinate, soak, or cook any of the ingredients in advance. Yes, you have to actually *have* the ingredients, but in the pantry section, we'll go over what you should have on hand at all times so that you can make something wonderful. The goal of this book is not only to solve the problem of lack of time, but to show you faster ways to carry out many tasks as well as to demystify much about cooking. Needless to say, I worked thoughtfully to develop quick recipes that are still healthful and downright delicious. These are recipes my students have learned and loved, and ones I feed my own family.

Just as in my last book, I have provided ways to adapt almost every recipe to be gluten-free, dairy-free, vegetarian, and/or vegan. Not only do I believe that there is no one diet that works for everyone, but I also believe that each individual has different needs as we go through various life phases. I want this book to be one you keep for the ages, not just while you audition a plant-based or Paleo diet.

Furthermore, I want this book to show you ways to adapt recipes based on the season or based on what you have in your pantry. Food waste is a huge global problem with negative implications for the environment. And what is bad for the environment is ultimately bad for us and our health. These recipes are meant to be flexible, for you to adapt to your tastes and what's in your fridge, as well as your budget. If you are on a limited budget, planning meals, learning how to adapt recipes, and having a strategy for stretching leftovers, can make the difference between cooking a wholesome meal from scratch versus ordering more costly and less healthful takeout. And, regardless of budget, we can all benefit from cooking at home more.

Wherever you find yourself, I am grateful for the trust you have put in me and this book, for bringing me into your kitchen and your life, and for paying it forward. Your act of cooking a meal for your family and loved ones not only expresses love and caring, but a way to influence the health and well-being of others. And now you can do it that much more quickly.

GETTING STARTED

Cooking More Quickly and Efficiently

First off, to make the most of this book, read through every section. Some people may not think it's necessary to read through a whole cookbook, especially if there's a recipe they want to try right away! (If that's you, go ahead—but be sure to read through the recipe first!) The reason I suggest you read through the entire book is that in every chapter I've included great tips and tricks that apply not to just the recipes in this book, but cooking in general. They truly will make your time in the kitchen faster—and more enjoyable.

Second—but equally important: If you want to cook more often and more efficiently, one of the most important strategies is setting up your kitchen with a few great tools, and your pantry with the essential building blocks of many recipes. You will have your own go-to items, but these are things I keep close in my kitchen, and ones I recommend to my students.

The Well-Stocked Kitchen

I have taught in hundreds of home kitchens, so I consider myself somewhat of a kitchen expert! I can cook the same recipes sixteen to twenty times in a month and have a different experience every time, based on the environment I am in and tools I am working with. My efficiency, speed, and overall enjoyment is very much tied to not how large or fancy the kitchen is, but how well it is set up and edited. By that I mean, clutter-free countertops, a well-lit workspace, and organized drawers and cabinets with functioning tools. One of my favorite kitchens to teach in happens to be one of the smallest, but it is perfectly organized and has a small drawer with a few very sharp knives, just the right amount of space where I can set up a large cutting board, and a place for everything else. Find another spot for mail, organize like items with like items, and position appliances that you want to use (such as a food processor) in an accessible spot in your kitchen. In *Kitchen Matters*, I provided a more comprehensive list of kitchen equipment and tools. In this book, I am focusing on features of certain products that aid in more efficient cooking, starting with larger appliances and moving to smaller tools.

OVEN. I have come to the conclusion that there is no perfect oven, so get to know yours and its flaws and work around them. For example, some ovens have hot spots in the back or on the bottom, which means that if you are baking more than one sheet pan of cookies, you should rotate the pans at the halfway point of the cooking process. In general, it is best to cook in the center of the oven. If you need to use more than one rack, position the cookware in the upper third and the lower third of the oven.

Most ovens, but not all, have a CONVECTION setting. It uses a fan to circulate heat throughout the oven, which results in a more even heat distribution. The CONVECTION setting can cook food more quickly and can dry excess moisture in the oven better than the traditional heating element. I especially like to use convection for roasting vegetables or for cooking multiple sheet pans or multiple chickens, for example. Since recipes are not tested with the CONVECTION setting, my rule of thumb is to *decrease* the temperature in any recipe by 25°F when using convection. The cook time should still be the same, but it's never wrong to check a few minutes early.

> *Quick tip:* If you need to preheat your oven in a hurry, set it to BROIL. When you are ready to bake or roast, change the setting to the normal BAKE or CONVECTION setting and it will likely be at your desired temperature.

STOVE. I much prefer gas over electric, since gas heat adjusts much faster to changes in the dial. I also really like the stoves with extra-wide burners so I can use multiple large skillets next to each other and keep them perfectly centered over the flame. I have also never met a perfect stove, so I just get to know their quirks and work around them the best I can.

EQUIPMENT

You don't need every gadget on the market to be a good cook or a quick cook. But you do need at the minimum a few basics, and I believe in quality over quantity. I have many staple workhorses in my kitchen that I have had for decades. In general, I favor nontoxic materials, such as Pyrex, glass, ceramic, enameled cast iron, cast iron, stainless steel, and black baker's steel. Try to avoid nonstick coatings and untreated aluminum, both of which when heated leach into your food. If that's what you have, grease your bakeware and then line with unbleached parchment paper before using. To determine the size of the pan, measure from the top as opposed to the bottom. I have provided a cheat sheet of volumes on page 329 so you don't have to compare the volumes and areas of all your cookware each time when you are adjusting the yield of a recipe either up or down.

BAKING PANS (RECOMMENDED NUMBER)

9- or 10-inch **pie plate** (1 or 2)
9- or 10-inch **springform pan** (1)
9-inch **round cake pan** (1 or 2)
Standard 12-well **muffin tin** (1), plus **unbleached parchment liners** or **reusable silicone liners**
8-inch square baking pan (1)
8½ x 4½-inch or 9 x 5-inch **loaf pan** (1)

BAKING DISHES

9 x 13-inch (1 or 2)
7 x 11-inch (1)

BAKING SHEETS. I suggest at least two 13 x 18-inch half sheet pans, and if you also have a smaller oven, two 10 x 13-inch quarter sheet pans. If your oven is wide enough, it is ideal to have at least one 15 x 21-inch three-quarter sheet pan. This larger size can fit more food in one layer,

making it a more efficient way to roast and bake. Check the width of your oven to make sure it will accommodate this size.

BLENDER. A good blender is so useful for making smoothies, nut milk, dressings, and creamy desserts. The stronger your blender, the more creamy and smooth the results will be. If it is in your budget, go for a Vitamix, which is a professional-strength blender that can turn cashews into cream and blitz rock-hard fruit into the smoothest puree. I use mine daily. If you are typically making smoothies for one or two people only, or are blending small quantities, a NutriBullet would be a more cost-effective option. You don't need both a standard blender and a Vitamix, however.

COFFEE GRINDER. I keep a small electric coffee grinder for grinding seeds (e.g., flax), grains, spices, and freeze-dried fruit. It's not an essential tool, but I find it handy. You can also use a Vitamix to grind these items.

COLANDERS AND SIEVES. I use colanders for draining pasta and veggies, but a fine-mesh sieve is what you need for rinsing itty-bitty quinoa or straining stock to be ultraclear.

COOLING RACKS. I can't believe how many kitchens I work in without cooling racks! It may seem optional, but honestly, if you bake, you need a wire rack onto which you transfer cookies, cakes, muffins, and quick breads so that they cool properly. These racks are also handy for drizzling doughnuts!

CUTTING BOARDS. You need at least one large cutting board, preferably with grooves on the edges to catch drippings from cooked meat, and a small one for smaller jobs.

I prefer wood or bamboo; either is naturally antibacterial and won't dull your knives the way plastics do. Wood requires a bit more maintenance, so be sure to dry your boards well before putting them away, and every couple of months, rub a little coconut oil into the surface. I clean mine with a rough sponge, dish soap, and the hottest water possible.

FOOD PROCESSOR. If I had to pick only one appliance to keep in my kitchen, it would be a food processor. I use it constantly for pureeing, chopping, ricing vegetables, making pastry dough and pesto, and more. Sometimes a blender can stand in for a food processor, but more often than not, it can't. In general, I prefer a blender for liquids, such as smoothies, soups, and dressings, and a food processor for everything else.

I recommend at least an 11-cup capacity. My favorite is the 16-cup Breville Sous Chef, which I find powerful and easy to use. I am obsessed with the adjustable slicing disk and the reversible shredding disk. (Check out my YouTube video for how to use a food processor.) No matter which brand you have, you must keep it in prime real estate in your kitchen, or you will never use it! You can buy additional disks from the manufacturer or online.

INSTANT POT. An Instant Pot is one brand of multicooker, an appliance that is a pressure cooker, slow cooker, rice cooker, and yogurt maker all in one. I have the 6-quart unit. Most people use it for its quick pressure-cooking function and these machines are all the rage for that reason. I do think multicookers, including the Instant Pot, have their limitations, but I have included a short chapter of Instant Pot recipes in this book, since the theme is quicker cooking. Read more about the Instant Pot on page 191.

KITCHEN TIMER. I am usually cooking multiple things at once and I am often helping someone with homework or working on the computer at the same time. Therefore, I have a triple timer by OXO to keep me from getting distracted; I find it invaluable.

KITCHEN SCALE. When you need to be accurate, there's no other way than with a kitchen scale. Choose one that can measure in pounds and ounces and can weigh at least up to 5 pounds.

KNIVES. You need decent, not the most expensive, but sharp knives. You only need four knives to complete your kitchen. These include:

A **chef's knife**, either a 6-inch or 8-inch, or both
A **4-inch serrated knife** for slicing tomatoes
A **paring knife** for trimming, poking beets, and coring fruits
A **serrated bread knife**

Please, please, please keep your knives sharp. Prep work will be so much more fun, efficient, and safe with sharp knives. All knives, even if they are expensive, need regular sharpening. You can use a honing steel to sharpen your knives at home, but I would still take them every six months to a professional. Check your area for cutlery stores or ask your local cookware store whether it does sharpening.

Hand wash your knives and dry them right away, to make them last longer.

MEAT THERMOMETER. This is nonnegotiable, since this is the only way to determine whether your poultry or meat is cooked to the perfect temperature. If you aren't sure your thermometer is accurate, put an oven mitt on your hand and dip the tip of the thermometer into a pot of boiling water. If the temperature goes up to 212°F, it's a keeper!

MICROPLANE GRATER/ZESTER. I have a larger grater for ginger, Parmesan cheese, and garlic, plus a finer zester for citrus and nutmeg.

MIXER. A stand mixer keeps me free to do other things while it creams butter or beats egg whites. My favorite is the 5-quart KitchenAid tilt-head stand mixer. Make sure you have the paddle and whisk attachments, and large bowl. You can buy additional accessories that connect to the mixer to make pasta or ice cream or grind meat. A handheld mixer is fine, but not as efficient.

MIXING BOWLS. I like a set of nesting glass bowls, which are easy to keep clean and easy to store. You need at least one large bowl, one medium-size, and one small.

PEPPER MILL. You can elevate your cooking simply by swapping freshly ground pepper for preground. Big flavor boost. Trust me.

POTS AND PANS. I only use stainless steel, enameled cast iron, or cast iron. Avoid untreated aluminum or nonstick containing PTFEs and PFOAs. If you must own a nonstick skillet, look for one with a ceramic coating. They tend to scratch easily, but they are not terribly expensive, so replace them as needed. Here are the basics:

> **Butter warmer** (although a 1-cup stainless-steel measuring cup can be used on the stove to melt small quantities)
>
> **Small: 2-quart saucepan with lid**
>
> **Medium: 3- to 4-quart saucepan with lid**
>
> **Large: 5- to 6-quart pot with lid**
>
> **Extra-large: 10-quart stockpot with lid** if you want to make a huge amount of stock or chili for a crowd
>
> **Stainless-steel or enameled/cast-iron skillets** (8-, 10- and 12-inch)
>
> **Dutch oven** (7-quart) for soups and stews

RULER. If, like me, you are terrible at guessing measurements, whether it is a 2-inch cube of squash or figuring out whether the pan is 8 or 10 inches, a standard 12-inch ruler is an essential piece of equipment. It's also handy for leveling off flour.

TOASTER OVEN. Most people use their toaster ovens for, not surprisingly, toast. For sure, it is a luxury, not a necessity, for a kitchen to be complete. But I do use my toaster oven quite often for toasting nuts and for baking small, flat items, such as a couple of cookies, a frittata, or my salty snack bars. Toaster ovens preheat much more quickly than a wall oven and use less energy, but mine also has a timer so I can pop in a baking dish before I go out for a run, and it will turn off automatically.

UNBLEACHED PARCHMENT PAPER. I line all my baking sheets and loaf pans with unbleached parchment paper, and many of my baking pans, too. (Bleached parchment paper may contain a toxin called dioxin, so I always use unbleached.) It makes clean up easy and protects your food from heavy metals and toxins, but it also enables you to remove breads and cakes in one piece, so you can avoid cutting them inside the pan and scratching the pan. Another option for baking sheets is Silpat reusable silicone baking mats. Silicone is an inert substance that does not leach, so it is safe to use in an oven. I have one mat that I use for baking, but not for foods with strong odors, such as fish, which might transfer to the mat.

WATER FILTRATION SYSTEM. Clean water is a basic necessity. Unfortunately, most municipal water is tainted with chlorine, fluoride, and other undesirable toxins. A water filter for the kitchen sink is a great investment. Or, if you can manage, a filtration system for the whole house is even better.

SMALL TOOLS

Measuring spoons. You need at least one set, preferably in stainless steel. But it's nice to have a second set if you bake a lot. I have one set with elongated, narrow spoons that fit into spice jars.

Dry measuring cups (individually sized ones that you can level off). I prefer stainless steel with the measurement imprinted into the metal, as opposed to a decal that will wear off.

Liquid measuring cups (with a pouring lip). 1-cup, 2-cup, and 4-cup, all made of glass. You can always use your blender jar to measure larger quantities. Be sure to read the increment markings at eye level, not from above, for accuracy.

Vegetable peeler

Can opener

Wine opener

Scalloped tongs (buy ones that are self-locking and are stainless steel on the bottom)

Citrus juicer

Silicone pastry brush (easier to clean than boar's hair and heat resistant)

Stainless-steel ladle

Pot holders (I like fabric-lined silicone ones)

Wooden spoons and wooden turners (a.k.a. wooden spatulas)

Metal spatula

Silicone spatulas

Whisks

NICE TO HAVE, BUT NOT NECESSARY

IMMERSION BLENDER. You can use a blender to puree soups, but a handheld immersion blender is so much more convenient, since you just stick it right in the pot and blend everything right in there. I use the Breville, which has a nonscratch guard on the bottom to protect my stainless-steel pots. It is very easy to clean.

SPLATTER GUARD. Place this on top of your skillet when searing protein in oil. The mesh allows heat to escape, but also prevents oil from splattering all over your stove.

CLEANING UP

Another way to speed up your time in the kitchen is clean up as you cook, so you're not left with a countertop full of dirty dishes before you sit down. Here are a couple of quick tips for cleaning:

○ Use the hottest water possible. It cleans your dishes more quickly, and they'll dry faster, too.

○ Use rubber gloves so that you can use the hottest water possible.

○ To remove burnt-on food fast, immediately sprinkle the pan with baking soda and about an inch of water. Simmer on the stove and scrape with a wooden spatula until all the stuck-on bits come off.

○ To clean cast iron, remove all food scraps first. Sprinkle the pan with a handful of kosher salt and rub surface with a dry rag or sponge. Wipe clean and rub the surface with a thin layer of neutral oil.

○ To clean your blender, add a drop of dish soap to the blender and fill a third of the way with warm water. Blend on medium speed until all nooks and crannies are free of food.

A Quicker Pantry

One of the most important strategies to be able to cook more quickly is having a pantry stocked with certain basic ingredients. Everything in the following list is something I almost always have on hand and these are the ingredients that are used in the recipes to follow. I do have preferred brands of products, ones that I have had success with over and over again and ones that I consider "clean"; that is, as close to their natural state as possible, minimally processed with no added chemicals or preservatives. Of course, I have not tried every single brand of rolled oats or quinoa out there, so feel free to use what you like. Everything listed here can be found at your local health food store, and many items can also be found at Trader Joe's and larger markets, such as superstore-size supermarkets Costco and Walmart, as well as online sources, such as Amazon.com, ThriveMarket.com, and Vitacost.com. Many items, you'll only need to buy two or three times a year.

As I always say to my students, recipes are just road maps and guidelines. If you don't have an ingredient or two, there is likely a perfectly good substitute.

FATS AND OILS

We need high-quality fats in our diet to support our brains, hormones, satiety, and more. I use unrefined, saturated, or monounsaturated fats that are more stable when heated. Refined versions of these fats have gone through a chemical and/or heat process to strip the fat of its healthful natural fatty acids, and oxidize it in the process (which means they have more free radicals, not good for us!). In my opinion, the best oils are unrefined and whole food–based, such as avocado, coconut, and olive.

You may have heard about the smoke point of oils; the smoke point is the temperature at which an oil will start to burn and, yes, smoke!—and diminish some of the healthy benefits. I try not to heat my fats and oils to a temperature that's too high. I am happy to finally see evidence that it is fine to cook with olive oil (which my Italian parents and family have been doing my whole life!). But we still don't want to burn it. Sometimes, I mix oils together if I am trying to raise the smoke point of one (e.g., olive oil) or balance the flavor of another (e.g., sesame oil).

Whenever you have a choice, purchase fats and oils in dark glass jars or bottles. Store all oils, except nut and seed oils, in a cool, dark place, such as the pantry. Nut and seed oils are more perishable and should be refrigerated.

Avocado oil

Butter, unsalted and grass-fed, or good-quality vegan butter

Coconut oil, virgin

Ghee, grass-fed (clarified butter with the milk solids removed, therefore it is lactose-free. It has a stronger, nuttier flavor than butter but is more stable at higher temperatures.) Fourth and Heart brand has a lovely ghee with vanilla and another with garlic added. I also like Countertop Foods' ghee with Ayurvedic spices.

Olive oil, cold-pressed extra-virgin

Sesame oil, toasted

Truffle oil (not necessary, but a nice finish on the vegan mushroom pasta and also great to drizzle on salads or popcorn)

VINEGARS

Vinegar is not just for salad dressing, but a wonderful ingredient that can round out the flavors of many dishes from soups to meats. Raw (apple) cider vinegar contains antibacterial, antioxidant, and digestive benefits that the others do not. Vinegars have different acidity levels, which is why I keep all of these in my pantry. Mirin (technically a rice wine) and balsamic vinegars are a little sweeter, but I have used wine vinegars plus a little honey or maple in their place. If you have a choice, purchase vinegar in glass bottles. I keep all these vinegars at room temperature in the pantry.

Balsamic vinegar
Cider vinegar, raw and unpasteurized
Red wine vinegar
Rice vinegar
Unseasoned rice vinegar
White balsamic vinegar (not aged) *or* Trader Joe's white Modena vinegar
White wine vinegar

SWEETENERS

Most of the time, I use unrefined, minimally processed sweeteners, which I think taste more interesting and are not quite as acid-forming to the body as refined sweeteners. Concentrated sweeteners are still not health foods, no matter how natural they are, and should be consumed sparingly. Sweeteners cannot always be swapped one-to-one with each other. Things to consider are the flavor, color, and whether the sweetener is wet or dry. I find maple syrup and maple sugar

to be the most versatile, although they are pretty expensive.

Unrefined sweeteners: coconut palm sugar, maple sugar, mild raw honey, pure maple syrup
Refined sweeteners: brown sugar, natural cane sugar, powdered sugar (look for one with tapioca starch instead of cornstarch)

FLOURS

You won't find too many recipes in this book that call for refined flour or even a gluten flour, but I keep a couple of small bags of whole-grain flours in the fridge for times that I don't want to make a grain-free dessert or I just need a tiny amount for dredging. The best option for grain flours is to buy them sprouted, which means the hard-to-digest phytic acid has been neutralized resulting in a more nutritious, digestible flour. Any flour that contains fat (whole-grain, nut, coconut) should be stored in a tightly sealed bag in the refrigerator to prevent rancidity. I have always used arrowroot as a thickening agent that is more natural than cornstarch. Now I use it more often in baking as a starch to combine with high-protein flours, such as almond.

Gluten-Containing Flours
Whole wheat pastry flour
Whole spelt flour
All-purpose flour (in small amounts)
Einkorn flour

Gluten-Free Flours
Arrowroot flour/powder
Almond flour, blanched fine
Chickpea (a.k.a. garbanzo) **flour**
Coconut flour
Cornmeal

Cassava flour or tapioca flour
Gluten-free flour blends
Oat flour; check for gluten-free certification label

QUICKER-COOKING WHOLE GRAINS

There's something so satisfying to me about a simple bowl of warm, tender grains; beans; and some sautéed greens. A few whole grains, such as brown rice, do take much more than thirty minutes to cook, so I am focusing here on the ones that are faster but still contain nutrients. The only grain that is a bit controversial is white rice, since it is very starchy and without much fiber or protein. I limit white rice to ½ to 1 cup at a meal and I pair it with high-fiber foods so that it doesn't affect my blood sugar. But there are advantages to white rice over brown such as less arsenic; better digestibility; and, of course, a quicker cook time. In every recipe in this book, you can substitute riced vegetables in place of a grain (see page 142 for ricing vegetables basics).

Gluten-Free Grains

Rice: black/forbidden, sushi, white basmati, or white long-grain
Millet
Quinoa
Puffed cereal (millet, rice, or quinoa)
Old-fashioned rolled oats: look for gluten-free certification label

Gluten-Containing Grains

Farro
Semipearled barley (may be labeled "pearled" but has beige color)
Bulgur

QUICKER-COOKING LEGUMES

If I had to choose grains or legumes, I would choose legumes every time. They have more protein, more fiber, and usually more antioxidants than grains. Although it is not difficult to cook dried beans and lentils from scratch, it's definitely not instant. Jarred or canned cooked beans are a convenience I can get behind and they are staples in my kitchen.

Canned, cooked beans/legumes: black-eyed peas, black beans, chickpeas, French lentils, pinto beans, white beans, such as cannellini or great northern
Dried red lentils (these do cook very quickly)

PASTA/NOODLES

A last-minute pasta dinner is in everyone's back pocket. I always have many different types of whole-grain or legume-based pastas on hand; these newer pastas provide extra nutrition and fiber. There are many wonderful pasta alternatives, too. Any pasta recipe can also use low-carbohydrate options, such as shirataki noodles (made from an indigestible fiber from the konjac root, which is full of prebiotic fiber to feed the good bacteria in the gut); kelp noodles (a clear, mineral-rich noodle made from a sea vegetable); and of course, vegetable-based alternatives, such as spaghetti squash, zucchini noodles, and butternut squash noodles, among others. Any pasta or noodle recipe in this book can use any of the options mentioned here.

Couscous
Pastas (my favorites are einkorn, brown rice, lentil, buckwheat, and quinoa)
Shirataki noodles
Kelp noodles

BREADS/WRAPS

There are so many high-quality bread and flour-based products on the market now. Organic, sprouted bread and tortillas are some of my go-to quick staples that I can turn into a sweet or savory quesadilla, roll-up, pizza crust, or dipper for soup. There's a clean version of these products to suit every diet. That said, if you need to ensure they are gluten-/dairy-free or vegan, read product ingredient labels carefully for undesired trace ingredients. If you want something lighter to use as a wrap or in place of a tortilla, consider sheets of toasted nori, lettuce, or cabbage leaves.

Tortillas (grain-free, brown rice, or sprouted, including sprouted corn)
Whole-grain bread
Lavash
Dried whole-grain bread crumbs or **panko bread crumbs**
Whole wheat naan bread
8-inch rice paper rounds
Nori sheets

BAKING ESSENTIALS

I have great memories of my friends and me in the kitchen when we were young, poring over cookbooks and magazines in search of a delicious cake or cookie recipe to whip up and devour. When the craving strikes, it's helpful to have the basics on the shelves.

Baking soda
Baking powder, aluminum-free non-GMO
Pure vanilla extract (check to make sure there's no added sugar or corn syrup)
Pure almond extract
Unsweetened cocoa powder for baking and raw cacao powder for raw desserts and smoothies

Dark chocolate bars, vegan if necessary
Chocolate chips, semisweet or dark, mini and regular size, vegan if necessary
Unsweetened coconut flakes
Unsweetened shredded coconut

Salt

It is no secret that I love salt and that I use it in almost every recipe. I highly recommend ditching table salt and all its additives for a high-mineral sea salt with a clean, pure flavor. Good salt can enhance the flavor of your cooking and baking and can increase the digestibility of your food. I use fine-grain sea salt for almost everything. I use flaky sea salt for finishing some vegetables, salads, and desserts. And I use an additive-free kosher salt for things that I will end up throwing away, such as pasta water and marinades. No sense wasting money on sea salt in those cases.

Fine-grain sea salt
Flaky sea salt
Kosher salt

NUTS AND SEEDS

I have a plethora of nuts and seeds on hand to add protein, good fat, crunch, and texture to so many dishes. Plus, they make a great whole food snack. Do seek out the freshest source for nuts and seeds, since their oils can make them spoil quickly. I buy all my nuts and seeds organic and store them in glass jars. Some, such as walnuts and hazelnuts, can go rancid quickly, so I store them in the freezer. If a recipe calls for nuts or seeds as an optional element, such as in a salad, feel free to omit them.

Flaxseeds (I prefer these ground fresh at home and not purchased already ground. Once the seed is opened, the oils are susceptible to rancidity from exposure to air.)

Hemp seeds, a.k.a. hemp hearts

Chia seeds

Black or tan sesame seeds

Gomasio (a Japanese condiment made with sesame seeds)

Roasted skinned hazelnuts (so much faster than roasting and skinning at home!)

Walnuts

Pine nuts

Cashews, raw and roasted

Almonds, whole raw and sliced

Pecans

Peanuts, roasted and salted

Pistachios, shelled

NUT AND SEED BUTTERS

I love nut and seed butters and use them in so many different preparations other than on toast. They are added to smoothies and dressings, spread on tortillas and pancakes, stirred into baked goods, and more. I purchase all nut and seed butters in glass, since the oils can cause plastics to leach. I store opened nut butters in the refrigerator.

Peanut butter, unsweetened crunchy or creamy

Almond butter, unsweetened crunchy or creamy

Tahini (sesame paste)

Sunflower seed butter

Raw cashew butter

SPICES/SEASONINGS

Spices infuse lots of flavor into food very quickly. Although I am listing the individual spices I use in these recipes, there's nothing wrong with buying premade spice blends. Just read the ingredient lists and make sure there are no preservatives or chemical additives. As with many food items, I prefer organic spices in glass jars. I like to toss spices once they have been around for one year.

Allspice, ground

Basil, dried

Bay leaves, dried

Black peppercorns, whole

Cayenne

Ceylon cinnamon, ground

Chipotle powder

Chives, dried

Coriander, ground

Cumin, ground

Curry powder

Dill, dried

Everything but the Bagel Seasoning

Garam masala

Ginger, ground

Granulated garlic (I prefer this over powder.)

Herbes de Provence

Kitchari spices (a turmeric-based Indian spice mix; or use curry powder or make your own)

Marjoram, dried

Mint, dried

Mustard seeds

Nutritional yeast

Nutmeg, ground

Onion, granulated

Oregano, dried

Paprika

Parsley, dried

Red pepper flakes, crushed

Smoked paprika

Turmeric, ground

Thyme, dried

CONDIMENTS AND OTHER BASIC INGREDIENTS

Unsulfured dried fruits: currants, green raisins, Medjool dates, dark raisins

Plantain chips

Freeze-dried fruits (raspberries, bananas, strawberries), see photo on page 2

Granola

Whole garlic

Garlic chili paste

Yellow curry paste or Thai green curry paste, such as Mae Ploy

Chicken, veggie, and mushroom stock

Dried mushrooms

White wine, dry

Harissa

Yellow and red onions

Limoncello (optional for Meyer Lemon–Olive Oil Cake, page 299)

Apple cider or apple juice, unsweetened

Soy-free Vegenaise or Primal Kitchen mayonnaise

Pomegranate molasses

Wakame/sea vegetables

SUPERFOODS

Superfoods are nutrient-dense foods, plants, and herbs that can be effective as supplements to an already good diet. They are usually available to us in their most natural state.

Adaptogens are Chinese herbs that are nontoxic to the body and combat stress. They are used to improve the health and quality

functioning of your adrenal system, the system that is in charge of your body's reactions to stress. For more on adaptogens, see page 27.

Collagen peptides

Barley grass juice powder

Maqui

Pitaya powder

Bee pollen

Raw cacao nibs

Raw cacao powder

Maca

Ashwagandha

SAUCES

Marinara sauce (see following note about glass jars)

Tomato paste (see following note about glass jars)

Hot sauce (I like sriracha)

Asian fish sauce (neither vegan nor vegetarian)

Salsa

CANNED GOODS

Crushed tomatoes, preferably in glass jars. Tomatoes are very acidic and cause materials, such as BPA and aluminum, to leach into the tomato product.

Roasted tomatoes, jarred

Full-fat coconut milk, typically sold in cans (not refrigerated coconut milk beverage)

Sun-dried tomatoes, packed in oil

Wild tuna, preferably in glass jars

Capers, jarred

Unsweetened applesauce

No-sugar-added preserves, such as peach or apricot, and fig

Pitted olives

Pimiento-stuffed olives

REFRIGERATOR

Organic pastured eggs

Miso paste (lighter misos are milder in flavor)

Firm or extra-firm tofu, preferably organic and sprouted

Pesto

Shoyu, gluten-free tamari, or coconut aminos

Worcestershire sauce, vegan if necessary

Whole-grain and **Dijon mustard**

Dairy/nondairy milk

Cheese

Pastured poultry

Grass-fed beef

FREEZER

Artichoke hearts

Cauliflower rice

Corn, plain and fire-roasted

Shelled edamame

Fruit (berries, cherries, peaches)

Peas

Stock (chicken, vegetable, fish)

Wild fish and **seafood**

A PRIMER ON ANIMAL PRODUCTS

Animal products can be a part of a healthful diet. But most animal foods, especially when eaten in large quantities, create inflammation in the body, which is the basis for most chronic disease. So, if we choose to eat animal foods, my opinion is that we should limit our animal products to a few ounces at a time, a few times per week.

Meat, poultry, and seafood are high in protein; contain vitamin B_{12}, which is hard to get from plant-based sources; and are nonglycemic, which is good. But not all animal products are high quality or are equally as nutritious. With all the labels and confusing marketing terms, it's no wonder consumers have a hard time making the best choice for their health. Here's what you need to know:

"Natural"

The word *natural* really means very little with respect to ethics, health, organics, or sustainability. It is one of the most overused, empty labels in food. "Natural" only implies that the product has been minimally processed with no artificial ingredients.

"Organic"

The "organic" label is associated only with the food the animal ate and the lack of hormones, drugs, genetically modified feed, animal by-products, and antibiotics. The animals could have eaten grains, but those grains were certified organic. "Organic" does not mean the animals were treated ethically or have been allowed to roam freely, however. I still recommend buying organic poultry and meats over nonorganic as much as possible.

Poultry

According to the USDA, *free-range* means the poultry has had access to the outdoors. Unfortunately, what this translates to is that the birds, for a very limited time each day, are permitted to exit the barn through a small opening and graze outside if they choose to. The USDA considers five minutes of open-air access each day to be adequate for it to approve the use of the free-range claim. Regardless, the reality is that the birds are so used to being in the barn, they rarely leave.

Pastured, on the other hand, implies animals (namely, chickens and pigs) have been raised in open fields and woods, foraging for food (primarily seeds and insects, with the occasional small rodent or reptile, if they can get them), and going back into a henhouse (in the case of chickens) at night to roost, nest, and lay eggs.

Beef

Cows are biologically designed to graze on grass, not grains. Meat from cows that have been raised exclusively on grass contains more omega-3 fats, less saturated fat, and a health-supportive fatty acid called conjugated linoleic acid (CLA) than is meat from grain-fed cows. It's like comparing a health-food-eating, fit person to a fast-food-eating couch potato. Which meat would you rather eat?

Grass-fed is technically supposed to mean that the cows have had a partial grass diet and access to pasture year-round. There is no third-party verification of this, however, and it is possible the cows are fed grains before they go to slaughter. You want to look for a label of "100% grass-fed" or "grass-finished."

Furthermore, another downside is that meat consumption has a serious negative impact on the environment—more than planes, trains, and automobiles combined.

Fish and Seafood

I personally favor fish and seafood over meat and poultry, but I am concerned about sustainability, mercury, nuclear radiation from Japan, industrial chemicals, and pesticides in our waters. So, I limit my fish consumption to a few ounces two or three times each week and I only buy wild-caught fish that have lived in an environment that is natural to the fish and that have eaten plankton, algae, and other small fish. Wild fish have higher concentrations of anti-inflammatory omega-3 fats, which are critical for brain and heart health.

Since it is impossible to generalize about the practices in the farmed fish industry, I look to seafoodwatch.org, published by the Monterey Bay Aquarium, as my go-to source for helping me make choices that lower my risk and maximize the potential health benefits of eating fish.

Dairy

Human beings weren't designed to regularly digest milk. And it is certainly not essential for good health. If you find that you cannot tolerate dairy, you should most definitely not eat it. If you can tolerate dairy, I recommend enjoying it in small quantities with these tips in mind for better digestibility and nutrition:

Try sheep or goat dairy over cow, since its fat composition is closer to humans' than cows' and it is easier to digest. I tend to use more grated pecorino (sheep's milk) over Parmesan (cow's milk.)

Choose cultured dairy, such as yogurt or kefir, which contain health-supportive good bacteria for gut health.

I recommend consuming raw dairy over pasteurized. Raw also contains beneficial bacteria and is more digestible. There is much discussion about raw dairy and its safety; I understand that some people may not be comfortable with or have access to raw dairy, so if you do choose pasteurized, please buy organic and preferably nonhomogenized.

Opt for full-fat instead of low-fat or nonfat. Studies have shown that people who eat full-fat dairy are more satisfied, snack less, and weigh less than people who eat low-fat dairy. Also, without the presence of fat, our body cannot absorb the important fat-soluble vitamins A, D, E, and K.

Easy Swaps and Substitutions

I have been asked for a substitution for every single ingredient I have ever used, from the most common allergens, including gluten, dairy, soy, nuts, and eggs, to seemingly innocuous foods, such as olive oil and peaches. I am very conscientious that there are many people who need to know basic substitutions due to intolerances, but it's good to know these swaps in the event you are out of something.

BUTTER. Butter does add a unique flavor to recipes and helps promote browning. But if you are dairy-free, you can substitute Miyoko's Cultured Organic Vegan Butter, unrefined virgin coconut oil, or organic Earth Balance vegan butter in any recipe. Keep in mind that coconut oil may impart a slight coconut flavor to the recipe. Miyoko's and Earth Balance vegan butters contain some salt, so you may consider reducing the salt in the recipe slightly.

BUTTERMILK.

1 cup of buttermilk

Swap: ½ cup plain, unsweetened whole yogurt (dairy or nondairy) + ½ cup milk (dairy or nondairy)

or 1 cup plain, unsweetened kefir (not dairy-free)

or place 1 tablespoon cider vinegar in a 1-cup measuring cup and add dairy or nondairy milk to make 1 cup

CRUSHED RED PEPPER FLAKES, CAYENNE, CHIPOTLE POWDER, HOT SAUCE, SRIRACHA, OR FRESH CHILES. If you cannot tolerate any heat or spiciness, just omit any of the above, or reduce the amount. They are not equal in terms of heat level, so you cannot substitute them one-for-one for one another. I prefer my food spicier than my family does, so I usually add a little sriracha or hot sauce to my dish.

Chipotle powder is derived from the chipotle pepper, which is a ripened, smoked, and dried jalapeño pepper. You can swap in smoked paprika (no heat at all) for all or some of the chipotle powder.

EGG. Eggs that are used as a binder in baked goods or to add leavening can be replaced with these substitutes:

1 egg

Swap: 1 flax egg or 1 chia egg: In a small bowl, combine 1 tablespoon of flax meal or ground chia seeds with 3 tablespoons of water and stir. Let the mixture sit, stirring it occasionally, for about 10 minutes, or until the mixture has the consistency of a raw egg white.

or: aquafaba (a.k.a. liquid from canned, cooked chickpeas—the thicker, the better, and it has to be from a can, not homemade). Use 3 tablespoons of aquafaba for each whole egg, 2 tablespoons for each egg white, and 1 tablespoon for each egg yolk. You'll get the best results if you beat the aquafaba with ¼ teaspoon of cream of tartar to stabilize it. It will take 8 to 9 minutes to achieve what will resemble meringue.

Actual egg

In the case of actual egg in a frittata or a scramble, there are substitutes for that, too:

For 2 eggs, substitute 7 ounces of extra-firm tofu, preferably organic and sprouted + 1 tablespoon of nutritional yeast + ¼ teaspoon of ground turmeric.

For 1 egg in custard or cheesecake, swap in ¼ cup of pureed silken tofu.

FLOUR.

1 cup gluten-containing flour, such as wheat

To make a recipe gluten-free, I recommend substituting 1 cup of Jovial Foods Multigrain Gluten-Free Pastry Flour for the original flour. I also recommend adding xanthan gum. Xanthan gum mimics the elasticity of gluten and will help provide structure to your batter. Refer to the xanthan gum package instructions for how much to add per cup of flour, because it varies according to what you are making. You do not need to add xanthan gum to gluten-free pancake or waffle batter, or if the flour is being used to thicken a pie or for dredging meat.

If you are wheat-intolerant but not gluten-free, you may be able to substitute spelt flour, which is a subspecies of wheat, one-for-one for wheat flour. The only exception is pancake batter, which can take about ⅞ cup of spelt flour for 1 cup of wheat flour.

If a recipe calls for oat flour, you may use a certified gluten-free oat flour.

You cannot substitute a nut flour or coconut flour for a grain flour, or vice versa.

HONEY. Honey is neither vegan nor should it be given to babies under the age of twelve months because it can cause a rare type of botulism (food poisoning). Maple syrup may be substituted in equal amounts in any recipe in this book.

MILK. Unsweetened and unflavored nut, seed, or oat milks can be substituted for dairy milk in any recipe in this book. You may also substitute ½ part canned coconut milk + ½ part nut milk for dairy milk. See specific substitution suggestions for buttermilk (page 16).

NUTS. If you have a nut allergy and a recipe calls for nuts, you have a couple of options. If the nuts are being used for crunch, you can either omit the nut altogether or substitute seeds, such as pumpkin or sesame seeds, or roasted chickpeas. For pesto recipes, replace nuts one-for-one with seeds, such as hemp or sunflower.

If a recipe calls for nut milk, substitute unsweetened hemp milk, oat milk, or flax milk.

If you are allergic to a specific nut, feel free to substitute another nut in its place.

Almond extract may be omitted in any recipe.

SHOYU/SOY SAUCE. Gluten-free tamari can be substituted one-for-one for shoyu if you are trying to avoid wheat or gluten. If you are trying to avoid soy, you can substitute coconut aminos one-for-one.

THE RECIPES

Here are some of my "best practices" tips for these recipes:

- It's good practice to follow a new recipe exactly the first time you make it, unless you feel very comfortable making substitutions that you have made with success before. You can always tweak the recipe to suit your taste the next time you make it.

- I know there are ingredients that are not tolerated by many people; therefore, I have tested out substitutions for almost all the recipes containing gluten grains and animal products, including dairy and eggs. If a suggestion is not offered within the specific recipe, you can check the Substitutions (pages 16-17) and try to make a substitution based on my go-to swaps. Obviously, it would be an impossible task and a very cluttered book to offer suggestions for a substitute for every

RECIPE CODES

Vg **Vegan:** Contains no products derived from an animal, including honey or bee pollen.

Ve **Vegetarian:** Contains no meat, poultry, game, fish, or shellfish; may contain animal-derived dairy or eggs.

GF **GF (gluten-free):** Contains no wheat, spelt, rye, barley, Kamut, or farro. If oats or other grains that may be contaminated with gluten are required, those ingredients will be clearly noted.

DF **DF (dairy-free):** Contains no products derived from the milk of an animal (all recipes coded Vegan are by definition dairy-free).

Vg-a **Vegan-adaptable:** Ingredients may be substituted or omitted to create a vegan recipe (see "make it vegan" tips).

Ve-a **Vegetarian-adaptable:** Ingredients may be replaced or omitted to create a vegetarian recipe (see "make it vegan" tips; may contain dairy or eggs).

GF-a **GF-adaptable:** Ingredients may be replaced or omitted to create a recipe free from gluten (see "make it gluten-free" tips).

DF-a **DF-adaptable:** Ingredients may be replaced or omitted to create a recipe free from dairy (see "make it vegan" tips; no need to avoid animal protein/eggs).

single ingredient. Feel free to connect with me to ask me for advice if one is not listed in a particular recipe. I will most likely have a recommendation.

- You might be surprised in a book about cooking more quickly that I did not provide prep and cook times for each recipe. I think those times can be very misleading. When I had my recipe testers cooking these recipes, a wide range of times was reported. Those with limited cooking experience predictably took longer to prep a recipe than those who had been cooking for years. For the average cook, almost all of these recipes should take less than thirty minutes from start to finish.

15 QUICKER THAN QUICK COOKING TIPS

1. Have a well-stocked pantry (see page 8).

2. Become friends with your food processor and learn how to use it (see page 5).

3. Organize your pantry, refrigerator, and freezer by category, so that it is easier to find ingredients. For example, baking items are stored together, canned goods are stored together, etc.

4. Use your toaster oven for baking or roasting smaller items, such as a 9-inch cake or a few vegetables, since it will preheat more quickly.

5. Take some time once a week to do a little prep for daily cooking: e.g., peel garlic cloves, wash salad greens, wash fresh herbs.

6. Preheat the oven in a hurry: set the oven to BROIL while you prep, and then change it over to BAKE or CONVECTION.

7. Keep a pot covered when trying to bring water or contents to a boil.

8. Chop or cut ingredients into small and uniform sizes—the smaller the ingredients, the quicker they'll cook.

9. Choose stovetop over oven when you can; stovetop requires more hands-on time, but still is quicker than the oven.

10. Buy and use a large, shallow stovetop pan/pot over a narrow, tall one. The wider the surface area, the more ingredients come into contact with the heat, and the faster the ingredients cook.

11. Take a minute to come up with a weekly plan and write it down.

12. Have someone (e.g., partner, spouse, children) help you.

13. Practice your knife skills—and make sure to get your knives sharpened regularly.

14. Cook once and eat twice—later in the week or freeze for another time.

15. Love your leftovers.

Breakfast

Your first meal can set the tone for the day. It is a prime opportunity to fuel your brain and provide the nutrients your body needs to perform at its best. Unfortunately, most of us are pressed for time in the morning and rely on what is already ready-to-eat: packaged cereals, sugary bars, white bread, or worse—nothing at all. There are plenty of healthful make-ahead breakfasts that you can prepare the night before. But the following recipes are ones you can turn to any day when time is tight or even when it's not, since they are all well balanced, delicious, and don't feel like an "instant" breakfast. But just as with any other meal, the morning will go more smoothly if you plan your breakfast the night before.

I will also make a plug for foods that aren't traditional breakfast foods. Don't overlook last night's leftover lentil soup, any version of not-fried rice (page 190) or quinoa with an egg or some almonds, or some leftover chicken with vegetables. As long as your plate contains a balance of good-quality protein, fats, and complex (slow-burning) carbohydrates, you have what you need to jump start your day with long-lasting energy and stable blood sugar.

LOW-FRUCTOSE SMOOTHIES

GF DF Vg-*a* Ve-*a*

Smoothies are easy, and once you get the hang of the proportions, you don't really need to follow a recipe. You also don't need to dump cup after cup of fruit into your blender and follow it with fruit juice. What you'll end up with is a sugar bomb.

To make your smoothie lower in fructose, try lower-glycemic fruits, such as berries; use just enough fruit for sweetness; replace some of the fruit with protein and good fats; or try no fruit at all. These smoothie recipes are designed to be lower in carbohydrates and higher in good fats, making them a great meal unto themselves. (If your kids need more sweetness and they aren't bothered by a little extra fructose, try adding a pitted date or half of a frozen banana to the blender. My son blends his smoothies all the way and then pulses in a handful of granola for extra sweetness and texture.)

Blueberry Delight

SERVES 1

1 cup unsweetened nondairy milk of choice (I use almond milk or flax milk)

½ cup frozen blueberries (see whether you can find wild—the antioxidant capacity is off the charts!)

¼ cup frozen cauliflower (florets or rice)

1 tablespoon nut or seed butter (I like almond butter or raw cashew butter)

1 tablespoon coconut butter (or just use more nut butter)

1 scoop collagen peptides, or 2 tablespoons hemp seeds

¼ teaspoon pure vanilla extract

SWEETENER OF CHOICE: 2 drops stevia, or 1 teaspoon monk fruit or raw honey

↓

tips

———

Feeling adventurous? Blend in a couple of small fresh basil leaves for an herbal, grassy flavor.

MAKE IT VEGAN

Use hemp seeds instead of collagen.

Combine all the ingredients in a blender and blend until smooth. Taste for sweetness.

Mint Cacao Chip

SERVES 1

1 cup nondairy milk of choice (I like ½ cup almond milk + ½ cup canned coconut milk)

1½ tablespoons raw cacao powder

¼ pitted and peeled avocado

Handful of fresh spinach (don't worry if you don't have it; you can also use mild greens, such as Swiss chard or romaine lettuce)

1 scoop collagen peptides, or 2 tablespoons hemp seeds

1 tablespoon nut or seed butter (I like almond or raw cashew)

1 tablespoon coconut butter or coconut oil (or more nut butter)

⅛ teaspoon peppermint extract

¼ teaspoon pure vanilla extract

6 ice cubes

SWEETENER TO TASTE: a couple of drops of stevia or 2 teaspoons monk fruit or honey

1 tablespoon raw cacao nibs

Combine all the ingredients, except the cacao nibs, in a blender and blend until smooth. Taste for sweetness. Add the cacao nibs and blend for a couple of seconds to break them up a little.

↓

tips

EVEN QUICKER

Make smoothie packs in advance by placing all the nonliquid ingredients in a resealable plastic bag or freezer-safe glass container and storing them in the freezer. When you want to make a smoothie, empty the packet into the blender with the liquid and blend!

MAKE IT VEGAN

Use hemp seeds instead of collagen.

ASK PAMELA

What is your favorite protein powder?

People ask me this all the time and my response is, "None!" I don't use protein powders because they usually rely on isolated proteins, which have been highly processed and denatured, making them hard for the body to recognize and assimilate. Furthermore, they often contain preservatives, synthetic flavors, sweeteners, heavy metals (yes, heavy metals—check out the *Consumer Reports* study from July 2010 titled "Health Risks of Protein Drinks"). I prefer to add natural protein: a scoop of collagen, a few tablespoons of hemp seeds, or a big spoonful of nut butter.

SUPERFOOD MORNING TONICS

Ve **GF-a** **Vg-a** **DF-a** | SERVES 1

My body and digestion are happier when I start the morning with warmth. When I wake up, I begin the day with warm water either plain or with fresh lemon juice. Then, with my breakfast or later in the morning, I make myself a warm superfood tonic that contains healthful boosts called adaptogens (see box on page 27 for information on specific adaptogens and their powers and flavors). Many of these powders can also be added to smoothies or porridges as well. I've listed a few of my favorites, but I often change it up according to how I'm feeling, what my body needs, or what I crave. I usually leave any powders that are too calming for the evening, lest I feel I have no energy to teach my classes! I don't use protein powders, but you could also take your favorite protein powder as a base and create a warm tonic from that.

Cacao Superfood Tonic

1 cup water or unsweetened nondairy milk

1½ tablespoons cacao powder (if you're sensitive to cacao, use carob powder)

▶ *Optional Add-Ins*

ADAPTOGENS: ½ teaspoon maca, lucuma, or ashwagandha

FLAVORS: pinch of ground cinnamon, or ⅛ teaspoon peppermint extract

Chai Superfood Tonic

1 cup water or unsweetened nondairy milk

1½ tablespoons chai spice

▶ *Optional Add-Ins*

ADAPTOGENS: ½ teaspoon ground turmeric, plus a pinch of freshly ground black pepper or maca

FLAVORS: pinch of ground cinnamon, pinch of ginger, a few drops of pure vanilla extract

Matcha Superfood Tonic

1 cup water or unsweetened nondairy milk

1½ tablespoons matcha powder

▶ *Optional Add-Ins*

ADAPTOGENS: ½ teaspoon ground turmeric, plus a pinch of freshly ground black pepper, maca, or ashwagandha

FLAVORS: ½ teaspoon barley grass juice powder, a few drops of pure vanilla extract

recipe continues →

↓

tips

You can also put everything into a frother to heat and dissolve all the powders. A frother creates a nice foamy texture, too. Just be mindful of the maximum amount of liquid recommended, plus some frothers will only work with room-temperature or cold ingredients to start.

MAKE IT GLUTEN-FREE

Omit barley grass juice powder.

MAKE IT VEGAN

Do not use collagen.

OPTIONAL BOOSTS THAT GO WITH
   ANYTHING: 1 scoop collagen
   peptides, coconut milk powder,
   frothed nondairy milk

To make any tonic: Heat the water or nondairy milk in a small saucepan over medium heat until hot, but not boiling. Pour into a glass blender and add the other ingredients, including your choice of add-ins.

Blend until the powders are dissolved and the liquid is foamy, about 30 seconds.

Pour into a cup and top with frothed nondairy or dairy milk, if desired.

WHAT ARE ADAPTOGENS?

Adaptogens are Chinese herbs that are nontoxic to the body and combat stress. They are used to improve the health and quality functioning of your adrenal system, the system that is in charge of your body's reactions to stress. Here are a few of my favotites:

Reishi is a mushroom that has a bitter, earthy flavor. It is known to strengthen the immune system, support improved memory and concentration, and ease anxiety. Reishi is also being used to help counteract the negative effects of chemotherapy.

Maca has an earthier taste that is mildly nutty with a hint of butterscotch. It's a good source of calcium, vitamin C, amino acids, phytonutrients, and healthy fatty acids.

Lucuma has a flavor profile resembling maple, caramel, or pumpkin. With lots of beta-carotene, it's good for the skin and eyes, and antiaging. It also has iron, zinc, vitamin B_3, and calcium.

Ashwagandha's scent and flavor are often described as "earthy." While it may not be the most attractively smelling adaptogen, its benefits include reducing anxiety and depression, stabilizing blood sugar, and improving learning, memory, and reaction time.

ZUCCHINI BREAD PORRIDGE

Ve **GF-*a*** **Vg-*a*** **DF-*a*** | SERVES 1

You could say I'm obsessed with riced vegetables. I've added them seamlessly to smoothies, soups, grains (page 142), and even as a quick stir-fry (page 141). They cook quickly, add extra nutrition and phytonutrients, and take seconds to prep if you have a food processor (see page 142 on ricing vegetables). But oatmeal? Have I gone too far? I started adding a ¼ cup of cauliflower to my oats a few years ago and never looked back. Believe me when I tell you, you don't taste them in small amounts and it just adds bulk and fiber without adding too many extra calories. Try frozen or fresh riced cauliflower if you're unsure, and then try this version with riced zucchini. I added all the yumminess that goes into zucchini bread for an extra-nutritious twist on oatmeal.

1 small or ½ medium-size zucchini, unpeeled

1 cup water (if you use hot water from an Instant Hot faucet, just add everything at the same time)

¼ cup unsweetened milk of choice, plus more to taste

½ cup old-fashioned rolled oats (you can also use a combo of grains, such as rolled oats, millet, and quinoa, and cook covered for 30 minutes)

1 tablespoon unsulfured raisins

1 tablespoon chopped walnuts or pecans (optional)

½ teaspoon ground cinnamon

Pinch of ground nutmeg

Pinch of sea salt

2 teaspoons pure maple syrup or honey, or to taste

Rice the zucchini: Trim the ends and cut the zucchini into very large chunks. Place in a food processor fitted with the metal S blade and pulse until the zucchini resembles rice.

In a small saucepan, bring the water to a boil. Stir in the remaining ingredients, including the riced zucchini, and cook over medium-low heat until the oats are tender, about 10 minutes.

Add additional milk to achieve your desired consistency. Taste for sweetness and serve.

↓

tips

Instead of maple syrup, add ½ ripe banana with the rest of the ingredients and cook together.

Swap in riced cauliflower or carrots for the zucchini, for a different version.

If you want to add some superfoods, try flax meal, hemp seeds, lucuma powder, or healthy fats, such as coconut butter. Add these at the end, after you've cooked the oats and have added any additional milk.

MAKE IT GLUTEN-FREE

Use certified gluten-free oats.

MAKE IT VEGAN

Use nondairy milk, such as almond or oat milk; maple syrup.

STRAWBERRY MINT TABBOULEH

Vg Ve GF | SERVES 4

Tabbouleh is a parsley salad with bulgur, cucumber, tomato, and mint mixed in. It's super refreshing and healthful, and I love eating it in the summer for a cooling breakfast. I gave tabbouleh a major twist by swapping in strawberries for the vegetables and using quinoa in place of bulgur. The result is a surprising explosion of flavors and textures that makes for a light yet filling breakfast, packed with protein and antioxidants.

3 cups cooked quinoa (see tips)

2 tablespoons unrefined cold-pressed extra-virgin olive oil

2 tablespoons freshly squeezed lemon juice

½ teaspoon sea salt

⅛ teaspoon freshly ground black pepper

¼ cup small fresh mint leaves

¼ cup chopped fresh parsley

1 cup hulled and chopped fresh strawberries

¼ cup toasted sliced almonds or chopped pistachios

Place the quinoa in a medium-size bowl. Mix in the olive oil, lemon juice, salt, and pepper.

When ready to serve, mix in the mint, parsley, and strawberries. Top with the almonds.

↓

tips

So many fruits go well in this recipe! Try any berry, stone fruit, kiwi, pineapple, mango, figs, or grapes.

If you are not using leftover quinoa for this recipe, try this: cook 1 cup of quinoa with ¾ cup of apple juice and 1 cup of water to give it a sweeter flavor. Bring to a boil, lower the heat to a simmer, and cook, covered, for 15 minutes, or until all the liquid is absorbed.

GRAIN-FREE PEANUT BUTTER–BANANA BREAKFAST COOKIES

| Ve | GF | Vg-*a* | DF-*a* | | MAKES 10 COOKIES |

These cookies are healthful enough to be eaten at breakfast, but sweet enough to be enjoyed as a treat. They're an ideal way to start the day, since they're loaded with protein, fiber, and healthy fats. You can make a batch at the beginning of the week, keep them refrigerated, and enjoy them all week long. These are also flavor-adaptable: you can split the base batter and add different things to each batch, such as chocolate chips and freeze-dried bananas in one batch and dried blueberries and crystallized ginger in another. You'll keep things interesting without creating a lot of extra work.

1¾ cups blanched almond flour (not almond meal)

2 tablespoons coconut flour

½ teaspoon baking soda

½ teaspoon sea salt

½ teaspoon ground cinnamon

¼ cup unsweetened shredded coconut or coconut flakes

¼ cup unrefined virgin coconut oil, unsalted butter, or ghee, at room temperature

¾ cup unsweetened peanut butter, creamy or crunchy (any nut butter or tahini can be used)

2 large eggs, flax eggs (see page 16), or 6 tablespoons whipped aquafaba (see page 16)

1 medium-size ripe banana, mashed

¼ cup pure maple syrup or honey

1 teaspoon pure vanilla extract

6 tablespoons chopped unsweetened freeze-dried banana (not essential, just for fun)

¼ cup unsulfured raisins

¼ cup raw cacao nibs or mini chocolate chips

tips

If you swap in sunflower butter, know that the chlorogenic acid in sunflower butter and baking soda cause a reaction that will turn your baked goods green. This is not toxic, but the color may not be what you are expecting. One way around it is to swap in a little unsweetened cocoa or cacao powder for some of the flour to mask the green color. In this recipe, you could use 2 tablespoons of cocoa powder and remove 2 tablespoons of almond flour.

MAKE IT VEGAN

Use coconut oil; flax eggs, or whipped aquafaba; maple syrup; cacao nibs or vegan chocolate chips.

Preheat the oven to 325°F. Line a large baking sheet with unbleached parchment paper or a silicone mat.

recipe continues →

In the bowl of a stand mixer, combine the almond flour, coconut flour, baking soda, salt, cinnamon, coconut, coconut oil, peanut butter, eggs, mashed banana, maple syrup, and vanilla. Mix well.

Stir in the freeze-dried banana, raisins, and cacao nibs.

Use a large ice-cream scoop or a heaping ¼ cup to transfer the batter, spaced 1 inch apart, onto the prepared baking sheet. Lightly press down on each mound, using your fingers. Bake until the cookies are golden on the outside and no longer soft on the inside, 20 to 25 minutes. Allow to cool on the baking sheet for 5 to 10 minutes. Then, transfer to a wire rack to cool completely. Store in an airtight container for 1 day at room temperature and up to 1 week in the refrigerator.

GRAINS AND GLYPHOSATE

Glyphosate is the active ingredient in Roundup, the herbicide technically patented as an antibiotic, and the most heavily sprayed pesticide in the United States. Glyphosate has been linked to cancer by California state scientists and the World Health Organization. Studies show it destroys the good bacteria in the gut, is an endocrine disruptor, is associated with leaky gut, drives heavy metals into the body, and causes fertility problems.

Glyphosate is not only used on genetically modified crops, but as a desiccant on conventional wheat, oats, barley, and rye as well. (And it's not just our food supply; I'm not even getting into the issue of Roundup being sprayed on grass at parks and in schools, and by landscapers.) There have been many independent tests done to determine the levels of glyphosate found in packaged foods, and the results are upsetting. The Environmental Working Group is one agency that has tirelessly investigated the depth of glyphosate's contamination in our food supply. I encourage you to search ewg.org for the organization's findings and contact manufacturers directly to ask whether their products have been tested and what the results were.

In general, seek out organic, non-GMO certified products, although even those may contain trace amounts of glyphosate.

I encourage you to email the customer service department of any product to know if and what the levels of glyphosate are that are contained in that product.

For further information, check out detoxproject. org or read *Whitewash: The Story of a Weed Killer, Cancer, and the Corruption of Science*, by Carey Gillam.

BLENDER POWER PANCAKES

Ve **Vg-*a*** **GF-*a*** **DF-*a*** | MAKES 8 PANCAKES

You might think that pancakes are only for the weekend. But with the help of a blender, this batter can be whipped up in no time. In fact, you can even blend the ingredients the night before and store it in the fridge to really make breakfast a breeze. These pancakes have a solid amount of fiber, protein, and healthy fats—all my requirements to start the day. Add fresh spinach for an extra boost of nutrition.

These pancakes freeze well. Let the pancakes cool and place a square of parchment or waxed paper between each one. Place in a resealable plastic bag and freeze for up to one month. Pop into a toaster oven to reheat.

1¼ cups mashed banana, or 3 small bananas (see tip)

2 tablespoons room-temperature unrefined virgin coconut oil, unsalted butter, or vegan butter, plus more for skillet/griddle

1 tablespoon cider vinegar, distilled white vinegar, or freshly squeezed lemon juice

1 teaspoon pure vanilla extract

2 large eggs or flax eggs (see page 16)

1¼ cups old-fashioned rolled oats

½ teaspoon aluminum-free baking powder

½ teaspoon baking soda

½ teaspoon sea salt

Pinch of ground nutmeg

OTHER NUTRITIONAL BOOSTS YOU CAN BLEND IN: ground flax, collagen peptides, fresh spinach, hemp seeds (hemp seeds can be stirred into the batter for texture, if desired)

Pure maple syrup, for serving (optional)

Place all the ingredients, except the nutritional boosts and maple syrup, in a blender and blend until just smooth; if using spinach, flax, or collagen, add while blending. Stir in your choice of any other nutritional boosts (if using).

Heat a large skillet or griddle over medium heat (or to 400°F). Brush with coconut oil. Scoop ¼ cup of the mixture onto the hot pan and cook for about 4 minutes on each side, flipping when the underside is golden brown, the edges are dry, and the top shows some bubbles. Repeat until you've used up the entire mixture.

Serve with maple syrup, if desired.

↓

tips

Replace the banana with applesauce: use ¾ cup of applesauce + 1 tablespoon of pure maple syrup.

This pancake batter holds up well in the refrigerator for a few days. Store it in the smallest container possible, so there is no air to oxidize the batter and turn it an unappealing color.

Try Pancake Tacos! Hold a pancake, spoon yogurt down the center, then top with chopped fruit and nuts. Eat taco-style!

MAKE IT GLUTEN-FREE

Use certified gluten-free oats.

MAKE IT VEGAN

Use coconut oil or vegan butter; flax eggs; do not add collagen.

SWEET BREAKFAST QUESADILLAS

`Ve` `Vg-a` `GF-a` `DF-a` | **SERVES 1**

Think of this as an alternative to making filled crepes! Tortillas are the secret ingredient that replaces whipping up and cooking crepe batter. And while tortillas are not hard to make, there are so many interesting and high-quality tortillas available that they're a convenience I can get behind. I always stock several types in my fridge (I especially like grain-free, brown rice, or sprouted, including sprouted corn) for last-minute meals or snacks. One of my family's go-to quick breakfasts is any variation on the theme of a warmed tortilla + something creamy + something crunchy. As long as it has some protein and good fat, anything goes!

1 high-quality tortilla

Unrefined virgin coconut oil, unsalted butter, or ghee with vanilla added

SOMETHING CREAMY: 2 tablespoons nut or seed butter, cream cheese (dairy or vegan), Greek yogurt (dairy or vegan), or a combo

FRUIT: sliced or caramelized bananas (see page 38), frozen or fresh blueberries or raspberries, thinly sliced strawberries, thinly sliced stone fruit, freeze-dried fruit

FEELING DECADENT: add 1 tablespoon mini dark chocolate chips, or 1 ounce dark chocolate shavings (whatever will melt quickly)

ADD SOME SUPERFOODS: stir maqui (purple) or pitaya powder (bright pink) into the cream cheese or yogurt; sprinkle in some hemp seeds, chia seeds, raw cacao nibs, bee pollen

ADD A FLAVOR BOOST: a pinch of ground cinnamon, cayenne pepper, or ground ginger

Heat a skillet or a griddle over medium heat. Spread one side of the tortilla lightly with coconut oil. Spread your creamy base on the other side. Top with fruit (don't overfill—keep everything in one layer) and sprinkle with chocolate chips and/or seeds, then your choice of superfoods or flavor boost. Fold the tortilla over to cover the filling, or for small tortillas, leave open-faced.

Place the tortilla on the heated skillet and cook until the underside is golden, 3 to 4 minutes. Carefully flip the tortilla over if it's folded and cook until

↓

tips

EVEN QUICKER

Heat the tortillas over a gas flame for 30 seconds on each side, spread with condiments, top with fruit, and serve.

MAKE IT GLUTEN-FREE

Use gluten-free or grain-free tortillas.

MAKE IT VEGAN

Use coconut oil; vegan cream cheese or yogurt; vegan chocolate; do not use honey or bee pollen.

recipe continues →

the other side is golden and the filling is warmed through, especially if you used frozen fruit. (Do not flip if you left the tortilla open-faced.) Cut into manageable wedges and serve.

Some of My Family's Favorite Combinations

Me: Grain-free tortilla with almond butter, cinnamon, caramelized bananas, bee pollen, and raw cacao nibs or dark chocolate

Hubs: Sprouted whole-grain tortilla with vegan cream cheese, fresh or frozen peaches, honey, sliced almonds

Daughter #1: Brown rice tortilla, sliced strawberries, chocolate hazelnut butter

Daughter #2: Spelt tortilla, Greek sheep's milk yogurt sweetened with honey, plus pitaya powder, berries, chia seeds

Mr. Picky: Spelt tortilla with peanut butter, freeze-dried fruit, strawberry preserves, and mini chocolate chips

---

CARAMELIZED BANANAS

In a couple of minutes' time, you can take bananas to the next level. Caramelized bananas are absolutely divine on porridge, yogurt, on toast or a tortilla, pancakes, you name it. Peel and slice a ripe yet firm banana into ½-inch-thick rounds. Warm about 1½ teaspoons of coconut oil, butter, or ghee (use coconut oil for DF or vegan) in a skillet over medium heat and cook the banana for a couple of minutes, or until golden on the underside. Flip over with a fork and cook until just golden on the other side. Don't overcook the bananas, or they will be mushy. After you try this once, the next time, you can add a pinch of ground cinnamon, nutmeg, or cardamom. Vanilla ghee, which you can purchase, is also wonderful.

SHEET PAN EGGS, TWO WAYS

Ve **GF** **DF-*a*** | MAKES FOUR THIN 4-INCH SQUARES

Of course, it only takes a minute or two to cook a couple of eggs in a skillet. But this is how I make a lot of eggs either for a crowd or for the week ahead. They are superversatile: cut into thin squares, these sheet pan eggs are great for breakfast sandwiches; slice them into strips for a last-minute protein addition to a salad.

2 teaspoons unsalted butter, ghee, or vegan butter

5 large eggs

1 tablespoon water

¼ teaspoon sea salt

Chopped fresh chives or parsley (optional)

Preheat the oven to 375°F (I actually use my toaster oven for this; see tip).

Place the butter in an 8 x 8-inch baking dish and place in the oven to melt the butter. Once the butter is melted, tilt the pan to coat the bottom with the butter or use a pastry brush.

In a medium-size bowl, beat the eggs really well with the water and pour into the prepared pan. Sprinkle with the salt and fresh herbs (if using). Bake for 8 to 10 minutes, or until set. Serve immediately or refrigerate for up to 3 days. The eggs can also be sliced and rolled into tortillas and frozen for later, if desired. I like to individually wrap each rolled egg and tortilla in parchment and then place all of them in an airtight container or resealable plastic bag.

To prepare in a quarter sheet pan, double all the ingredients, line with unbleached parchment paper, and cook for 11 to 12 minutes, or until set.

↓

tip

These eggs bake beautifully in a toaster oven. Just make sure ahead of time that your pan fits. My toaster oven can accommodate an 8 x 8-inch pan easily. Remember to position the rack on the bottom level for baking and roasting.

recipe continues →

Sunny-Side Up Sheet Pan Eggs

MAKES 12 EGGS

12 large eggs

1 tablespoon avocado oil, unsalted butter, or ghee

Sea salt

Freshly ground black pepper

↓
tip

MAKE IT DAIRY-FREE

Use vegan butter or avocado oil.

Preheat the oven to 425°F. Place a half sheet pan in the oven to preheat for 10 minutes. In the meantime, carefully crack all the eggs into a large measuring cup or mixing bowl with a spout.

Remove the sheet pan from the oven and drizzle with the oil or place a pat of butter or ghee on the pan. Brush the pan with the fat. Carefully pour the eggs into the pan.

Bake until the yolks are at your desired doneness, 5 to 6 minutes for runny yolks and 8 minutes for firm yolks. Sprinkle lightly with salt and pepper.

To serve, cut each portion, using a thin spatula.

BROCCOLI and MUSHROOM STOVETOP FRITTATA

Ve **GF** **Vg-a** **DF-a** | SERVES 3 OR 4

I love a superthick frittata and I love even more how it provides me with the opportunity to use up virtually any leftovers I have. I use the formula of six large eggs to 1½ cups of vegetables + sautéed shallot or onion + salt and pepper for a thinner, but just as delicious, stovetop frittata. Broccoli and mushrooms are one of my favorite combos because I often keep frozen versions of these vegetables on hand. But any cooked vegetable (remember that frozen vegetables have previously been blanched) will work, as well as chopped fresh herbs and bits of shredded or crumbled cheese. Although this frittata is in the breakfast section, eggs are an inexpensive source of high-quality protein and can be enjoyed for lunch or dinner as well. If you have time, consider topping this with a basic mixed green salad or tucking it into a warm pita or tortilla.

4 teaspoons ghee, unrefined cold-pressed extra-virgin olive oil, or vegan butter

2 medium-size shallots, sliced

1 cup small broccoli florets (or frozen/defrosted)

½ cup sliced mushrooms (or frozen/defrosted)

6 large eggs

½ teaspoon sea salt

Freshly ground black pepper

In a 10-inch skillet, melt 1 teaspoon of the ghee over medium heat.

Add the sliced shallots and sauté until tender and translucent, about 4 minutes.

Add the broccoli and mushrooms and sauté for an additional 4 minutes, or until the vegetables start to soften up.

In a separate bowl, whisk the eggs. Mix the vegetable mixture, salt, and pepper to taste into the eggs.

Heat the remaining 1 tablespoon of ghee in the same pan over medium heat and then pour in the egg mixture.

Lower the heat to low, cover, and cook for about 12 minutes, or until set on top. If desired, broil the top of the frittata to achieve a golden color, 1 to 2 minutes.

tips

EVEN QUICKER

Preheat the broiler. Cook the eggs in the ghee in an ovenproof skillet over medium heat, using a silicone spatula to carefully lift up the outside edges so that the uncooked egg can flow underneath. Once the eggs are mostly set, 5 to 6 minutes, transfer the pan to the broiler and broil 6 inches from the broiler for a minute, or until cooked through.

MAKE IT VEGAN

Use olive oil or vegan butter. To replace the eggs, process 14 to 15 ounces of firm tofu, 2 tablespoons of chickpea flour, 1½ teaspoons of olive oil, ¾ teaspoon of sea salt, ¼ teaspoon of ground turmeric, and freshly ground black pepper to taste in a food processor until smooth. Stir the cooked vegetables into the pureed tofu mixture and pour into an oiled 9- or 10-inch pie plate. Bake in a 350°F oven for 30 to 40 minutes, or until the frittata is set and the surface is dry and slightly golden.

EGGS IN PURGATORY
with WHITE BEANS

| Ve | GF | Vg-*a* | DF-*a* | SERVES 6 |

I can't take credit for the name of this recipe, which is basically an Italian version of shakshuka, a Middle Eastern spiced, tomato-saucy baked egg dish. I like to cook this dish on the stovetop so that I can prepare the eggs to order, removing the runny ones early for those who prefer them that way and keeping others in the skillet longer for people like me who like the yolks cooked all the way through. Different skillets and different burners will affect the cook time for the eggs, so be mindful and check the yolks often. Eggs in Purgatory is a dynamite brunch dish, but don't overlook it for lunch or dinner, served with polenta or a cauliflower puree.

2 tablespoons unrefined, cold-pressed, extra-virgin olive oil

1 medium-size onion, sliced thinly

4 garlic cloves, chopped finely

½ teaspoon crushed red pepper flakes, or more to taste

½ teaspoon dried oregano

½ teaspoon paprika

Pinch of ground nutmeg

28 ounces jarred crushed or pureed tomatoes

¼ cup fresh flat-leaf parsley, chopped

1 teaspoon sea salt

Freshly ground black pepper

1½ cups cooked white beans, such as cannellini or great northern, or 1 (15-ounce) can, drained and rinsed (see tip)

6 large eggs, cracked into individual ramekins or small bowls, if possible

Freshly grated Parmesan or Pecorino Romano cheese, for garnish (optional)

In a 12-inch skillet, heat the oil over medium heat.

Add the onion and sauté until tender and translucent, 5 to 6 minutes.

Lower the heat to medium-low and add the garlic, red pepper flakes, oregano, paprika, and nutmeg. Sauté until fragrant, about 1 minute.

Stir in the tomatoes, half of the parsley, the salt, and black pepper to taste. Increase the heat to medium and bring to a simmer. Stir in the beans and

recipe continues →

↓

tips

If you don't eat beans, try sautéing a diced fennel bulb with the onions.

EVEN QUICKER

Warm an equal amount of prepared marinara sauce and add the spices, parsley, and white beans. Bring to a simmer and start at the final step.

MAKE IT VEGAN

Omit eggs and cheese (or use vegan cheese); add more beans, or small cauliflower florets, or diced potato while sautéing the onion. Make sure the cauliflower or potato are tender before serving.

simmer for another 5 minutes. If the tomato mixture looks too thick and not as loose as you'd like, add a tablespoon of water.

Make six wells in the tomato sauce with the back of a wooden spoon. Pour each egg into a well and try to keep the whites from escaping. Do not stir. Cover the skillet and cook for 3 to 6 minutes, or until your desired yolk consistency is achieved. I press the center of the yolks with my fingertip to determine doneness. Serve immediately with freshly grated cheese (if using) and a sprinkle of fresh parsley.

IS SOY GOOD OR BAD FOR YOU?

According to NutritionFacts.org, one of my favorite websites for science-backed information:

Soybeans naturally contain a class of **phytoestrogens** called isoflavones. People hear the word *estrogen* in the word *phytoestrogens* and assume that means soy has estrogen-like effects. Not necessarily. **Estrogen** has positive effects in some tissues and potentially negative effects in others. For example, high levels of estrogen can be good for the bones, but can increase the likelihood of developing breast cancer. Ideally, you'd like what's called a "selective estrogen receptor modulator" in your body that would have proestrogenic effects in some tissues and antiestrogenic effects in others. Well, that's what soy phytoestrogens appear to be. Soy seems to lower breast cancer risk, an antiestrogenic effect, but can also help reduce menopausal hot-flash symptoms, a proestrogenic effect. So, you may be able to enjoy the best of both worlds.

BREAKFAST TOFU SCRAMBLE

Vg **Ve** **GF-*a*** | SERVES 4 TO 6

Tofu and soy are controversial, so I buy the highest-quality tofu I can find, which is not only organic and non-GMO, but sprouted as well, which improves digestibility and nutrient absorption. Tofu is very bland and takes on any flavor you pair it with, so the sky's the limit for ingredients you add to it. Just treat this like scrambled eggs and you won't go wrong. I love this with a splash of hot sauce, sautéed spinach, and sautéed leftover potatoes.

2 (14-ounce) containers firm or extra-firm tofu (I like Wildwood Organics sprouted), drained and crumbled

2 tablespoons nutritional yeast

1 teaspoon sea salt

1 teaspoon ground turmeric (gives the scramble a yellow color)

½ teaspoon garlic powder

Freshly ground black pepper

1 tablespoon unrefined, cold-pressed, extra-virgin olive oil or avocado oil

3 scallions, chopped

1 red bell pepper, seeded and chopped

Chopped fresh chives or your favorite green herb, for garnish

In a large bowl, mix together the tofu, yeast, salt, turmeric, garlic powder, and black pepper to taste.

Heat the oil in a large skillet over medium heat. Add the scallions and bell pepper and sauté until the onion is tender and translucent, about 4 minutes. Add the tofu mixture. Mix until well combined.

Cook the tofu scramble until heated through and slightly golden brown, about 2 minutes.

Serve warm with your desired accompaniments or rolled up in a tortilla for a breakfast burrito.

↓

tips
———

Try a Tex-Mex flavor profile: add 1 teaspoon of ground cumin and add to the sauté ½ diced bell pepper and 1 diced tomato; serve with cilantro, avocado, and a tortilla.

EVEN QUICKER

You can complete the first two steps the night before and keep refrigerated.

MAKE IT GLUTEN-FREE

Serve with gluten-free tortillas.

MINI SWEET POTATO TOASTS

Ve **GF** **Vg-*a*** **DF-*a*** | **MAKES 4 TO 5 SLICES TOAST OR 12 TO 16 DISKS**

Even though sweet potatoes are one of my favorite foods, and one of the most nutritious foods out there, I wasn't sure about the sweet potato toast trend... until I tried it. Just to be clear, sweet potato rounds are the toast rather than sweet potato on toast. Slice them up and pop them into your toaster and top them however you would top toasted bread. What I appreciate about sweet potatoes for breakfast versus bread is the slow-burning fuel they provide versus the flour in bread, which can turn into sugar pretty quickly in the body. For me, toast is all about the toppings anyway!

1 sweet potato, unpeeled, scrubbed clean and cut into ⅛-inch-thick disks or lengthwise into slices

TOPPING SUGGESTIONS: nut butter plus cacao nibs and fruit or honey drizzle; or cream cheese (dairy or vegan) and herbs, avocado, and sea salt

Toast the slices of sweet potatoes in a toaster or toaster oven for two cycles, or 10 minutes. Top with anything you would put on toast.

↓

tips

Make sure the rack in your toaster oven is positioned in the correct place. The top level is for broiling, the middle is for toasting, and the bottom is for baking.

MAKE IT VEGAN

Use vegan cream cheese; do not use honey.

MICROWAVE FRENCH TOAST CUP

| Ve | Vg-*a* | GF-*a* | DF-*a* | SERVES 1 |

I came up with this recipe for a segment I did on a local morning show and everyone on the set went crazy for it. These French toast cups are a great breakfast and couldn't be quicker to prepare. The key with French toast for a healthy breakfast is using the most nutrient-dense bread you can find and keep the added sweeteners low to avoid the sugar roller coaster. It's worth teaching your kids how to make this, as long as you set the rules for how many chocolate chips they can add!

1 teaspoon unsalted butter, vegan butter, or unrefined virgin coconut oil

¼ cup milk of choice

1 large egg, beaten, or 1 flax egg (see page 16)

¼ teaspoon ground cinnamon

½ teaspoon pure maple syrup

¼ teaspoon pure vanilla extract

2 slices whole-grain bread or bread of choice, cut into cubes or torn by hand

OPTIONAL ADD-INS/TOPPINGS: raisins, chopped nuts, chocolate chips, blueberries

Butter the inside of a large (or two small) microwave-safe mug.

Whisk together the milk, egg, cinnamon, maple syrup, and vanilla in a bowl. If adding toppings to the mug, place half of the bread cubes in the mug and top with a pinch of your desired toppings. Add the remaining bread cubes and top with another pinch of toppings.

Pour the milk mixture over the bread.

Microwave on HIGH until set, 1 minute 15 seconds to 1 minute 30 seconds. French toast will puff in the microwave, so make sure you do not fill the mug up to the top.

↓

tips

EVEN QUICKER

Prepare the cups to the point of microwaving the night before and refrigerate. Microwave the next morning.

MAKE IT GLUTEN-FREE

Use gluten-free bread.

MAKE IT VEGAN

Use coconut oil or vegan butter; nondairy milk; flax egg; vegan bread.

Are microwaves safe?

If I had to guess without analyzing data or scientific studies, I would say microwaves aren't safe. But the data prove differently, according to multiple studies, including one from Harvard Medical School in February 2019. There is no more nutrition lost from microwaving food than from cooking it in an oven or on the stove. That said, plastic should never be microwaved since it will leach into the food. And I think the texture of certain foods is compromised in the microwave, such as rice and animal protein. Truth be told, I don't own a microwave because I just don't really have much use for one and I have limited space in my kitchen.

So, how do I reheat leftovers? I place my leftovers in a skillet or a saucepan with a little water over medium-low heat. Some food, such as grains, I keep covered; others, I do a quick sauté until everything is warmed through.

FAUX GRANOLA PARFAIT

I usually have homemade granola in the freezer (we actually like it better frozen). But for those times when I don't, I pull from the pantry and make an instant "faux granola" to top yogurt. Spoon your favorite (dairy or nondairy) yogurt into a jar or a glass, and top with a sprinkle of crunchy bits, such as raw cacao nibs, hemp seeds, sunflower seeds, pumpkin seeds, chopped nuts, and/or flaked unsweetened coconut. Add some dried, freeze-dried, or fresh fruit and eat—or add another layer of yogurt and crunchy bits. One of the reasons this is even better than regular granola is that there is no concentrated sweetener added!

Salads

I am crazy for salads and I almost always have one on every cooking class menu, which means I have many fabulous salad recipes tucked away in my repertoire. My approach toward salads is to use local, seasonal ingredients, which will be freshest and most likely more nutritious than ingredients that are imported and/or out of season. Salads also provide a lot of flexibility: I hardly ever stick to the proportions of a salad recipe exactly, but instead feel very comfortable making substitutions based on what I have in the fridge or pantry. I do like a salad with different textures and a good balance of acid and oil.

Most salads are quick by nature if you're fast at cleaning greens and chopping. Here are a few strategies to make salads QTQ:

❶ Always wash your greens as soon as you get home from the market so that they are always ready to go.

❷ Make your own dressings from scratch. They really don't take much time and are 100% worth making from scratch, since they are supereasy and simply taste better (I have never seen a commercial salad dressing that uses unrefined oils, is free from refined sugars and preservatives, *and* actually tastes good).

❸ Even quicker: use prewashed salad greens, or buy precut or precooked ingredients from the produce section or salad bar of a grocery store. Keep cooked grains and other protein toppings on hand!

EASY, BASIC SALAD DRESSING

To make a basic salad dressing on the fly, I like a proportion of 1 part acid to 2 to 3 parts oil. Start with 2 tablespoons of vinegar or lemon juice to mix with 4 to 6 tablespoons of oil. Once you have the correct ratio, then you can play with adding other flavors, such as mustard, shallots or garlic, salt and pepper, and perhaps a drop of sweetener.

OLIVE BAR CHICKPEA SALAD

Ve **GF** **Vg-*a*** **DF-*a*** | **MAKES 8 CUPS, ENOUGH FOR 4 TO 6 AS A MAIN OR 8 AS A SIDE DISH**

My parents always had a stash of delicious jarred pickled vegetables, roasted peppers, and olives for quick snacks or an easy antipasto platter for impromptu guests. I have followed suit keeping these staples on hand; and most of my local grocery stores have "olive bars" with more than a dozen varieties of olives, marinated vegetables, and some brined cheeses. For a really quick salad, I toss some of the olive bar ingredients with canned chickpeas (another pantry staple) and presto!—a healthful, easy salad that is fabulous for a potluck or to bring to work all week. You don't even need to follow the recipe below. Just combine what you have and season to taste with vinegar and dried oregano. I don't usually have to add olive oil, since many of these ingredients are already packed in oil.

3 cups cooked chickpeas, or 2 (15.5-ounce) cans, drained and rinsed

1⅓ cups chopped roasted sweet bell pepper

1⅓ cups chopped marinated or water-packed artichoke hearts

1⅓ cups chopped roasted or sun-dried tomatoes packed in olive oil

1 cup chopped pitted olives of choice

Sea salt (I usually use between ½ and ¾ teaspoon)

½ teaspoon dried oregano

2 tablespoons red wine vinegar

2 tablespoons chopped fresh flat-leaf parsley

OTHER NICE ADD-INS: marinated feta or mozzarella cheese, roasted garlic cloves, pickled onions, pepperoncini

Mix together all the ingredients in a large bowl. Taste for seasoning and adjust for salt and/or vinegar. Serve at room temperature or refrigerate for up to 4 days.

tips

White beans or a mix of kidney beans and chickpeas is also nice.

MAKE IT VEGAN

Omit cheese or use vegan cheese.

AVOCADO TOAST SALAD

Vg-*a* **Ve-*a*** **GF-*a*** **DF-*a*** | SERVES 6

Just when I think I should be tired of avocado toast, I can't resist that combination of crunchy bread and creamy fat, especially with the punchy flavor of Trader Joe's Everything but the Bagel Seasoning. One day, after I found myself layering too many ingredients onto a piece of avocado toast and making it impossible to eat neatly, I realized I had an avocado toast salad on my plate. Lightbulb!

This recipe was part of a breakfast/brunch class. I aim to have a good balance of sweet and savory when I serve brunch, so I always plan on a wonderful seasonal salad. To serve as a main course, add some smoked wild salmon and/or hard-boiled or poached eggs for an extra-special treat!

Dressing

Zest of ½ lime

1 tablespoon fresh lime juice

1 tablespoon unseasoned rice vinegar

1 teaspoon Dijon mustard

1 teaspoon pure maple syrup or raw honey

½ teaspoon sea salt

Freshly ground black pepper

3 tablespoons unrefined, cold-pressed, extra-virgin olive oil, or more to taste

———

2 small ripe but firm avocados, pitted, peeled, and lightly mashed

2 English muffins, split and toasted, or equivalent slices of sturdy bread

2 teaspoons Everything but the Bagel Seasoning or more to taste

12 cups sturdy lettuce of choice, such as baby Gem or butter lettuce

1 cup thinly sliced radish

⅔ cup pickled red onions or shallots (recipe follows)

½ cup microgreens (optional)

↓

tips

If you start this recipe without having done any prep, start with the pickled onions. Then, wash your greens, and proceed with the recipe as written.

MAKE IT GLUTEN-FREE

Use gluten-free English muffins or bread.

MAKE IT VEGETARIAN

Do not serve with salmon.

MAKE IT VEGAN

Use vegan English muffins or bread; maple syrup; do not serve with salmon or eggs.

Prepare the dressing: Place all the dressing ingredients in a screw-top jar. Shake to emulsify and set aside.

Prepare the avocado toast: Divide the mashed avocado among the toasted English muffin halves and spread evenly. Sprinkle with Everything but the Bagel Seasoning. Cut into bite-size pieces and set aside.

Place the lettuce on a large platter and drizzle lightly with some of the dressing. Toss to coat. Add the sliced radishes, pickled onions, microgreens

recipe continues →

(if using), and avocado toast pieces to the lettuce mixture. Drizzle with additional dressing. Serve immediately.

Pickled Red Onions or Shallots

2 tablespoons red wine vinegar

1 tablespoon unbleached cane sugar

½ teaspoon kosher salt

1 small red onion or 2 medium-size shallots, sliced thinly

Combine 1 cup of water and the vinegar, sugar, and salt in a small, nonreactive saucepan and bring to a boil. Stir in the onion and simmer for 15 minutes. Remove the onion from the liquid and set aside to cool.

CABBAGE, CARROT, and BEET SALAD with MAPLE-CURRY DRESSING

| Ve | GF | DF | Vg-a | | SERVES 6 |

A restaurant chain in my neck of the woods, called Mendocino Farms, has a side salad called the Healthiest Salad Ever. Not only is it teeming with nutrients, it's also super delicious. I am going to make a bold statement and say that I think my version of the salad is even more delicious, with the addition of some curry powder and massaged kale. Make this ahead and enjoy it all week. Sooooo good with a piece of salmon (omit for vegetarian)!

3 cups thinly sliced purple cabbage

3 cups thinly sliced stemmed kale, any variety (about 6 large leaves)

2 tablespoons unrefined, cold-pressed, extra-virgin olive oil

¼ teaspoon sea salt

Dressing

2 tablespoons unrefined, cold-pressed, extra-virgin olive oil

½ teaspoon sea salt

2 tablespoons freshly squeezed orange juice

2 tablespoons unseasoned rice vinegar

1 tablespoon pure maple syrup or raw honey

Freshly ground black pepper

4 teaspoons peeled and minced fresh ginger (a medium-grate Microplane can do this easily)

½ teaspoon curry powder

___

1½ cups grated carrot (about 4 carrots, peeled)

1½ cups grated raw beet (about 2 beets, peeled)

1 large or 2 small oranges, peeled and cut into chunks

⅓ cup toasted cashews or almonds, chopped

¼ cup unsulfured golden or green raisins

___

OPTIONAL ADD-IN: ½ cup cooked black rice

↓

tips

Use the slicing disk of your food processor to prep the cabbage and the grating disk to prepare the carrots and beets.

Massaging the kale leaves with your hands is an essential step in making a more tasty kale salad. The leaves tenderize and even taste less bitter.

MAKE IT VEGAN

Use maple syrup.

Place the cabbage and kale in a large bowl. Drizzle with the olive oil and salt and massage the leaves until softened.

recipe continues →

Prepare the dressing: In a screw top jar or a small bowl, combine all the dressing ingredients. Shake or whisk well.

Add the carrot, beets, orange, nuts, and raisins to the bowl of greens. If using the black rice, add it here. Drizzle with enough dressing to coat lightly and toss. Taste for seasoning. You will likely have too much dressing if you don't add the black rice. Serve immediately or refrigerate and serve the next day.

ASK PAMELA

What kind of kale do you like best?

First and foremost, I like whatever variety is organic and looks the freshest! Sometimes, such as in a stew or something saucy, I like the curly kale varieties (green or purple), which trap the sauce in the leaves. I find dinosaur kale (a.k.a. lacinato or Tuscan kale) to be the easiest to wash. If you're new to kale, I would start with the dinosaur kale, which has flat leaves and is easier to tenderize.

BRUSSELS SPROUT SLAW

Ve **GF** **DF** **Vg-*a*** | SERVES 6

↓

tips

I have quite a few slaw recipes in my repertoire, and when I was thinking about creating a new variation, I immediately thought about using Brussels sprouts, which to me are like baby cabbages. Whatever cabbage can do, Brussels sprouts can do; so, why not turn them into a slaw? Raw Brussels sprouts are actually quite mild and sweet, and when sliced thinly make an ideal base for a slaw or salad.

This one is so flavorful and loaded with nutrition. I can easily make it for a weeknight dinner with a simple piece of fish or braised lentils.

Dressing

¼ cup high-quality mayonnaise, such as Primal Kitchen or soy-free Vegenaise

3 tablespoons cider vinegar, preferably unpasteurized

1 tablespoon tahini

1 tablespoon pure maple syrup

Zest of 1 large lemon

¾ teaspoon sea salt

Freshly ground black pepper (I like a generous amount here)

———

12 to 14 ounces whole Brussels sprouts, trimmed (see tip)

1 (4-ounce) wedge red cabbage (or swap in carrots)

1 large or 2 small, tart apples, unpeeled, cored, and cut into small sticks or slices

Prepare the dressing: In a large serving bowl, whisk together the dressing ingredients.

Place the Brussels sprouts in a food processor fitted with the slicing disk (for Breville machines, set the disk at 1⅔) and process until all are thinly sliced. Repeat with the cabbage. Place the sliced sprouts, shredded cabbage, and apple pieces in the serving bowl. Toss well to combine. Taste for seasoning.

You can also use 3½ cups of preshredded Brussels sprouts. The bag of organic Brussels sprouts at Trader Joe's is 14 ounces, hence the strange quantity listed.

The slaw is also nice with fresh jalapeño pepper, sliced very thinly.

If you want the visual of chopped nuts or seeds, pistachios or toasted sunflower seeds are good.

MAKE IT VEGAN

Use egg-free mayonnaise, such as soy-free Vegenaise, or instead of mayo blend 2 tablespoons of raw cashew butter and 2 tablespoons of water for an easy, rich dressing.

CHINESE CHICKEN SALAD

GF **DF** **Vg-a** **Ve-a** | SERVES 6 TO 8

The most nutritious versions of this classic L.A. salad have a base of cabbage instead of iceberg lettuce. Not only is cabbage one of the most underestimated vegetables and one of the best cancer-fighters, there are so many varieties to choose from. I love savory in this salad. But who am I kidding? It's all about the dressing and this one is amazing. We also enjoy it for dipping summer rolls (page 121).

Salad

2 bone-in, skin-on chicken breasts

4 garlic cloves, smashed

½ teaspoon black peppercorns

1 (1-inch) piece fresh ginger, peeled and sliced into rounds

1 tablespoon kosher salt

6 cups chopped savoy or napa cabbage

4 cups chopped romaine lettuce

2 cups thinly sliced red cabbage (about ⅛ medium-size head)

1 large carrot, grated or julienned

1 cup mandarin orange segments

½ cup slivered almonds, lightly toasted

Dressing

6 tablespoons unseasoned rice vinegar

3 tablespoons unrefined, cold-pressed, extra-virgin olive oil

3 tablespoons pure maple syrup, mild raw honey, or cane sugar

1½ tablespoons raw cashew butter (or add an extra 1½ tablespoons of olive oil or mayonnaise)

¾ teaspoon toasted sesame oil

¾ teaspoon chili-garlic sauce or sriracha

1¼ teaspoons sea salt

¾ teaspoon minced garlic (about 1 medium-large clove)

⅜ teaspoon ground ginger

↓

tips

You can also add sliced avocado and purchased chow mein noodles (not exactly nutritious, but fun [omit noodles for gluten-free]).

While the chicken is cooking, prep the rest of the ingredients and the dressing.

EVEN QUICKER

Use precooked rotisserie chicken instead of poaching your own.

MAKE IT VEGAN

Use maple syrup or cane sugar; omit the chicken. The salad is still wonderful without it, and you can add shelled edamame and some extra almonds, if you like.

Prepare the salad: Place the chicken in a saucepan with the garlic, peppercorns, ginger, and salt and add water to cover. Bring to a boil over high heat, lower the heat to low, cover, and simmer until the chicken is cooked through, about 25 minutes. If you have time, allow the chicken to cool in the poaching liquid for 20 minutes. Remove the skin and bones and shred the meat into bite-size pieces.

Combine the chicken and remaining salad ingredients in a large serving bowl.

Prepare the dressing: Whisk together all the dressing ingredients in a bowl or shake in a glass jar with a screw-top lid.

Pour enough dressing over the salad to coat lightly and toss.

MEXICAN CHOPPED SALAD with CREAMY CHIPOTLE DRESSING

Vg Ve GF | SERVES 6

Whenever I serve a Tex-Mex meal, I always include a healthy dose of veggies. This salad was a class favorite and I made it differently each time, changing the ingredients depending on what looked good at the market that week. Just remember that creamy dressings need sturdy lettuces, not flimsy ones like baby field greens. Speaking of dressing this one is a little spicy, but that heat can be toned down by removing some of the chipotle in favor of smoked paprika.

Salad

2 heads mini romaine lettuce or ½ large head romaine, leaves chopped into bite-size pieces (4 to 5 cups)

2 cups chopped red cabbage

4 cups of any combination of the following, chopped:

   Radishes

   Peeled jicama

   Cucumber

   Avocado

   Pinto or black beans (not chopped)

   Grilled or fresh, raw corn (kernels)

Dressing

6 tablespoons unrefined, cold-pressed, extra-virgin olive oil

2 tablespoons raw cashew butter or vegan mayonnaise

3 tablespoons unseasoned rice vinegar

1½ teaspoons pure maple syrup

1 medium-size garlic clove, minced

¾ teaspoon sea salt

¼ teaspoon chipotle powder

¼ teaspoon smoked paprika, or more to taste

Freshly ground black pepper

Prepare the salad: Place the lettuce in a large bowl and layer the remaining salad ingredients on top.

Prepare the dressing: Place all the dressing ingredients, plus 2 to 4 tablespoons of water, depending on the consistency of the cashew butter, in a screw-top jar and shake to combine or blend in a blender until smooth.

Drizzle just enough dressing to coat lightly and toss together. Leftover dressing can be stored in the refrigerator for up to 4 days. The dressing can be made ahead of time, but it will thicken considerably in the refrigerator. Thin it out with a little warm water.

ENDIVE and CITRUS SALAD with SPICY RED ONIONS

Ve **GF** **Vg-*a*** **DF-*a*** | SERVES 6

Don't underestimate the health benefits of the Allium family, which includes onions and garlic. These vegetables have important detoxification benefits, have anti-inflammatory effects, protect the cardiovascular system, and contain a wide array of antioxidants and anticancer properties. The spicy red onions happen to be my favorite part of this salad—tangy, spicy, and packed with flavor. I adapted the onion recipe from Chef Dan Kluger whose restaurant Loring Place is one of my favorites in New York City.

The rest of the salad is very simple and can come together quickly while the onions are in process. I've served this in the winter and spring for brunch, lunch, or dinner. It's divine with Perfect Seared Scallops (page 258) or Branzino Fillets (page 252).

Spicy Red Onions

2 tablespoons unrefined, cold-pressed, extra-virgin olive oil

1 medium-size red onion, sliced into ¼-inch rounds

Sea salt

1 teaspoon crushed red pepper flakes

¼ cup freshly squeezed lime juice (remember to always zest before juicing)

2 teaspoons pure maple syrup or honey

1 teaspoon finely grated lime zest

Dressing

1 medium-size garlic clove, minced

1 tablespoon red wine vinegar

1 teaspoon freshly squeezed lemon juice

1 teaspoon pure maple syrup or honey

¼ teaspoon sea salt

Freshly ground black pepper

3 tablespoons unrefined, cold-pressed, extra-virgin olive oil

recipe continues →

↓

tips

See my blogpost "How to Segment Citrus" for a visual: http://pamelasalzman .com/how-to-segment-citrus-fruit/.

EVEN QUICKER

Many of the recipes in this book call for freshly squeezed citrus juice or, less commonly, apple juice. If you don't normally have orange or apple juice, for example, buy some today and freeze the juice in an ice cube tray in 1-tablespoon measurements. Then, you don't have to worry about buying it just for the recipe. Tablespoon-size ice cubes melt remarkably fast at room temperature.

MAKE IT VEGAN

Use maple syrup; omit the cheese (or use vegan cheese).

Salad

3 large or 4 small heads endive, trimmed, leaves separated

2 small bunches frisée, or 1 (5-ounce) container baby arugula

3 blood oranges or small navel oranges, or 1 large grapefruit

½ cup Parmesan cheese shavings (I do this with a vegetable peeler) (about ¼ pound; optional)

Maldon or flaky sea salt

Prepare the spicy onions: Heat the olive oil in a large skillet over medium-high heat. Cook the onion, stirring often, until lightly charred and softened but not falling apart, 5 to 7 minutes, seasoning lightly with salt. Add the red pepper flakes and toss to combine. Remove the pan from the heat and mix in the lime juice and maple syrup. Let cool, then mix in the lime zest. Taste and adjust the seasonings. The spicy onions can be made 3 days ahead and stored in the fridge. Cover and chill, then bring to room temperature to serve.

Prepare the dressing: In a glass jar with a tight-fitting lid, combine all the dressing ingredients, shake until emulsified, and set aside.

Prepare the salad: Place the greens in a serving bowl or platter. Drizzle with a little dressing to coat very lightly.

With a sharp knife, remove the peel and pith from the blood oranges and segment the slices (see tip). Tuck the citrus into the greens.

Scatter the cheese shavings on top. Drizzle with the remaining dressing or only as much as is needed.

Sprinkle with flaky sea salt.

MARRAKESH SALAD
with **BULGUR** and **DATES**

`Ve` `DF` `Vg-a` `GF-a` | SERVES 6

Okay, I'll fess up—I've never been to Morocco and I have never studied Moroccan cuisine. But that didn't stop me from combining some of my favorite Moroccan ingredients in this fabulous salad. I will forever love anything salty and sweet together, but the addition of sour is the icing on the cake. Drop the bulgur and swap in cooked and cooled quinoa for a gluten-free option or cauliflower rice for a grain-free variation. I've eaten this as an entrée salad as is or with a simple roasted piece of fish. I taught this salad in my classes many years ago and people still tell me they make it on the regular.

⅓ cup bulgur or quinoa (for Basic Quinoa, see page 323)

Dressing

1 tablespoon freshly squeezed lemon juice

1 tablespoon red wine vinegar

½ teaspoon sea salt

A few twists of freshly ground black pepper

1 to 2 teaspoons raw honey or pure maple syrup

3 tablespoons unrefined, cold-pressed, extra-virgin olive oil

Pinch of cayenne pepper (optional)

Pinch of ground cinnamon

Salad

½ cup raw almonds

2 teaspoons unrefined, cold-pressed, extra-virgin olive oil

Pinch of sea salt

Zest of 1 large lemon or 1½ small lemons

3 heads Baby Gem lettuce or equivalent amount of greens, large leaves torn in half

4 scallions, sliced

6 Medjool dates, pitted and chopped

½ cup pitted green olives, sliced lengthwise

Handful of fresh mint leaves, roughly torn

1 avocado, pitted, peeled, and sliced lengthwise

In a medium-size saucepan, cook the bulgur in plenty of boiling water until tender, about 20 minutes. Drain in a fine-mesh sieve and spread out on a baking sheet to cool.

recipe continues →

↓

tips

This salad is also good with cooked, diced beets. Pistachios can be subbed for almonds. Feta is a nice addition.

Refrigerate the dates to make them easier to chop.

EVEN QUICKER

Take your favorite basic vinaigrette (e.g., My Favorite Everyday Salad Dressing [page 320] and add a pinch of cayenne pepper and a pinch of ground cinnamon.

MAKE IT GLUTEN-FREE

Use quinoa.

MAKE IT VEGAN

Use maple syrup; do not add feta.

Prepare the dressing: Place all the dressing ingredients in a screw-top jar and shake until combined. Set aside.

Prepare the salad: Sauté the almonds in olive oil in a medium-size skillet over medium heat until they are lightly toasted, about 4 minutes. Chop coarsely, then sprinkle with the salt and lemon zest. Set aside.

Arrange the lettuce in a large bowl or on a platter. Add the cooled bulgur and scallions. Drizzle lightly with the dressing and toss gently.

Arrange the dates, olives, mint, and chopped almonds on top of the greens. Arrange the avocado slices on top of the salad. Drizzle with the remaining dressing.

MARKET SALAD with CREAMY LEMON CASHEW DRESSING

Ve **GF** **Vg-*a*** **DF-*a*** | SERVES 6

I know this is going to come off as a very bold statement, but this is my favorite salad dressing at the moment and, for sure, in my top three favorite salad dressings of all time. I love a great vinaigrette, but sometimes I want the substance of a creamy dressing. The secret ingredient here is raw cashew butter, which has almost no flavor but adds a luscious, dairylike silkiness to the dressing, plus extra protein! It's a great hack in recipes that call for soaking and blending raw cashews. The way I wrote the recipe is how I teach it in my classes and how I most often make it, but you can use so many different vegetables here, such as cucumbers, blanched green beans, carrots, and beets, to name a few. The dressing also makes an amazing dip for crudités!

tip

MAKE IT VEGAN

Do not add cheese.

Salad

4 heads mini romaine lettuce, or 1 large head romaine, leaves torn into bite-size pieces (about 10 cups)

2 cups sugar snap peas, trimmed and cut on the diagonal into ½-inch pieces

6 radishes, sliced thinly (halved or quartered before slicing if large)

½ (1.75-ounce) container microgreens (optional; not easy to find)

1 bunch fresh chives, or a handful of fresh mint leaves, chopped

1 large avocado, pitted, peeled, and cubed or sliced

Dressing

6 tablespoons unrefined, cold-pressed, extra-virgin olive oil

2½ tablespoons raw cashew butter

Zest of 1 lemon

2½ tablespoons freshly squeezed lemon juice

1 small garlic clove, minced

½ teaspoon Dijon mustard

½ teaspoon sea salt

Freshly ground black pepper

OPTIONAL ADD-INS/SUBSTITUTIONS: a few kumquats sliced crosswise, cooked quinoa or millet, edible flowers, walnuts, flaky sea salt, feta or goat cheese

recipe continues →

Prepare the salad: Place the lettuce in a large bowl and layer the remaining salad ingredients on top.

Prepare the dressing: Place all the dressing ingredients plus 2 tablespoons of water in a bowl or screw-top jar and whisk or shake to combine.

Drizzle the salad with just enough dressing to coat lightly, then toss together. Leftover dressing can be stored in the refrigerator for up to 4 days. The dressing can be made ahead of time, but it will thicken considerably in the refrigerator. Thin it out with a little warm water.

ASK PAMELA

Are prewashed greens safe to eat without washing?

There are a couple of brands in LA that I trust and I have had no issues with eating prewashed greens without giving them another wash. But if it makes you feel more comfortable, feel free to wash them one more time.

WARM WINTER SALAD

Ve **GF** **Vg-*a*** **DF-*a*** | SERVES 6

I love my salads; but in the winter, fresh, raw produce options are limited, and I also tend to favor warm, cooked foods. This salad gives me the best of both worlds with warmed cauliflower and shallots plus heartier winter greens that hold up nicely without getting soggy. Sometimes I add toasted pine nuts and sun-dried or roasted tomatoes to this, if I am looking to make it even more substantial.

6 tablespoons unrefined, cold-pressed, extra-virgin olive oil

½ medium-size head cauliflower, cut into florets and sliced thinly through the stems (see tip)

Sea salt and freshly ground black pepper

4 large shallots, peeled and sliced

¼ cup balsamic (not aged) or sherry vinegar

10 cups mixed winter greens, such as radicchio, endive, arugula, and frisée (or baby spinach)

1 (3-ounce) block Parmesan or Pecorino Romano cheese, grated (with a Microplane, if you have one) (optional)

Heat 2 tablespoons of the olive oil in a medium-large skillet over medium heat. Add the cauliflower slices with a pinch of salt and pepper. Sauté just until warmed through and no longer raw, about 3 minutes. Transfer to a plate and set aside.

If the skillet seems dry, add a little oil from the remaining 4 tablespoons. Whatever is left will be used for the dressing. Add the shallots and season with a big pinch of salt and pepper to taste. Sauté until softened, about 5 minutes. Add the vinegar and remaining oil to the skillet and warm through over medium heat, about 1 minute.

Place the greens in a large salad bowl or platter. Top with the cauliflower and the shallot mixture. Grate as much Parmesan cheese as you'd like all over the top, if desired.

↓

tips

This is a really quick way to prepare cauliflower with a result that is similar to roasted, but without turning on the oven.

You can replace the cauliflower with 1½ cups of white beans, drained and rinsed if canned.

MAKE IT VEGAN

Omit the cheese or use vegan cheese.

SPRING SALAD with STRAWBERRIES and CACAO NIBS

Ve **GF** **Vg-*a*** **DF-*a*** | SERVES 6

The classic combination of a seasonal fruit, cheese, and nut in a salad is a formula I rely on often when coming up with new salad recipes. But one day, I challenged myself to reinvent the wheel by finding a different yet still healthy ingredient swap for the dairy and nut. Avocados always satisfy my craving and raw cacao nibs turned out to be a new favorite crunchy topping in salads. The nibs are unsweetened and actually kind of bitter. They have loads of antioxidants and minerals, and they're the perfect contrast to the sweetness of the fruit. In the late summer, this salad is amazing with fresh figs.

Dressing

¼ cup unrefined, cold-pressed, extra-virgin olive oil

2 tablespoons white balsamic vinegar (not the thick, syrupy aged kind—see tip)

2 teaspoons pure maple syrup or mild raw honey

¼ teaspoon sea salt

Freshly ground black pepper

Salad

1 large head butter lettuce, larger leaves torn, smaller leaves left whole

2 tablespoons thinly sliced basil

2 cups strawberries, hulled and sliced

1 ripe, but firm avocado, halved, pitted, peeled, and cut into ¼-inch slices

1 cup microgreens, any variety (optional)

2 tablespoons raw cacao nibs

Flaky sea salt, to finish (optional)

Prepare the dressing: Place all the dressing ingredients in a screw-top jar and shake until combined. Set aside.

Prepare the salad: In a large bowl, toss the lettuce and basil with just enough dressing to coat lightly, then arrange on a platter. Arrange the strawberry slices, avocado, microgreens (if using), cacao nibs, and flaky sea salt (if using), on top and drizzle with enough dressing to coat lightly. Serve immediately.

↓

tips

Make sure herbs are completely dry before chopping. If you don't have a sharp knife, tear the basil with your hands to prevent bruising.

I have also made this salad with 2 to 3 ounces of goat cheese, crumbled; if using, add to the salad when you arrange all the ingredients.

Trader Joe's white balsamic vinegar is labeled white Modena vinegar.

MAKE IT VEGAN

Use maple syrup; do not add cheese.

TACO SALAD

Ve **GF** **Vg-*a*** **DF-*a*** | SERVES 6

There's a taco salad at a local fast-casual Mexican chain that my kids love. This is a vegetarian version of it; but what really makes it great is the creamy, tangy, spicy dressing: it's key to making all the ingredients in the salad taste so good together. My version here uses chickpeas, but you can use any taco protein or even cooked rice and beans. My son does not think the tortilla chips should be optional, however!

Chickpeas

2 tablespoons unrefined avocado oil or cold-pressed extra-virgin olive oil

3 cups cooked chickpeas, or 2 (15-ounce) cans, drained and rinsed

2 teaspoons chili powder

2 teaspoons ground cumin

¾ teaspoon smoked paprika

½ teaspoon garlic powder

½ teaspoon onion powder

½ teaspoon dried oregano

¼ teaspoon chipotle powder, or to taste

½ to ¾ teaspoon sea salt, depending on whether chickpeas are salted

Dressing

½ cup plain, unsweetened whole Greek yogurt, coconut yogurt, or good mayonnaise

½ cup sour cream (or use all Greek yogurt, coconut yogurt, or good mayonnaise)

½ cup fresh cilantro leaves and tender stems

1 jalapeño pepper, stem and seeds removed (see tip)

1 large or 2 small tomatillos, husked, rinsed, and chopped (see tip)

1 scallion, white and green parts

Juice of ½ lime

1 large garlic clove

¾ teaspoon sea salt, plus more to taste

¼ teaspoon freshly ground black pepper

Salad

1 medium-size head romaine lettuce, chopped

1 to 2 ripe, but firm avocados, pitted, peeled, and cubed

½ red onion, chopped finely, or 4 scallions, sliced

1 cup cherry or grape tomatoes, halved

1 cucumber, diced

————

Tortilla chips, for garnish (optional)

tips

You can replace the tomatillos and jalapeño with ½ (16-ounce) jar of tomatillo salsa.

To reduce the harshness of raw onion, soak the diced or chopped onion in ice water for 15 minutes. Drain well and pat dry before adding it to a salad.

If you don't like a creamy dressing, try this vinaigrette instead: ¼ cup of olive oil, 2 tablespoons of red wine vinegar, 1 tablespoon of freshly squeezed lemon juice, 1 teaspoon of Dijon mustard, 1 minced small garlic clove, ¼ teaspoon of sea salt, ¼ teaspoon of freshly ground black pepper, and 2 tablespoons of chopped fresh cilantro.

MAKE IT VEGAN

Use coconut yogurt or vegan mayonnaise or make the vinaigrette above; vegan tortilla chips.

Prepare the chickpeas: Heat a large skillet over medium heat. Add the oil and when hot, add the chickpeas and stir to coat with the oil. Add the spices and sauté until fragrant, 2 to 3 minutes.

Prepare the dressing: Place all the dressing ingredients in a blender and blend until combined.

Assemble the salad: Mix together the chickpeas and the salad ingredients in a large bowl. Garnish with tortilla chips (if using). Serve the dressing on the side.

TOSSED NIÇOISE SALAD

GF **DF** **Vg-*a*** **Ve-*a*** | SERVES 4 TO 6

A Niçoise salad is traditional composed salad that I change up many different ways, swapping in canned or roasted salmon for the tuna, or avocado for the potatoes. Even though I love the idea of keeping all the components of this salad separate for picky eaters, it's so much easier to just toss it altogether in a big bowl and not have to worry about presentation. In the summer, a big Niçoise salad makes the perfect light, one-dish meal—it's also flexible in that you can vary ingredient amounts based on preferences. Even better, if you plan ahead, all the components can be prepped the day before.

tip

MAKE IT VEGAN

Use avocado instead of hard-boiled eggs; omit the tuna.

Dressing

½ teaspoon sea salt

Freshly ground black pepper

1½ teaspoons Dijon mustard

2 tablespoons Champagne vinegar or white wine vinegar

⅓ cup unrefined, cold-pressed, extra-virgin olive oil

Salad

1 pound baby potatoes

2 tablespoons kosher salt

8 ounces haricots verts (thin French green beans) or string beans, trimmed

3 or 4 hard-boiled large eggs, peeled and quartered (see page 318 for how to hard-boil eggs)

½ cup pitted olives, preferably Niçoise

1 pint cherry tomatoes, halved

4 radishes, trimmed and sliced thinly

1 head butter lettuce, leaves used to line serving bowl or platter or torn and tossed with salad ingredients

1 to 2 (6-ounce) cans high-quality tuna, preferably packed in olive oil, drained and broken into pieces

Prepare the dressing: Whisk all the dressing ingredients together in a medium-size bowl or shake in a screw-top jar. You can also make this while the potatoes cook.

Prepare the salad: Place the potatoes and kosher salt in a medium-size saucepan and cover by a few inches with water. Bring to a boil over high heat, lower the heat to a simmer, and cook until tender, about 15 minutes. Remove from the saucepan with a slotted spoon and bring the water back to a boil. Prepare a bowl of ice water for the green beans. Once the water comes back to a boil, add the beans to the saucepan and set a timer for 3 minutes. They should be crisp-tender, but not taste raw. Drain and immediately submerge in the ice water bath. Drain after 5 minutes or so and pat dry. Cut in half or into thirds.

To assemble the salad, toss everything except the tuna, in a bowl along with the dressing. Finally, add the tuna and lightly toss once more.

Soups

Soups are cozy, warm hugs in a bowl. I prepare them at least twice a week during the school year and I make sure there are leftovers for easy portable lunches. What I like best about soups is their digestibility and how they lend themselves to versatility. Plus, I can generally add riced vegetables and/or leafy greens to almost any soup (more nutrients!). Soups can absolutely be a full, balanced meal unto themselves with the inclusion of hearty legumes, small amounts of animal protein, or fiber-rich whole grains.

You would be surprised how much depth of flavor you can create in a short amount of time. For these quicker-than-usual soups, I rely on good homemade stocks, a gentle sauté of aromatic vegetables to start, and my arsenal of herbs and spices. If you tend to be short on time most days, consider cooking a double batch of soup or stew and freezing one for another time.

INSTANT MASON JAR SOUPS

Oh, how I wish I knew about these healthy, "instant" soups when I worked a traditional nine-to-five office job. You can prep a bunch of these at the beginning of the week and bring them to work. All you need to do is add boiling water, which will warm everything through in a couple of minutes. To make up your own soup jar, the key is to include an ingredient that packs a lot of flavor, such as premade tomato sauce, pesto, or salsa, plus components that don't really need cooking, as much as warming through. This would make a great travel meal, as well! Just make sure your glass jar is nice and thick, such as a canning jar, and it's a minimum pint-size capacity.

Minestrone

`Ve` `Vg-a` `GF-a` `DF-a`

3 tablespoons good-quality marinara sauce

1 tablespoon prepared pesto, preferably homemade

¼ teaspoon sea salt, plus more to taste

Small handful of raw spinach

2 tablespoons grated zucchini

⅓ cup cooked white beans, such as cannellini or great northern

⅓ cup cooked farro or other hearty grain, such as barley, wheat berries, etc.

OPTIONAL ADD-INS: frozen vegetables, such as green beans, carrots, and peas

↓

tips
———

MAKE IT GLUTEN-FREE

Use cooked rice, millet, or quinoa.

MAKE IT VEGAN

Use dairy-free pesto.

Miso Noodle

`Vg` `Ve` `GF-a`

1 tablespoon white miso

1 teaspoon toasted sesame oil

1 teaspoon shoyu, tamari, or coconut aminos

¼ teaspoon sriracha or chili-garlic paste, or more if you like it spicy

¼ cup frozen or blanched shelled edamame

2 medium-size shiitake mushrooms, stemmed, caps wiped clean, and sliced thinly

4 sugar snap peas, trimmed and sliced thinly on the diagonal

½ cup cooked noodles (ramen, soba, whole wheat spaghetti, or shirataki)

1 tablespoon chopped fresh cilantro

1 tablespoon thinly sliced scallion

Sea salt

↓

tip
———

MAKE IT GLUTEN-FREE

Use gluten-free tamari or coconut aminos; shirataki noodles.

recipe continues →

Thai Curry

`Vg` `Ve` `GF-a`

3 tablespoons full-fat coconut milk (freeze the rest for another time)

1 teaspoon Thai green or yellow curry paste

Big pinch of coconut palm sugar

Big pinch of ground turmeric

Big pinch ground ginger

1 teaspoon shoyu, tamari, or coconut aminos

1 small carrot, peeled and julienned

¼ cup frozen cauliflower florets

¼ cup frozen peas

½ cup cooked white or brown rice

GARNISHES: fresh basil, fresh mint, and lime wedges

Mexican

`GF` `DF`

½ small avocado, pitted, peeled, and diced

⅓ cup prepared salsa (any variety you like)

Pinch of ground cumin

Pinch of chipotle powder

¼ cup cooked, shredded chicken

⅓ cup frozen fire-roasted or regular corn

⅓ cup cooked black beans

¼ teaspoon sea salt, plus more to taste

↓

tip

MAKE IT GLUTEN-FREE

Use gluten-free tamari or coconut aminos.

Place all the ingredients for one soup recipe, except the garnishes, in a 16-ounce or larger glass jar with a tight-fitting lid in the order that they appear. Store in the refrigerator overnight. It's fine if the frozen vegetables defrost.

When ready to consume, remove from the refrigerator, pour 1 cup of boiling water on top, and close the lid. Allow the soup to heat up and the flavors to meld (about 5 minutes).

Open the lid and stir well to combine. Taste for seasoning and add salt or desired flavors accordingly. Garnish with your desired accompaniments.

HOMEMADE RAMEN NOODLE SOUP

| DF | Vg-*a* | Ve-*a* | GF-*a* | SERVES 4 |

I understand the lure of an instant soup, especially one that is dirt cheap. But you get what you pay for. Packaged ramen noodle soups are not only low in nutrition but, I would argue, detrimental to your health. The list of ingredients reads like a scary chemistry experiment and I am here to tell you that we can do better. In minutes, you can cook ramen noodle soup from scratch with high-quality (baked, not fried) ramen noodles and DIY seasonings. Add loads of healthful, quick-cooking vegetables and also a generous squirt of sriracha, and you've got a meal that's healthier and way more delicious than a packaged sodium bomb. This soup is a great vehicle for leftover cooked chicken, pork, or shrimp (even turkey). If you don't do grains, add shirataki (see page 183) or kelp noodles (see page 183).

5 cups vegetable or chicken stock, preferably homemade

2 ramen noodle cakes (look for baked, not fried; see tip)

3 tablespoons shoyu, tamari, or coconut aminos

Pinch of maple sugar, coconut palm sugar, or cane sugar

¾ teaspoon onion powder

¼ teaspoon plus a pinch of garlic powder

¼ teaspoon plus a pinch of ground ginger

2 tablespoons dry wakame flakes

2 tablespoons white or yellow miso

Handful of baby spinach leaves

¼ cup sliced scallion, green and white parts

OTHER SUGGESTIONS: thinly sliced mushrooms or bok choy (add to pot with noodles), bean sprouts, halved hard-boiled egg, cooked shredded chicken or pork, cooked shrimp (add to the soup bowl), chili-garlic sauce

Place the vegetable stock in a stockpot and bring to a boil over high heat.

Add the noodles, shoyu, sugar, onion powder, garlic powder, ground ginger, and wakame flakes and cook for 3 to 4 minutes, or until the ramen noodles are soft.

recipe continues →

↓

tips

Cook gluten-free noodles separately, as they release too much starch.

Miso is a live food. To preserve its beneficial enzymes, do not boil it.

MAKE IT GLUTEN-FREE

Use gluten-free noodles; gluten-free tamari, or coconut aminos; gluten-free miso.

MAKE IT VEGAN

Use vegetable stock and do not add animal protein or eggs; edamame makes a good protein substitute.

Pour a ladleful of stock into a bowl and add the miso (see tip), whisk until smooth, then pour back into the stockpot.

Stir in the baby spinach leaves until wilted.

Ladle into bowls and garnish with the scallions. Serve as is or with additional accompaniments as suggested.

CREAMLESS MUSHROOM SOUP

Vg-*a* Ve-*a* GF-*a* DF-*a* | SERVES 6

I had the privilege of teaching a culinary retreat in southwest France many years ago and this recipe was part of the menu. I felt strongly about demonstrating and sharing recipes that would highlight the local produce, yet still keep true to my style of cooking. So, instead of pouring a quart of heavy cream into this soup, I used cooked and pureed leeks, onions, and mushrooms. The result? A very creamy and luxurious soup that feels rustic and elegant at the same time. This soup always gets rave reviews and tastes as if you slaved over the stove for hours instead of minutes.

2 tablespoons unsalted butter or unrefined, cold-pressed extra-virgin olive oil

½ large onion, diced

1 large leek, washed, white and light green parts sliced (see tip)

2 medium-size carrots, peeled and diced

2 medium-size celery stalks, diced

3 garlic cloves, chopped finely

1 large sprig thyme

2 pounds whole cremini or white mushrooms, wiped clean with a damp paper towel, sliced

5 to 6 cups (depending on how thick you like your soup) chicken, vegetable, or mushroom stock

1 tablespoon shoyu, tamari, or coconut aminos

1 to 2 teaspoons sea salt (depending on saltiness of the stock)

Freshly ground black pepper

OPTIONAL ACCOMPANIMENTS: minced fresh chives, vegan Kite Hill cream cheese, crème fraîche, truffle oil, a few sliced, sautéed mushrooms

Melt the butter over medium heat in a large stockpot with a capacity of at least 5½ quarts. Add the onion, leek, carrots, celery, and garlic, and sauté until the onion is tender and translucent, 7 to 8 minutes.

Stir in the thyme and mushrooms and cook until the mushrooms have softened, about 5 minutes. Add the stock, shoyu, salt, and pepper to taste and simmer, covered, for 20 to 30 minutes.

Remove the thyme sprig. With an immersion blender, puree half of the soup (or all of it, if you want a smooth soup) in the pot or carefully puree in batches in a blender. Taste for seasoning. Serve with the suggested accompaniments.

↓

tips

Wash and save the dark green part of the leeks in the freezer for the next time you make chicken or vegetable stock.

For additional nutrition and creaminess, cook 1 cup rice or cauliflower rice in the soup. Add with the stock.

For additional flavor, add 1 ounce of dried wild mushrooms, ground in a coffee grinder or spice grinder, to the pot when you add the stock. This will also thicken the soup, so go with the 6 cups of stock.

Finish with a nice drizzle of wine, such as Madeira or sherry.

EVEN QUICKER

Buy precleaned and presliced mushrooms or slice in a food processor with the slicing disk.

MAKE IT GLUTEN-FREE

Use gluten-free tamari or coconut aminos.

MAKE IT VEGAN

Use olive oil; vegetable or mushroom stock; vegan cream cheese; do not use crème fraîche.

CREAMY TOMATO SOUP

GF **Vg-*a*** **Ve-*a*** **DF-*a*** | SERVES 6

My husband's favorite comfort food is tomato soup and grilled cheese. He inevitably asks for it on the first chilly day of the year. Most tomato soups contain heavy cream or thickening agents to add body; my secret ingredient here is cooked white beans that, when pureed, add creaminess and protein. This is one of the easiest soups you'll ever make and beats canned tomato soup every time.

- 2 tablespoons unrefined, cold-pressed, extra-virgin olive oil
- 2 tablespoons unsalted butter, ghee, or vegan butter (or use all oil, but butter really makes the soup)
- 1 medium-size onion, chopped
- 2 small carrots, peeled if desired and diced
- 2 (18-ounce) jars crushed tomatoes or tomato puree

- 2½ teaspoons sea salt, plus more if your stock is unsalted
- Freshly ground black pepper
- 1½ cups cooked white beans, such as cannellini or great northern, or 1 (15-ounce) can, drained and rinsed
- 4 cups chicken or vegetable stock, preferably homemade

Heat a medium-size pot over medium heat and add the olive oil and butter. Add the onion and carrots and sauté until the onion is tender and translucent, about 6 minutes.

Add the tomatoes, salt, and pepper to taste, and stir until fragrant, about 5 minutes.

Add the white beans and stock, bring to a boil, and simmer, partially covered, for 20 minutes.

Puree the soup in the pot using an immersion blender, or in batches using a regular blender. Taste for seasoning and serve.

↓

tip
—

MAKE IT VEGAN

Use all oil or vegan butter; vegetable stock.

ZUCCHINI-LEEK SOUP

Vg **Ve** **GF** | SERVES 4

Zucchini is a wonderful low-starch summer squash but can be lacking a little in the flavor department. Of course, that's what many children love about it! This soup gives zucchini a boost with good-quality fat, a pinch of red pepper flakes, and some tang from vinegar. Even though I prefer not to blend hot ingredients in my plastic high-speed blender pitcher, I use it for this soup because it makes the creamiest consistency, almost as if there's cream in it. This soup is equally good hot or cold, making it perfect for summer entertaining.

¼ cup unrefined, cold-pressed, extra-virgin olive oil, plus more for finishing

2 large leeks, washed white and light green parts sliced thinly, dark green parts washed and saved for stock if desired

2 large sprigs thyme

3 large garlic cloves, chopped

Pinch of crushed red pepper flakes

1½ tablespoons white wine vinegar

4 medium-size zucchini, (about 1½ pounds) sliced into ¼-inch-thick rounds; do not peel

1½ teaspoons sea salt

2 cups homemade vegetable stock or water

In a large saucepan or soup pot, heat the olive oil over medium heat. Add the leeks and sauté until tender, 8 to 10 minutes.

Add the thyme, garlic, and red pepper flakes and sauté for a minute more. Add the vinegar and cook until most of the liquid has evaporated, 4 to 5 minutes.

Add the zucchini and salt and stir to combine. Cover the pan, and cook over medium-low heat until the zucchini is just tender, 8 to 10 minutes. Remove and discard the thyme sprigs.

Transfer the mixture to a high-speed blender, add the vegetable stock, and blend until very smooth. Taste for seasoning and serve as is, or transfer back to the pot and warm through until your desired temperature is achieved.

Serve in bowls with an extra drizzle of good olive oil.

tips

If you don't have a high-speed blender, use an immersion blender or a standard blender. The result will not be quite as creamy, but it will still be delicious.

Use kitchen twine or a tea bag to keep the thyme sprigs together, to make them easier to find and remove.

RED LENTIL and VEGETABLE SOUP

Vg Ve GF | SERVES 6

I am crazy about lentils and I don't know what took me so long to branch out past the typical brown and green varieties. While whole lentils (e.g., green, black, and French) hold their shape and are perfect for salads and as a substitute for ground meat, the texture of split lentils (e.g., red and yellow) isn't great for those dishes since they fall apart to mush. Split lentils do, however, cook in less time than whole lentils—perfect for this book! This soup is quick and hearty, without being heavy.

2 tablespoons unrefined, cold-pressed, extra-virgin olive oil or virgin coconut oil

1 yellow onion, diced

1 large carrot, diced

4 garlic cloves, minced

1 teaspoon smoked paprika

½ teaspoon ground cumin

2 tablespoons tomato paste

6 cups vegetable stock, preferably homemade (if vegetarian or vegan is not necessary, use chicken stock)

1½ cups dried red lentils

1 teaspoon sea salt, plus more to taste

¼ teaspoon freshly ground black pepper

2 cups chopped vegetables, such as fresh or frozen cauliflower, green beans and/or zucchini, fresh or frozen peas, chopped fresh greens, or any combination—my favorite is to use part frozen cauliflower and part peas

Heat the oil in a large stock pot over medium heat. Add the onion, carrot, and garlic and cook, stirring occasionally, until soft, about 5 minutes. Stir in the smoked paprika and cumin and sauté until fragrant, about 1 minute.

Add the tomato paste, stock, red lentils, salt, and pepper and bring to a boil. Cover, lower the heat, and simmer for 20 minutes.

Optional: If you like some of the soup a little smoother, stick an immersion blender into the pot and puree some of the soup. Or pour 1 to 2 cups of the soup into a regular blender and puree. Pour the soup back into the pot. Taste for seasoning.

Add the vegetables and simmer, partially covered, until the vegetables are tender and the soup is hot.

MEDITERRANEAN FISH STEW

GF **DF-*a*** | SERVES 4

tip

MAKE IT DAIRY-FREE

Use olive oil; vegan baguette.

This is one of my older recipes that I continue to make on the regular because it's just so delicious and really fast. It's also one of the recipes I enjoy any time of the year. What makes it quicker is using a purchased fish stock (a confession: I really like making my own chicken, turkey, and vegetables stocks, but fish stock—not so much). Many markets have homemade fish stock in the freezer section of the fish department or with the other frozen foods. I keep a quart in my freezer at all times, as well as a few pieces of frozen wild fish, making this recipe a great back pocket staple.

2 tablespoons unsalted butter or vegan butter

1 tablespoon unrefined, cold-pressed, extra-virgin olive oil

1 onion, chopped

2 large garlic cloves, sliced

1 fennel bulb, halved and chopped

2 medium-size carrots, chopped

⅔ cup fresh flat-leaf parsley, chopped

1 bay leaf

1 sprig thyme

Pinch of crushed red pepper flakes, or more to taste

1 teaspoon sea salt, plus more to taste

Freshly ground black pepper

½ teaspoon ground turmeric (optional)

12 ounces fresh tomatoes, chopped (peeled and seeded, if desired) or jarred chopped tomatoes, drained

8 ounces Yukon Gold or other boiling potatoes, peeled if you like and diced

10 ounces (1¼ cups) fish stock (chicken or vegetable stock will also work)

1 cup dry white wine, such as pinot grigio, chardonnay, or sauvignon blanc

1¼ pounds fish fillets (use halibut, cod, sole, red snapper, sea bass), cut into 2-inch pieces (or use more fish and fewer vegetables)

1 dozen mussels or small clams, scrubbed clean (optional)

Heat the butter and olive oil in a heavy-bottomed large pot or Dutch oven over medium-high heat. Add the onion, garlic, fennel, and carrots and sauté for about 6 minutes, or until tender.

Add half of the parsley, the bay leaf, thyme, red pepper flakes, 1 teaspoon of the salt, black pepper to taste, and the turmeric (if using). Gently cook for 2 minutes, or until fragrant. Add the tomatoes and stir to combine.

Add the potatoes, stock, and white wine. Bring to a boil, lower the heat to a simmer, and cook, covered, until the potatoes are tender, about 10 minutes.

Add the fish and cook for another 5 minutes, uncovered, or until the fish is cooked through. (If you decide to use mussels or small clams, simmer in the pot, covered, until they open.) Add more salt to taste, if desired. Ladle into bowls and serve. Garnish with the remaining parsley. This is especially nice with a piece of toasted baguette rubbed with garlic.

SWEET POTATO and SAUSAGE SOUP

`GF` `DF` `Vg-a` `Ve-a` | SERVES 4

Good quality, fresh sausage is merely seasoned ground meat, such as pork or poultry, in an animal casing, usually pork (see tip). The sausage spices, such as fennel seed and garlic, season the soup nicely. And feel free to use a spicy sausage if everyone will go for it. Sweet potatoes are a great pair with all these flavors. To make this soup even heartier, you can add a cooked grain such as barley (not gluten-free), or a nongrain, such as wild rice.

2 tablespoons unrefined, cold-pressed, extra-virgin olive oil or avocado oil

1 large onion, chopped

2 celery stalks, chopped

12 ounces fresh (not precooked) Italian sausage (I use mild chicken or turkey sausage), sliced into ½-inch rounds

1 large sprig thyme

1 pound sweet potatoes (any variety), peeled if desired and cut into 1-inch cubes

2 teaspoons sea salt

Freshly ground black pepper

6 cups vegetable stock or chicken stock, preferably homemade

1 bunch kale, any variety, stemmed and roughly chopped

1 tablespoon cider vinegar, or more, to taste

In a large soup pot, heat the oil over medium heat. Add the onion and celery and sauté until tender and translucent, 5 to 6 minutes.

Add the sausage and sauté until fragrant, about 5 minutes. Add the thyme, sweet potatoes, salt, pepper to taste, and stock. Increase the heat and bring the soup to a boil, then lower the heat, cover, and simmer for 15 minutes.

Uncover and remove the thyme sprig. Add the kale and cook for 5 minutes, or until tender. Taste for seasoning and add the cider vinegar.

tips

If you do not eat pork, make sure you ask what the casing is made from, since it can be used even for poultry sausage. You can also ask for "bulk" sausage meat, which hasn't been put in a casing.

MAKE IT VEGAN

Use high-quality plant-based sausage or vegan "crumbles"; vegetable stock.

HARISSA VEGETABLE STEW

Vg-*a* **Ve-*a*** **GF-*a*** **DF-*a*** | SERVES 6

Don't be put off by the long list of ingredients here; it's mostly spices and things that take no prep. Harissa is a spicy Moroccan condiment made from chile peppers and layered with cumin, coriander, and caraway seeds, along with other possible ingredients. Harissa can be made from scratch, but many brands are available that make preservative-free versions packaged in glass. That's a convenience I'm into! This recipe is a huge hit with my students—with this kind of flavor, it's easy to see why!

2 tablespoons unrefined, cold-pressed, extra-virgin olive oil, ghee, or unsalted butter

1 onion, chopped finely

4 garlic cloves, chopped finely

2 carrots, chopped

2 celery stalks, diced

1 teaspoon harissa, or more to taste (see tip)

3 tablespoons tomato paste

1 teaspoon ground cumin

1 teaspoon paprika

½ teaspoon ground turmeric

1½ teaspoons sea salt (more if using unsalted stock)

Freshly ground black pepper

7 cups chicken or vegetable stock, preferably homemade

2 cinnamon sticks

1 bay leaf

½ cup uncooked medium-grain white rice, bulgur, or quinoa

1½ cups cooked white beans or chickpeas or 1 (15-ounce) can, drained and rinsed

2 (3-inch strips) lemon peel plus the juice of 1 lemon

¼ cup unsulfured golden or green raisins

2 cups leafy greens, such as spinach, baby kale, and/or baby Swiss chard

Fresh cilantro and/or flat-leaf parsley, for garnish (optional)

Turmeric-Greek yogurt (see tip), for garnish (optional)

↓

tips

The heat in harissa will vary from brand to brand. If the ingredients do not list bell peppers, it is very spicy, so use 1 teaspoon to start. If the ingredients contain bell peppers, you can probably try 2 tablespoons of harissa.

For turmeric-Greek yogurt, add 1 teaspoon of ground turmeric to ¾ cup of plain, unsweetened whole Greek yogurt; stir to combine.

MAKE IT GLUTEN-FREE

Use white rice or quinoa.

MAKE IT VEGAN

Use olive oil; vegetable stock; use nondairy yogurt + turmeric.

Heat the oil in a large soup pot over medium heat. Add the onion, garlic, carrots, and celery. Sauté until tender and translucent, 6 to 7 minutes. Add the

recipe continues →

harissa, tomato paste, cumin, paprika, turmeric, salt, and pepper to taste and sauté until fragrant, about 1 minute.

Add the stock, cinnamon sticks, bay leaf, rice, beans, lemon peel, and raisins. Bring to a boil, partially cover, and lower the heat to a simmer. Cook for 20 minutes, or until the rice is tender. Remove the bay leaf, cinnamon sticks, and lemon peel. Stir in the lemon juice, greens and cilantro, if using. Serve with turmeric-Greek yogurt, if desired.

ASK PAMELA

What else can you do with harissa?

- Replace hot sauce or cayenne in any recipe with a smidge of harissa to taste.

- Stir into mayonnaise and ketchup for a little kick.

- Blend harissa into hummus.

- Use it instead of hot sauce on eggs.

- Stir it into bland salsa.

- Add a dollop to marinades for a little zing.

- Add it to marinara sauce for instant arrabbiata.

TURMERIC and GINGER CHICKEN (NOODLE) SOUP

| DF | Vg-*a* | Ve-*a* | GF-*a* | | SERVES 6 |

Usually in the beginning of January, I receive a barrage of e-mails and messages from my students and clients about their families being hit hard with whatever virus is going around. I have come up with a few "immunity-boosting" soup recipes for them to have in their arsenal whenever their tribes are down for the count. This particular soup became a favorite even after flu season. An anti-inflammatory bowl of homemade soup—one that just screams comfort—is always welcome at my table any time of year.

2 teaspoons unrefined, cold-pressed, extra-virgin olive oil

2 carrots, sliced thinly

2 celery stalks, sliced thinly

1 (1-inch) piece fresh ginger, peeled and grated or sliced thinly

4 large garlic cloves, sliced thinly

2 teaspoons ground turmeric

⅛ teaspoon ground cumin

⅛ teaspoon ground coriander

⅛ teaspoon cayenne pepper, or to taste

1 teaspoon sea salt, plus more to taste (depending on saltiness of the stock)

A few grinds of black pepper, or to taste

8 cups chicken, vegetable, or miso-based stock, preferably homemade

Cooked, shredded chicken, preferably poached (see page 64), ½ cup per person (optional)

Cooked noodles (½ cup per person or as you prefer; see page 183 for noodle alternatives; optional)

Fresh herbs, such as dill, parsley, or cilantro (optional)

↓

tips

MAKE IT GLUTEN-FREE

Use gluten-free noodles.

MAKE IT VEGAN

Use vegetable or miso-based stock; omit the chicken.

Heat the oil in a large saucepan or soup pot over medium heat. Add the carrots and celery and sauté for 3 minutes. Stir in the ginger, garlic, turmeric, cumin, coriander, and cayenne and cook until fragrant, about 60 seconds. Add the salt, black pepper to taste, and stock and stir to combine.

recipe continues →

Bring to a boil, lower the heat to a simmer, and cook, partially covered, until the vegetables are tender, 18 to 20 minutes. If using chicken, add the cooked chicken to the pot after the soup has been simmering for 15 minutes (essentially, you are warming the chicken in the soup for 3 to 5 minutes). Taste for seasoning.

For those who want noodles, place the cooked noodles in each individual bowl and ladle the soup on top. Garnish with fresh herbs, if desired. Store leftover soup and any cooked noodles separately.

Appetizers and Light Bites

I absolutely love having friends over, whether it's for dinner or just drinks and light bites. I used to make a big deal out of hors d'oeuvres, but these days, I'd much rather spend my limited time focused on the main meal and enjoying my guests. Furthermore, I prefer that everyone doesn't fill up too much before the real food is served.

These recipes do double duty; not only are they great appetizers, they're perfect for times when my family doesn't want a full meal. Not every dinner, for example, needs to look like a standard plate of animal protein, starch, and vegetable. Many times, I have put out a "grazing board" for lunch or dinner if we just need a smaller meal.

BAKED FETA

Ve **Vg-a** **GF-a** **DF-a** | SERVES 6 TO 8

If there's one appetizer that I make more than any other, it is this baked feta. Soft, salty, dripping with juicy flavors, it can be spooned on anything. It takes no more than five minutes to assemble, about fifteen minutes to bake, and it is one of the best things you'll ever eat. But you must use real-deal feta made with sheep's or goat's milk, which is creamy and flavorful, as opposed to cow's milk feta, which I don't even consider to be authentic feta. The bonus is that sheep and goat dairy are more digestible than cow dairy. There are too many combinations of possible toppings to list here, but the way it's written is my go-to.

1 (7- to 8-ounce) block Greek or Bulgarian feta cheese (see headnote)

1 cup cherry tomatoes, halved, or ½ cup jarred roasted tomatoes or prepared marinara sauce (see tip)

⅓ cup pitted olives, such as kalamata, chopped if desired

2 large garlic cloves, sliced thinly

A good glug (more than a drizzle) of unrefined, cold-pressed, extra-virgin olive oil

2 sprigs oregano, or a couple of pinches dried

Strip of lemon peel and juice of ½ lemon

Pinch of crushed red pepper flakes

Freshly ground black pepper

SERVING SUGGESTION: your favorite crackers or toasted bread, endive leaves, or roasted sweet potato slices (page 177)

Preheat the oven to 400°F. Place the block of feta in a baking dish or a small cast-iron skillet (something equivalent to an 8-inch square or a 9-inch round works well, but whatever it is, it will be your serving dish). Add the remaining ingredients, including black pepper to taste. Bake until the feta is soft and creamy, 15 to 20 minutes.

Serve immediately with bread or crackers, endive leaves, or roasted sweet potato slices.

↓

tips

Cast iron will hold its heat for longer, thereby allowing the feta to stay warmer for longer. Leftovers (what leftovers??) are great on top of pasta or eggs.

I recommend using cherry tomatoes in the summer when they're in season. When tomatoes are out of season, use jarred roasted tomatoes or marinara sauce.

In the fall, I love to change up the recipe by omitting the tomatoes, olives, garlic, and oregano and using halved grapes or quartered figs, a drizzle of honey, 2 teaspoons of fresh thyme leaves plus a couple of sprigs for garnish, and only optionally the lemon peel and juice.

MAKE IT GLUTEN-FREE

Serve with gluten-free crackers or bread.

MAKE IT VEGAN

Use a vegan soft cheese (roast until soft and adjust the seasonings accordingly); serve with vegan crackers or bread.

DECONSTRUCTED DEVILED EGGS

| Ve | DF | Vg-*a* | GF-*a* | SERVES 6 |

Deviled eggs are a throwback food for me, something that my mom served in the '70s. They have made a comeback, with lots of interesting flavor combinations and even the use of beets to dye the egg whites. I have found that deconstructing the traditional recipe and serving the eggs sliced on a schmear of mayo, mustard, and cayenne gives an equally tasty and familiar bite in a fraction of the time.

3 large eggs

3 tablespoons good-quality mayonnaise (I like soy-free Vegenaise)

1 teaspoon Dijon mustard

⅛ teaspoon cayenne pepper, or a dash of hot sauce

15 round crackers with a diameter slightly bigger than that of an egg (I like the Trader Joe's round rice crackers)

Paprika, for dusting

Flaky sea salt

Coarsely ground black pepper

Chopped fresh chives

↓

tips

MAKE IT GLUTEN-FREE

Use gluten-free crackers.

MAKE IT VEGAN

Use vegan mayonnaise; vegan crackers. Cauliflower is a great substitute for the eggs: Take a head of cauliflower; slice the cauliflower florets through the stem into thin slices. Roast, drizzled with olive oil, in a 400°F oven, or pan sauté in olive oil until tender.

Hard-boil the eggs: Fill a medium-size saucepan with at least 4 inches of water and bring to a boil over high heat. Lower the heat and carefully place the eggs, one at a time, in the water (I do this with a large spoon, lowering the eggs to the bottom of the saucepan and gently removing the spoon). Set your timer for 12 minutes and cook the eggs at a simmer. In the meantime, prepare a medium-size bowl of ice water.

At the 12-minute point, remove the eggs from the saucepan with a slotted spoon and transfer to the ice water bath to stop cooking. Allow them to sit in the ice water for at least 10 minutes. The eggs can be prepared several days in advance at this point and kept in a covered container in the refrigerator.

While the eggs cook, or when you are ready to add them to the ice water, in a small bowl, whisk together the mayonnaise, Dijon mustard, and cayenne.

recipe continues →

Tap the top and bottom of the eggs on a hard surface, such as a countertop or cutting board, and peel the shell away. Give the eggs a rinse to remove any particles of shell and pat dry. Slice each egg crosswise into ¼-inch-thick rounds. I have a handy mozzarella slicer to make the most perfect slices of egg.

Arrange the crackers on a small platter. Spoon a small dollop (about a scant teaspoon) of the mayonnaise mixture onto each cracker. Top with a slice of egg.

Dust with paprika (I do this with a tea strainer or a fine-mesh sieve). Sprinkle with the salt and black pepper. Garnish with chopped chives.

LOADED BLACK BEAN DIP

Ve **Vg-*a*** **GF-*a*** **DF-*a*** | SERVES 6

*Crudités (or chips) and dip are my favorite light snack, and when I am
entertaining or trying to make a dip look more appealing to the kids, I always
spread it out on a plate or a shallow bowl and go crazy with the toppings. That
way, when you scoop up a bit of dip, you also get lots of texture and flavors at the
same time. You can even serve this dip like a salad, with extra toppings covering
the whole plate! Leftovers? Use them in a quesadilla!*

1½ tablespoons unrefined, cold-
    pressed, extra-virgin olive oil or
    avocado oil

1 onion, diced

½ jalapeño pepper, seeded and diced

3 cups cooked black beans, or
    2 (15-ounce) cans, drained,
    cooking or can liquid reserved

1 tablespoon freshly squeezed lime
    juice

½ teaspoon ground cumin

1 teaspoon sea salt

Suggested Toppings

⅓ cup fire-roasted corn, fresh or
    frozen/defrosted

1½ tablespoons chopped red onion or
    charred scallion

6 cherry or grape tomatoes, chopped

¼ avocado, peeled and chopped

3 tablespoons fresh cilantro

3 slices pickled jalapeño pepper

Toasted pepitas

Feta or queso fresco

Serve with tortilla chips, plantain
    chips, jicama or radish slices, sweet
    potato toasts (see page 48)

↓

tips

MAKE IT GLUTEN-FREE

Serve with gluten-
free tortilla chips or
vegetable slices.

MAKE IT VEGAN

Use vegan chips; do
not use cheese.

Heat the oil in a medium-size skillet over medium heat. Add the onion and
jalapeño and sauté until tender, about 6 minutes.

Transfer the onion and jalapeño to a food processor fitted with the metal S
blade. Add the remaining ingredients, except the toppings, and add ¼ cup
of the reserved bean liquid. Process and puree until smooth or your desired
consistency is achieved.

Spread the dip in a shallow bowl, plate, or platter. Top with your desired
toppings and serve with chips or crudités. The dip can be made 2 to 3 days in
advance. Bring to room temperature before serving.

TEXAS CAVIAR

Ve **DF-*a*** **Vg-*a*** **GF-*a*** | SERVES 6

If you're looking to change up your chips and salsa routine, try Texas caviar, which to me is like a heartier salsa with a base of black-eyed peas instead of all tomato. You can definitely use pinto or black beans if you don't have black-eyed peas. This is supercolorful and chock-full of flavorful ingredients. It will take a few minutes to pull together if you use good-quality precooked beans.

¾ cup cooked black-eyed peas

½ cup chopped yellow bell pepper

1 jalapeño pepper, seeded and chopped

¼ cup chopped red onion

½ cup chopped tomato

1½ tablespoons unrefined, cold-pressed, extra-virgin olive oil

2 tablespoons red wine vinegar

⅛ teaspoon garlic powder

1 teaspoon dried oregano

¼ teaspoon ground cumin

1½ teaspoons sea salt

¾ teaspoon freshly ground black pepper

1 tablespoon roughly chopped fresh cilantro

SERVING SUGGESTION: your favorite chips; sliced, peeled jicama; small romaine leaves

Combine the black-eyed peas and all the chopped ingredients in a medium-size bowl.

In a separate bowl, mix together the olive oil, vinegar, garlic powder, oregano, cumin, salt, and pepper.

Pour the dressing over the vegetable mixture and stir to combine. Allow to sit in the refrigerator for several hours or add fresh cilantro and serve immediately with your desired accompaniments.

↓

tips

I know you know this, but it would make me feel better to remind you that after you cut a chile pepper, you should not touch your eyes, mouth, or nose. And you should wash your hands, cutting board, and knife with soap and water. We don't need spicy heat transferred where it's not wanted.

MAKE IT GLUTEN-FREE

Use gluten-free chips.

MAKE IT VEGAN

Use vegan chips.

FARINATA with ROSEMARY and RED ONIONS

`Vg` `Ve` `GF` | **MAKES ONE 10-INCH PANCAKE; SERVES 2 TO 4**

Farinata is the Italian version of socca, a thin, savory flatbread made from chickpea flour and water and a superquick and easy appetizer/snack to whip up. I sometimes use farinata in place of tortillas or a pizza crust. It lends itself to unlimited toppings so you really can't go wrong. Even better, chickpea flour has much more protein and fiber than grain flours.

1 cup chickpea flour, a.k.a. garbanzo flour

1 teaspoon sea salt

Big pinch of smoked paprika

1 cup warm (not hot) water (use less for a thicker pancake)

1 tablespoon unrefined, cold-pressed, extra-virgin olive oil

½ cup very thinly sliced red onion

1½ teaspoons finely chopped fresh rosemary

¼ cup roasted tomatoes or rehydrated sun-dried tomatoes (optional)

OTHER NICE ADDITIONS: whole roasted garlic cloves, fresh thyme, thinly sliced roasted peppers

In a large bowl, whisk together the flour, salt, and smoked paprika. Pour in the water slowly and whisk until smooth. Cover and let sit for at least 15 minutes, or longer if possible. You can also make this many hours ahead and keep it covered in the refrigerator.

Preheat the oven to 450°F.

Place a 10-inch cast-iron skillet in the oven for 10 minutes.

Remove the pan from the oven, add 1 tablespoon of oil, and swirl the oil around to coat the bottom. Pour the batter into the hot pan and scatter the onion, rosemary, and tomatoes (if using) on top. Bake for 10 to 15 minutes, or until set. If you'd like to broil the top to char it a little, switch the oven setting to BROIL and broil 4 to 5 inches from broiler for 1 minute. Do not step away from the oven, otherwise it will burn. Cut into wedges and serve hot.

↓

tip

—

You can make ahead and freeze for later; simply store the slices between parchment or waxed paper and freeze in a container or resealable plastic bag. Reheat in your toaster oven or in a pan on the stovetop.

ROASTED RED PEPPER PESTO on GRILLED FLATBREAD

Ve | **Vg-***a* | **GF-***a* | **DF-***a* | SERVES 8 AS AN APPETIZER, OR 4 AS A LUNCH

I used to make homemade pizza dough and found the process to be uncomplicated and very satisfying. But it is a bit time-consuming waiting for the dough to rise; that is, it's not a quicker-than-quick project! I have found that prebaked, store-bought naan, an Indian flatbread, can be a great stand-in for pizza crust. You can find them in the bread section of the supermarket. Just top as you would a pizza, bake, and eat! Here's just one delicious way you can enjoy them.

4 whole red bell peppers, washed and dried (see tip)

4 garlic cloves

¾ cup walnuts, toasted if you like

1 tablespoon red wine vinegar

¼ cup fresh basil leaves

¼ cup freshly grated Parmesan cheese or Pecorino Romano

1 teaspoon sea salt

¼ teaspoon freshly ground black pepper

Pinch of cayenne pepper

6 tablespoons unrefined, cold-pressed, extra-virgin olive oil

4 whole wheat naan breads, or your favorite premade flatbread or tortillas

SUGGESTED TOPPINGS: sliced fresh basil leaves, jarred roasted or sun-dried tomatoes packed in oil, roasted or grilled eggplant, roasted or grilled thinly sliced zucchini

To roast the peppers, preheat the broiler to HIGH and position a rack 6 inches below the heat source. This is usually the second level. Place the whole peppers on a baking sheet and broil until blistered and blackened on all sides, turning every couple of minutes.

Set aside in a bowl and cover for at least 15 minutes, or until cool enough to handle. Remove the skin and seeds. You should have about 2⅔ cups of peeled and seeded roasted peppers. You can make this ahead of time and refrigerate in an airtight container for up to 4 days.

recipe continues →

↓

tips

An alternative to grilling the naan is heating it through in a toaster oven or regular oven.

If you don't want to roast your own peppers, use 12 ounces of jarred roasted peppers, drained.

MAKE IT GLUTEN-FREE

Use gluten-free flatbread or tortillas.

MAKE IT VEGAN

Omit cheese and salt; instead, sub in an equal amount of miso (the darker, the better, as the darker misos are less sweet); use vegan flatbread or tortillas.

In a food processor, process the garlic and walnuts until very finely chopped.

Turn off the processor and add the red wine vinegar, basil, Parmesan, salt, black pepper, cayenne, and roasted red peppers. Then, with the motor running, pour the olive oil through the feed tube. Process until well blended.

Taste for salt and acidity. Adjust the seasonings accordingly.

Grill the naan: Turn a grill or gas burner to medium heat or preheat a grill pan. Alternatively, see the tips for warming naan as opposed to grilling it. Spread the pesto on a piece of naan and top as you would like. Grill until warmed through and char marks have appeared on the bottom of the naan. Garnish with fresh basil leaves, if desired. Cut into pieces and serve.

ANYTIME SUMMER ROLLS

DF **Vg-a** **Ve-a** **GF-a** | MAKES 8 ROLLS

I really wanted to call these "Anything Anytime Summer Rolls" because I never follow a recipe when I make these. I just use whatever fresh and leftover cooked ingredients I have in the fridge—convenient and superfast. Whatever you would put on a sandwich, salad, or pizza can go into a rice paper wrapper. Here, I offer suggestions for ingredients, though you can customize with what's in your own fridge. You can put the sauce into the roll or leave it out to use as a dip. The only thing you need to learn is the technique for softening the rice paper and rolling them up. The key is not to overstuff them and not to use too many pointy ingredients, which could puncture the rice paper.

↓

tips

The sauce can be refrigerated for up to 5 days. Bring to room temperature and re-emulsify before using.

MAKE IT GLUTEN-FREE

Use gluten-free tamari or coconut aminos.

MAKE IT VEGAN

Use maple syrup; do not add animal protein.

Sauce

2 tablespoons creamy peanut butter, preferably organic, or cashew or almond butter

1 tablespoon unrefined, cold-pressed, extra-virgin olive oil

1 tablespoon unseasoned rice vinegar

1½ teaspoons raw honey or pure maple syrup

1½ teaspoons water

1½ teaspoons shoyu, tamari, or coconut aminos

Pinch of sea salt

Pinch of cayenne pepper

Summer Rolls

8 (8-inch) rice paper rounds, plus more in case some tear

Handful of fresh mint leaves

Handful of fresh basil leaves

Handful of fresh cilantro leaves

4 medium-size Brussels sprouts, sliced thinly or shredded

¼ head small red cabbage, sliced thinly or shredded

2 medium-size carrots, shredded, grated, or julienned

1 large avocado, pitted, peeled, and cut into thin slices

OTHER POSSIBILITIES: cooked shrimp, chicken, tempeh, or tofu, cooked rice noodles, leftover vegetables (roasted sweet potato is so good here)

Prepare the sauce: Whisk together all the sauce ingredients in a bowl or a glass jar and set aside (see tip).

recipe continues →

Prepare the summer rolls: Fill a shallow baking dish with warm water. Soak one rice paper round (make sure there are no holes) in the warm water until pliable, 30 seconds to 1 minute. Transfer to a plate or cutting board.

Spread 2 teaspoons of the sauce on the soaked rice paper round (or omit and use as a dip once the rolls are assembled) and top with two to three large mint leaves, one to two large basil leaves, and a pinch of cilantro leaves; a pinch each of the Brussels sprouts, cabbage, and carrot; and a couple of avocado slices, taking care not to overstuff. Roll up the rice paper tightly around the filling, folding in the sides as you continue to roll. Transfer the summer roll to a plate and cover with dampened paper towels.

Make the remaining rolls in the same manner. Serve the rolls sliced in half on the diagonal.

I prefer to serve these the same day, but they can be stored in the fridge, covered with a damp paper towel, for 2 to 3 days.

SUSHI HAND ROLLS

GF **DF** **Vg-*a*** **Ve-*a*** | SERLVES 6

We are major sushi fans, although considering how inconsistent fish quality is, we tend more toward veggie sushi, which is pretty easy to make at home. I've listed our favorite ingredients here, but this recipe is very flexible! The hardest part is making small, cut rolls that need to have just the right amount of rice on the nori, and not too much. Making hand rolls requires much less skill and patience. To make hand rolls even quicker, pick up some sushi rice (which has been seasoned with vinegar, sugar, and salt) at your local sushi restaurant.

2 cups uncooked sushi rice, rinsed

¼ cup unseasoned rice vinegar (if using seasoned rice vinegar, omit the mirin, salt, and sugar)

2 tablespoons mirin

¾ teaspoon sea salt

2 tablespoons unbleached cane sugar (optional)

6 sheets toasted nori

6 tablespoons tan or black sesame seeds or gomasio

1 cup julienned carrot

1 cup julienned cucumber

1 avocado, pitted, peeled, and sliced

8 ounces leftover cooked salmon or canned salmon or tuna

Leftover Sheet Pan Eggs (page 39)

Place the rice in a medium-size saucepan and add 2 cups of water. Bring to a boil and cover the pot with a tight-fitting lid. Lower the heat and simmer for 20 minutes.

While the rice cooks, combine the vinegar, mirin, salt, and sugar in a small saucepan and heat over medium heat until the sugar and salt are dissolved. Do not boil.

When the rice is done, transfer to a shallow glass or wooden container. Pour the vinegar mixture over the rice and combine gently. Allow the seasoned rice to cool to barely warm.

Once the rice is cool, place one nori sheet, shiny side down, on a dry surface and spread about ½ cup of the sushi rice on the left third of the nori. Lightly moisten the right-hand edge of the nori roll with water.

Sprinkle with the sesame seeds and lay the toppings over the sushi rice.

To roll, fold the bottom right corner of the nori over to form a cone shape and continue to roll the nori until the cone is fully formed. Repeat this process with the other nori sheets, rice, and toppings.

GREEN GODDESS QUESADILLAS

Ve **Vg-*a*** **GF-*a*** **DF-*a*** | SERVES 1

Quesadillas don't really need to have queso! I make them all time with vegetables and creamy ingredients, such as avocado, refried beans, or a vegan soft cheese. They're one of the quickest snacks or small meals I can pull together. If sautéing scallions and spinach is a little more than you bargained for, throw them into the tortilla uncooked and let it stay on the pan a little longer.

2 tablespoons unrefined, cold-pressed, extra-virgin olive oil or avocado oil

2 tablespoons chopped scallions

Handful of fresh spinach

1½ teaspoons freshly squeezed lemon juice

Pinch of sea salt

1 sprouted, whole-grain, or brown rice tortilla

¼ cup shredded or thinly sliced sharp white Cheddar cheese or crumbled vegan soft cheese (optional)

½ small ripe, but firm avocado, pitted, peeled, and mashed with a fork

In a medium-size sauté pan over medium heat, heat 1 tablespoon of the olive oil. Add the scallions and sauté until softened and translucent but not falling apart.

Add the spinach, lemon juice, and the salt and sauté until wilted.

Remove the spinach and onion from the pan and set aside. Wipe the pan clean with a dry paper towel.

On one half of the tortilla, layer half of the cheese (if using), then the spinach mixture, then the avocado, and then the rest of the cheese (if using). Fold the tortilla over.

Using the same sauté pan over medium heat, evenly coat the pan with the remaining 1 tablespoon of olive oil. Lay the folded tortilla on the heated pan and let it cook for 2 to 3 minutes, or until the cheese has started to melt.

Using a spatula and your hand to stabilize the top, flip the quesadilla over. Cook for another 2 to 3 minutes, or until the ingredients are warmed through and the cheese is fully melted.

↓

tips

For a twist on a quesadilla, stuff the ingredients into a split pita that has been brushed on both sides with olive oil and cook in the same way or on a preheated grill.

MAKE IT GLUTEN-FREE

Use a gluten-free or grain-free tortilla.

MAKE IT VEGAN

Use vegan cheese, or do not add cheese.

SAVORY GOAT CHEESE ROLL-UPS

Ve **Vg-*a*** **GF-*a*** **DF-*a*** | SERVES 2 AS A SNACK

I originally came up with this recipe as a way to keep my kids interested in the school lunch that I packed for them. I used to spread hummus on a lavash, sprinkle grated carrot or leftover grilled vegetables on top, and roll it up. When the rolls were cut, I used to call them pinwheels. I soon began experimenting with more grown-up flavors and ingredients and now I make these all the time for potluck meetings and casual happy hours.

3 tablespoons goat cheese or vegan soft cheese

1 (8- to 10-inch) tortilla of choice or lavash

¼ cup sun-dried tomatoes packed in oil, chopped

¼ cup fresh spinach leaves

Drizzle of unrefined, cold-pressed, extra-virgin olive oil

Pinch of sea salt

Freshly ground black pepper

Spread the goat cheese evenly across the entire tortilla. Make sure the cheese goes to each end of the tortilla.

Sprinkle the sun-dried tomato and spinach on the tortilla, making sure to leave about a 1-inch border so the tortilla will seal together when it is rolled.

Add the oil, salt, and pepper to taste.

Roll up the tortilla, slice into about 1-inch rounds, and serve.

↓

tips

MAKE IT GLUTEN-FREE

Use a gluten-free tortilla or gluten-free lavash.

MAKE IT VEGAN

Use vegan soft cheese, hummus, avocado, or Loaded Black Bean Dip (page 115) in place of the goat cheese.

PAN CON TOMATE

Ve **Vg-a** **GF-a** **DF-a** | MAKES 6 PIECES OF TOAST

On my last trip to Spain, I ate this addictive combination of toast rubbed with fresh tomato every single day for breakfast. Sometimes, I would add a thin sliver of Manchego cheese for protein, but pan con tomate is perfect in its simplicity. Of course, when you grill a high-quality bread and rub it with garlic, you can pretty much put anything on top and it will be delicious. For an even quicker snack, use toasted, not grilled, bread.

2 large ripe tomatoes, best you can find

3 large slices crusty peasant bread, about ½ inch thick

Best-quality unrefined, cold-pressed, extra-virgin olive oil

1 whole garlic clove

Flaky sea salt or fine-grain sea salt

Preheat a grill over medium heat (see tip).

With a box grater set over a medium-size bowl, grate the tomatoes. If there's a piece of skin left over, sprinkle it with salt and eat it, or discard.

Brush both sides of the bread with olive oil. I use a silicone pastry brush to do this. Grill the bread on both sides until toasted and slightly charred, about 3 minutes per side. Thinly slice the end off the whole garlic clove and rub one side of each piece of bread with the cut side of the garlic. Cut the bread in half crosswise and arrange on a platter.

Spoon the grated tomato on the grilled bread and sprinkle with flaky salt. Serve immediately.

↓

tips

I love the flavor of grilled bread, but feel free to toast it in the toaster oven or regular oven if that's easier.

MAKE IT GLUTEN-FREE

Use gluten-free bread.

MAKE IT VEGAN

Use vegan bread.

SUPERFOOD APPLE SANDWICHES or APPLE NACHOS

Ve | GF | Vg-*a* | DF-*a* | SERVES 4

It's funny how the snacks I made for my kids after school when they were little turned out to be the ones I continue to make for myself when I want something easy but with balanced nutrition. Apples, in particular, are a great base for protein. Don't skip the flaky salt; it makes all the difference.

2 crisp apples, cored and cut crosswise ¼ inch thick for sandwiches, or into 16 wedges each for nachos

¼ cup freshly squeezed orange juice

¼ cup creamy peanut butter, or nut or seed butter of choice, at room temperature, or warmed until drizzly

Big handful of sprouted buckwheat groats, puffed millet, granola, or hemp seeds

Flaky sea salt

2 ounces dark chocolate, shaved with a vegetable peeler, or chocolate chips or cacao nibs

Toss the cut apple pieces in a bowl with the orange juice and ¼ cup of water until the cut sides are very lightly coated. This is to prevent the apples from oxidizing.

For sandwiches: Spread the nut butter on one apple round and top with crunchy things, such as sprouted buckwheat groats, puffed millet, or granola. Top with another apple round.

For nachos: Spread the apples in one layer on a plate or platter. Drizzle with warm nut butter, then sprinkle with flaky sea salt, granola, or shaved chocolate or seeds. Bananas are also a good addition.

↓

tips

Being coated in some type of vitamin C–infused liquid is key for helping the cut apple look fresh and not oxidized. Lemon juice in water works well, but my kids prefer the sweeter flavor of OJ.

This would also be delicious with the Date Caramel Sauce from *Kitchen Matters*.

Make Crunchy Banana Bites: Peel and slice a banana into 1-inch rounds. Spread 1 teaspoon of nut or seed butter on each cut end of the banana and dip in finely shredded coconut, granola, puffed cereal, hemp seeds, crushed freeze-dried fruit, or a combo of these ingredients.

MAKE IT VEGAN

Use vegan chocolate; vegan granola.

PARMESAN ZUCCHINI CORN MUFFINS

Ve **Vg-*a*** **GF-*a*** **DF-*a*** | MAKES 12 MUFFINS OR ONE 8-INCH SQUARE PAN

I make corn muffins and corn bread all year to supplement soup and chili, for an on-the-go breakfast with nondairy cream cheese or as a quick snack. In my quest to balance out the sweet snacks with savory, I came up with this tasty quick bread that celebrates one of my favorite food combinations: zucchini, corn, and Parmesan cheese. Once you have the formula recipe down, you can play around with adding hot sauce or extra cayenne to give these a kick; green onions or chives for a mild onion tang; or basil to provide a burst of summer. The recipe works equally well for muffins as it does for a bread in a pan. Muffins are quicker, though!

1 cup whole wheat pastry flour, whole spelt flour, einkorn flour, or your favorite GF flour blend (see tip)

1 cup yellow cornmeal, preferably stone-ground (see tip)

2 teaspoons aluminum-free baking powder

½ teaspoon baking soda

½ teaspoon fine-grain sea salt

Pinch of cayenne pepper

¾ cup buttermilk (see tip)

½ cup unrefined, cold-pressed extra-virgin olive oil, avocado oil, or melted unsalted butter or vegan butter

2 large eggs or flax eggs (see page 16)

2 tablespoons pure maple syrup (optional)

¾ cup grated Parmesan or pecorino cheese

1½ cups shredded zucchini (about 8 ounces)

1 cup fresh or frozen/defrosted corn kernels (optional)

Preheat the oven to 375°F. Line a 12-well muffin pan with paper liners or butter an 8-inch square baking dish (I usually dip a pastry brush in the melted butter I'm using in the recipe and butter the pan that way).

tips

If you like a more tender, less grainy corn bread, increase the flour by ½ cup and decrease the cornmeal by ½ cup.

No buttermilk? No problem; see page 16 for substitutions.

MAKE IT GLUTEN-FREE

Use your favorite GF flour blend + ¾ teaspoon xanthan gum. I add xanthan gum even if the GF blend contains it.

MAKE IT VEGAN

Use oil or vegan butter; use flax eggs; omit the cheese; use nondairy yogurt or ¾ cup nondairy milk + 2 teaspoons of freshly squeezed lemon juice or cider vinegar in place of the buttermilk.

In a large bowl, whisk together the flour, cornmeal, baking powder, baking soda, salt, and cayenne. In a medium-size bowl or a blender, combine the buttermilk, oil, eggs, maple syrup (if using), and ½ cup of the grated cheese until well blended. Pour the wet ingredients into the dry and stir until just combined. Stir in the shredded zucchini and corn kernels (if using). Using an ice-cream scoop, divide the batter among the prepared muffin wells, or pour it into the prepared wells. Sprinkle the tops with the remaining ¼ cup of cheese.

Bake the muffins for 20 to 25 minutes, or until the tops are golden and a toothpick inserted in the center of a muffin comes out clean. Or bake the corn bread in the prepared 8-inch square pan for 35 to 40 minutes. Remove from the oven and let cool for 5 minutes on a wire rack before removing the muffins from the pan.

WHOLE WHEAT VEGGIE SKILLET PIZZA ROLLS

| Ve | SERVES 4 TO 6 |

This is one of the few recipes in the book that is over the thirty-minute mark, but it can still be done at the last minute if you have premade pizza dough. These rolls are so fun for a party with a bowl of warm marinara sauce on the side for dipping. I can't help but add vegetables to everything, but you can top the dough as you would a regular pizza; just don't add too much moisture, or the rolls will be undercooked.

3 tablespoons unrefined, cold-pressed, extra-virgin olive oil

2 teaspoons dried oregano

1 teaspoon garlic powder

Flour (any kind) for dusting countertop and dough to prevent sticking

1½ pounds fresh whole-grain pizza dough; allow the dough to sit out at room temperature while you preheat the oven and prep the ingredients

⅓ cup marinara sauce + more for dipping the rolls in

½ cup thinly sliced raw white or cremini mushrooms and/or baby spinach leaves (see tip)

1 large garlic clove, sliced thinly

¼ cup shredded mozzarella, plus more for sprinkling on top of rolls

1 tablespoon grated Parmesan cheese, plus more for sprinkling on top of rolls

Chopped fresh basil (optional)

Preheat the oven to 425°F.

Mix the olive oil, oregano, and garlic powder together in a bowl.

Lightly brush the bottom and sides of a 10-inch skillet with about 1 tablespoon of the olive oil mixture. Reserve the rest of the mixture. Preheat the skillet in the oven for 10 minutes (you can put it in the oven while the oven is preheating).

Generously flour your countertop and the top of the dough. Using a rolling pin, roll the dough into a long rectangular shape, about 24 x 4 inches.

recipe continues →

↓

tips
———

I also like to use any leftover sautéed veggies I have in the fridge. Frozen veggies can work as well if you defrost them and pat them dry before incorporating them into the pizza.

This is also great with pesto spread onto the dough instead of marinara sauce.

Brush half of the reserved garlic oil on top of the dough. Spread the marinara sauce evenly on top of the dough. Sprinkle the veggies, garlic slices, mozzarella, and half of the Parmesan on top of the sauce.

With the long edge of the dough, roll it onto itself, forming one long tube. Slice the tube into 1½ -inch-thick pieces.

Take the warmed skillet out of the oven and arrange the pieces of dough in the skillet in one layer.

Brush the remaining garlic oil on top and then sprinkle with a little more mozzarella and Parmesan. I don't go heavy on the cheese, but feel free to add what you like.

Bake for 25 minutes, or until the dough is puffed and golden brown on top.

Serve with warmed marinara sauce for dipping.

Vegetable Sides

Vegetables are where it's at. They give us so many vitamins, minerals, fiber, and phytonutrients for very few calories. Most people feel uninspired by vegetables—they remember the overboiled, mushy Brussels sprouts they had when they were a kid—or discouraged because their children won't eat them. Keep at it, because I promise eventually they (and you!) will come around. The recipes in this chapter have been approved by many a picky child—and picky adult! Use your judgment on how to be flexible with vegetables, whether it is leaving a sauce or herbs on the side or allowing children to use their favorite condiment to "enhance" the flavor of vegetables.

One of my default methods of cooking vegetables is roasting—and this is a great way to get vegetable-phobic people of all ages to eat the good stuff. It's easy to coat vegetables with oil, season them up, and walk away from the oven while they caramelize without any effort. Some vegetables cook faster than others (such as asparagus and leafy greens), so I keep a list in my head as to which ones are my go-to when time is short. For denser vegetables (such as winter squash and root vegetables), I rely on the stovetop method (see page 138), which has a bit more hands-on time involved but can help vegetables achieve tenderness more quickly.

In general, the smaller the vegetables are cut, the faster they will cook, which is why I love riced vegetables so much. Finally, don't overlook the convenience and nutrition of frozen vegetables, either. As I have mentioned elsewhere in this book, frozen vegetables have been blanched (flash-cooked in salted, boiling water before freezing), thereby allowing them to cook more quickly than their fresh counterparts.

WHITE BALSAMIC–BRAISED ROOT VEGETABLES

Ve | **GF** | **Vg-*a*** | **DF-*a*** | SERVES 6

For people with limited time to cook, braising vegetables on the stove is a great technique, especially for denser vegetables such as carrots, parsnips, rutabaga, butternut squash, and sweet potatoes. You can braise vegetables really simply with water, salt, and olive oil or butter; or for a little extra effort, add some white balsamic and herbs and you'll have a dish worthy of your Thanksgiving table.

3 tablespoons unsalted butter, vegan butter, or unrefined virgin coconut oil

2 pounds mixed root vegetables or peeled winter squash, cut into 1-inch cubes

1 shallot or ½ red onion, sliced into thin wedges, or ½ cup small frozen cipollini or pearl onions

2 garlic cloves, smashed with the flat end of a knife

⅔ cup homemade vegetable stock or water

5½ tablespoons white balsamic vinegar (not aged) or Trader Joe's white Modena vinegar

1½ teaspoons minced fresh rosemary, or 1 teaspoon minced fresh rosemary + 1 teaspoon minced fresh thyme

1 teaspoon sea salt

Freshly ground black pepper

In a large, heavy, deep skillet with a lid, melt the butter over medium heat. Add the cubed vegetables, onion, and garlic and sauté for about 1 minute, fully coating the vegetables with the butter.

Add the stock, balsamic, rosemary, salt, and pepper to taste and bring to a boil. Cover and lower the heat to medium. Cook until the vegetables are almost tender, 12 to 15 minutes.

Remove the lid and sauté over medium-high heat for 5 to 15 minutes to let the vegetables caramelize and the liquid evaporate. Turn off the heat and let the vegetables rest for 5 to 10 minutes. Taste for seasoning.

↓

tips

If your skillet does not have a lid, use aluminum foil or a sheet pan as a lid.

MAKE IT VEGAN

Use vegan butter or unrefined coconut oil.

CONFETTI VEGETABLE SAUTÉ

Ve | Vg | GF | SERVES 6

If you haven't noticed, I am crazy about riced vegetables of all kinds. What started with a cauliflower rice phenomenon has now crossed over to riced sweet potato, butternut squash, carrot, zucchini, and others. These little bits cook superfast and give the mouthfeel of a cooked grain. Here, I combined lots of different colors and flavors for a riced veggie extravaganza. These vegetables are mere suggestions. You know what I always say, use what you've got!

↓

tips
———

Other nonriced vegetables can include corn kernels, diced green beans, peas, or diced asparagus.

Scallions or leeks can be subbed for the red onion.

2 cups sugar snap peas, trimmed

2 large carrots, peeled and ends trimmed, cut into fourths

2 cups green or red cabbage chunks

½ red onion, peeled and cut into big chunks

1 medium-size sweet potato, peeled if desired, cut into big chunks (purple is pretty)

2 tablespoons unrefined oil of choice—olive, avocado, or coconut

6 garlic cloves, chopped finely

¼ teaspoon crushed red pepper flakes, or to taste

2 cups riced cauliflower or riced broccoli, fresh or frozen (does not need to be defrosted)

Sea salt and freshly ground black pepper

1 tablespoon unseasoned rice vinegar

1 tablespoon toasted black or tan sesame seeds, or Everything but the Bagel Seasoning (be conservative with salt if using this seasoning)

Fresh herbs, such as dill, flat-leaf parsley, or cilantro (optional)

Pulse the vegetables, one type at a time, in a food processor fitted with the metal S blade, until finely chopped. No need to clean the food processor in between. Transfer to a large bowl.

In a large sauté pan (or two medium-size sauté pans), heat the oil over medium heat. Add the garlic and red pepper flakes and sauté for 30 seconds, or until fragrant. Add all the vegetables and salt and black pepper to taste and sauté until just softened, 4 to 6 minutes. Taste the veggies after 4 minutes for your desired tenderness. Stir in the vinegar.

To finish, sprinkle with sesame seeds or Everything but the Bagel Seasoning and some fresh herbs. Serve immediately.

BEYOND CAULIFLOWER RICE

Cauliflower is a member of the cancer-fighting class of vegetables, the cruciferous family. It is one of the most nutritious vegetables with loads of fiber, vitamin C, choline (good for the brain), and antioxidants. Cauliflower rice or riced cauliflower, which has been all the rage for a few years now, is a great way to get more of this superhealthy vegetable into your life. It is basically cauliflower cut into pieces that are the same size as grains of rice. I use cauliflower rice in place of grains in soups and bowls, as well as in smoothies and oatmeal (just ¼ cup and you won't notice it), and as a substitute for rice or couscous. It cooks superfast and tastes pretty neutral.

Although it is perfectly easy to rice cauliflower at home with a food processor, I love having the frozen product in the freezer at all times for the convenience, also because frozen veggies cook more quickly than fresh (it's worth repeating that frozen vegetables have been parcooked prior to freezing). Just about every supermarket in America stocks frozen cauliflower rice—from Trader Joe's to Costco to Walmart to Target to your local health food store. I wouldn't be surprised if my local 7-Eleven had it!

If cauliflower rice wasn't life-changing enough, now there are so many more possibilities when it comes to riced vegetables. I've riced sweet potatoes, butternut squash, zucchini, beets (they do bleed color), carrots, broccoli stalks, and kohlrabi. Some vegetables can go both sweet and savory, such as zucchini and sweet potatoes. And others, I keep savory, such as broccoli and kohlrabi. No matter what you choose, here's a basic tip sheet on how to rice your favorite veggies.

HOW TO RICE VEGETABLES

1. Clean and dry the raw vegetables and remove any parts that you would not eat. I often peel broccoli stems if they seem tough.

2. Chop into large pieces (about 2 inches) and place in a food processor fitted with the metal S blade. I prefer to do one type of vegetable at a time in case they have different densities.

3. Use the PULSE button to process in quick motions. You'll just need to do this a couple of times to break down the vegetables until they have the shape of rice. Scrape down the sides of the machine, if necessary, and pulse again if the pieces are still too big. You now have riced vegetables.

HOW TO MAKE VEGETABLE RICE

1. Warm a skillet over medium heat.

2. Add your fat of choice (olive oil, avocado oil, coconut oil, and ghee are my favorites.)

3. Add the riced vegetables and a pinch of salt and pepper and sauté until tender. Add a few tablespoons of water or stock, if needed. Depending on how much is in the pan, this can take 5 to 10 minutes. Taste it to know for sure and adjust the seasonings accordingly. Next time you make it, try sautéing garlic and crushed red pepper or adding different spices.

4. Or add to actual rice without adjusting the water-to-rice ratio or the cook time. Add to soups and cook until tender; usually 10 minutes will do the trick, but you can leave it in there longer.

SAUTÉED VEGETABLES with CAPERS, ALMONDS, and DILL

`Ve` `GF` `Vg-a` `DF-a` | SERVES 4

When I need a quick vegetable side dish, I pull out the skillet and start sautéing whatever I have. I stick to my motto of "what grows together, goes together" and it never fails me. Use whatever you have in season and cut the vegetables uniformly so that they cook at the same rate. (I prefer my vegetables cooked crisp-tender, which also allows more nutrients to stay intact.) Feel free to steal this delicious combo of capers, almonds, lemon, and dill and use it on a simple piece of salmon or basic cooked grains. I do love this dish so much that I have made it for large groups and roasted the vegetables in the oven instead of sautéing. Roasting takes longer, but you can cook much more at once.

2 tablespoons plus 2 teaspoons unrefined, cold-pressed, extra-virgin olive oil

4 cups mixed vegetables such as:

   1⅓ cups asparagus pieces, cut on a diagonal to about ½ inch long, or small cauliflower florets

   1⅓ cups (about 6 ounces) sliced green beans, cut on a diagonal to about ½ inch long

   1⅓ cups sliced carrots or parsnips, cut on a diagonal about ½ inch long (about 3 carrots/parsnips)

Sea salt

Freshly ground black pepper

2 tablespoons capers, drained from their brine

1 tablespoon ghee, unsalted butter, or vegan butter (or use all olive oil)

¼ cup raw slivered almonds

Juice of ½ lemon

4 sprigs dill, chopped coarsely (see tip)

Large pinch of flaky sea salt, such as Maldon

Heat 2 tablespoons of the oil in a large skillet over medium heat. Add the vegetables with a pinch of salt and pepper and sauté until just starting to get tender, but still slightly crisp, 6 to 8 minutes.

Transfer the vegetables to a serving bowl.

recipe continues →

↓

tips

EVEN QUICKER

If you don't have time, don't sauté the capers or almonds; just add them raw on top of the cooked vegetables. It will still taste amazing!

Dill is my favorite herb to use in this recipe, but if you don't have any, fresh chives or parsley are also nice.

If you drain all the brine from the jar of capers, they will still last a long time in the fridge. Salt is a natural preservative and will keep the capers fresh.

MAKE IT VEGAN

Use vegan butter, or all olive oil.

To the same pan, add the remaining 2 teaspoons of oil (if the pan looks dry) and the capers and sauté until they pop open and are crispy, 1 to 2 minutes. Spoon the capers over the vegetables.

Again, in the same pan, sauté the ghee and slivered almonds, until the almonds are lightly browned. Transfer the almonds to the vegetables.

Squeeze the lemon juice over the vegetables and garnish with dill and flaky salt.

CURRIED SAUTÉED CABBAGE

Ve **GF** **Vg-*a*** **DF-*a*** | SERVES 6

The lowly cabbage needs more respect, in my opinion. It is one of the most nutritious vegetables, and pretty cheap, too. There is so much versatility to cabbage, and I love how the flavor mellows when it is sautéed. I'd be perfectly happy eating ribbons of cabbage sautéed with a little butter and salt all the time, but adding curry powder takes it to a whole new level. Even though curry powder has an Indian flavor profile, you don't have to pair it with other Indian dishes. This cabbage goes with any basic fish or poultry protein, as well as spooned over cooked grains. And the leftovers are amazing scrambled with eggs!

1 medium-size head green cabbage (about 2½ pounds)

2 tablespoons ghee, unsalted butter, or olive oil

2 teaspoons yellow or brown mustard seeds

2 teaspoons curry powder (not curry paste) or premade kitchari spices (see tip)

1 teaspoon sea salt

Cut the cabbage in half through the core and cut out the core. Place both halves, cut side down, on a cutting board. Slice the cabbage thinly (about ¼ inch thick).

Melt the ghee in a large skillet over medium-high heat. Add the mustard seeds and sauté for a few seconds until they pop. Add the cabbage, spices, and salt and sauté until the cabbage is softened, about 10 minutes, stirring occasionally. Taste for seasoning and serve.

tips

You can find high-quality premade spice blends with Ayurvedic spices. Countertop Foods has a wonderful blend of kitchari spices, based on the spices used in the Ayurvedic stew of split yellow lentils and rice.

MAKE IT VEGAN

Use olive oil or vegan butter.

SAAG (SPINACH) PANEER with TOFU

| Ve | GF | Vg-*a* | DF-*a* | SERVES 4 OR 5 |

Saag, a classic Indian dish of cooked leafy greens with fried paneer cheese, is thickened with cream or coconut milk, making it a rich and hearty vegetable-based meal. Here, I keep the spice profile, but swap in panfried tofu for the cheese. I love this over rice or scooped up with naan.

tip
___

MAKE IT VEGAN

Use coconut oil; coconut yogurt.

7 ounces firm tofu, drained

2 tablespoons unrefined virgin coconut oil or ghee

Sea salt

½ cup coarsely chopped shallot or red onion

1 (1 x 1-inch) piece fresh ginger, peeled and chopped or grated

¾ teaspoon ground cumin

½ teaspoon ground coriander

½ teaspoon garam masala

¼ teaspoon crushed red pepper flakes, or a pinch of cayenne pepper (optional)

¼ teaspoon ground turmeric

1 pound fresh baby spinach leaves

½ cup plain, unsweetened whole-milk yogurt or coconut yogurt

Place the tofu in between two pieces of paper towel on a cutting board or plate and press any excess moisture out. I usually do this first and then measure out all the spices. Remove and discard the paper towel. Cut the tofu into 1-inch cubes.

Heat 1 tablespoon of the oil in a large skillet over medium heat. Add the tofu cubes and cook, turning, until golden brown on several sides. Transfer to a plate and sprinkle with salt.

Place the shallot and ginger in a mini food processor and process to a paste. If you don't have a mini food processor, do your best to mince the shallot and ginger with a knife or large Microplane.

Heat the remaining tablespoon of oil in the skillet and add the shallot mixture. Sauté until tender, about 5 minutes.

recipe continues →

Add the spices and cook, stirring frequently, until fragrant and well combined with the shallot mixture, about 1 minute. You can add a few spoons of water to prevent the spices from burning, if necessary.

Add as much spinach as can fit in the pan and sprinkle with salt. Stir the spinach until wilted and add more spinach with another pinch of salt. Finish adding the spinach and stir until all of it is wilted.

Stir in the tofu and toss to combine with the spinach. Cook for a few minutes, until the tofu is heated through.

Turn off the heat and stir in the yogurt. Taste for seasoning and serve immediately.

CAULIFLOWER TIKKA MASALA

Ve **GF** **Vg-*a*** **DF-*a*** | SERVES 4 TO 6 AS A SIDE DISH OR
2 TO 3 AS AN ENTRÉE

There are a few recipes that can cross the borders between one category, such as vegetables, and another, such as mains. This is a twist on chicken tikka masala, where big chunks of cauliflower stand in for the poultry. For me, it's all about the creamy, spiced tomato sauce, which I could eat on anything from riced veggies to basmati rice to lavash. We very often eat this as a vegan main dish with a side of rice and no one leaves the table hungry!

1 large head cauliflower, green leaves removed

2 tablespoons ghee or unrefined virgin coconut oil

1 large onion, diced finely (you can do this in a food processor)

4 garlic cloves, minced

1 (2-inch) piece fresh ginger, peeled and grated

2 teaspoons sea salt

½ teaspoon ground coriander

½ teaspoon ground cumin

1½ to 2 tablespoons garam masala (depending on how much spice you like)

1 pound fresh, peeled, and seeded tomatoes, diced, or an 18-ounce jar

1 tablespoon maple sugar, coconut palm sugar, or natural cane sugar

1 cup coconut milk, preferably full-fat (see tip)

Chopped fresh cilantro, for garnish (optional)

Steamed basmati rice, for serving

↓

tips

If using canned coconut milk from a 14-ounce can, feel free to use all of it if you want a richer sauce.

Always shake a can of coconut milk before opening it, to combine the fat at the top with the thinner liquid at the bottom. If it's not combining well in the can, pour the contents into a blender and blend before using.

For a little extra kick, add a pinch of cayenne pepper.

MAKE IT VEGAN

Use unrefined virgin coconut oil.

Place the cauliflower, core side up, on a cutting board. Cut the cauliflower into quarters (cutting through the core horizontally and vertically).

In a large skillet over medium-high heat, melt the ghee. Sear the cauliflower wedges until golden brown on both cut sides, 5 to 7 minutes. Remove from the skillet and set aside.

Add the onion and cook until tender and slightly browned, about 5 minutes. Stir in the garlic, ginger, salt, coriander, cumin, and garam masala and sauté until fragrant, about 1 minute.

recipe continues →

Add the diced tomatoes and continue to cook for 5 minutes while scraping up the brown bits from the bottom of the pan, using a wooden spoon or turner.

Add the sugar, lower the heat, and simmer for about 5 minutes, or until the sauce has thickened. Pour in the coconut milk and add back the cauliflower wedges. Cover and simmer until the cauliflower is tender, about 5 minutes. Poke the core with the tip of a paring knife to be sure. Transfer the cauliflower to a platter and pour the sauce on top. Garnish with chopped cilantro, if desired, and serve with steamed basmati rice.

ROASTED ASPARAGUS with PECORINO DRESSING

Ve **GF** | SERVES 6

Asparagus holds a special place in my heart, because when I was a little girl, we could eat asparagus only when it came into season for a short time in the spring. We never saw it the rest of the year! After I endured those cold East Coast winters, asparagus was the first promise of sunnier and warmer days. My mom would make it once a week (or more) until it was gone from the markets. This creamy pecorino dressing is a breeze to prepare and jazzes up basic roasted asparagus. It would make a perfect Easter side dish.

2 bunches medium-thick asparagus, woody ends trimmed

1 tablespoon unrefined, cold-pressed, extra-virgin olive oil

½ teaspoon sea salt

Freshly ground black pepper

Dressing

½ cup plain, unsweetened, whole Greek yogurt (or half soy-free Vegenaise)

5 tablespoons grated Pecorino Romano cheese

1 medium-large garlic clove, minced or grated with a Microplane

Zest of 1 small lemon

2 tablespoons freshly squeezed lemon juice

Pinch of sea salt

Freshly ground black pepper

Preheat the oven to 400°F and line a baking sheet with unbleached parchment paper.

Arrange the asparagus in a single layer on the prepared baking sheet, drizzle with the olive oil, and toss to coat. Sprinkle with the salt and pepper to taste and roast for 12 minutes, or until tender.

Meanwhile, make the dressing: Place all the dressing ingredients in a medium-size bowl and whisk to combine.

Spread the dressing over the bottom of a platter and arrange the asparagus on top. Serve immediately.

ROASTED BROCCOLI
with TAHINI SAUCE, HAZELNUTS, and RAISINS

Ve   GF   Vg-*a*   DF-*a* | SERVES 4 TO 6

I will try to contain my enthusiasm for how much I love this side dish, but I fear you won't fully appreciate how supergood it is. You will just have to trust me that this tahini-hazelnut-raisin-caper-herb situation is ridiculously delicious and you'll want to add it to everything (cauliflower, carrots, and eggplant come to mind). To make this really quickly, just eyeball the ingredients and don't even measure anything. I cut the broccoli into smaller florets for the purposes of quicker cooking, but if you have time, you can make the pieces bigger. I especially love this with any basic fish or chicken dish, as well as any cooked grain, such as black rice or quinoa.

↓

tip

MAKE IT VEGAN

Use olive oil; maple syrup.

1½ pounds broccoli crowns, cut into florets and then sliced in half through the stem

2 tablespoons unrefined, cold-pressed, extra-virgin olive oil or melted ghee

¾ teaspoon sea salt

Freshly ground black pepper

⅓ cup tahini

2 tablespoons freshly squeezed lemon juice

1 garlic clove, minced

1 to 2 teaspoons mild raw honey or pure maple syrup (optional)

1 cup fresh dill leaves—leave the tender stems attached

1 cup fresh flat-leaf parsley leaves—leave the tender stems attached

¼ cup roasted and skinned hazelnuts, roughly chopped

¼ cup unsulfured green raisins or currants (if they are superdry, soak them in warm water for 15 minutes and then drain)

¼ cup capers, drained from brine

Preheat the oven to 400°F. Line a large, rimmed baking sheet with unbleached parchment paper.

Place the broccoli florets on the prepared baking sheet. Drizzle the broccoli with the oil and toss to coat. Sprinkle with ½ teaspoon of the salt and pepper

recipe continues →

to taste. Arrange in one layer on the baking sheet. Roast until tender and just starting to crisp up on the edges, about 15 minutes.

Prepare the sauce: In a medium-size bowl, combine the tahini, enough water to make a pourable sauce (start with ¼ cup and add more as necessary), the lemon juice, garlic, honey, and remaining ¼ teaspoon of salt.

Arrange the herbs on the perimeter of a small platter. Place the broccoli florets in the center. Sprinkle the hazelnuts, raisins, and capers on top and around the broccoli. Drizzle everything with the sauce and serve extra sauce on the side.

ROASTED RADISHES

Vg **Ve** **GF** | SERVES 4 TO 6

Radishes are a wonderful detoxifying vegetable that most people think of only eating raw. When I made this dish in class, the first question I got was, "You can roast radishes?" The answer is not just yes, but a loud yes, because roasted radishes are divine. Their flavor really mellows out and they taste a little like cooked cabbage. With the addition of oil and herbs, they take on a rich, buttery flavor. These are great served with roasted poultry or in a grain bowl.

2 bunches radishes, stems trimmed, radishes sliced in half lengthwise

2 tablespoons unrefined, cold-pressed, extra-virgin olive oil or avocado oil

¾ teaspoon sea salt

¼ teaspoon freshly ground black pepper

GARNISHES: chopped fresh organic herbs (I like dill or parsley), flaky sea salt, the juice from ½ lemon

Preheat the oven to 400°F. Line a rimmed baking sheet with unbleached parchment paper.

Place the radishes on the prepared baking sheet and toss with the olive oil, salt, and pepper. Roast for 10 to 12 minutes, or until tender.

Once the radishes are roasted, add the herbs, salt, and lemon juice. Or just enjoy them plain!

↓

tip

You can use a similar approach to other quick-cooking vegetables, such as very small cut cauliflower florets, green beans, asparagus, summer squash, and sugar snap peas.

ROASTED BELL PEPPERS with **GREEK TOMATO SALAD**

Ve | GF | Vg-*a* | DF-*a* | SERVES 6

These are like individual Greek salads in roasted pepper cups. I am not going to lie—I have eaten them like tacos. Kind of messy, but that's part of the fun. It's all about the salty, juicy, crunchy textures, so if you have capers but not olives, no problem; cucumber instead of shallot, great. This salad mixture would also be great chopped small and stuffed into roasted mini peppers for a tasty appetizer.

Peppers

6 sweet bell peppers (any type works; use a contrasting color to the cherry tomatoes for a visual pop)

2 tablespoons unrefined, cold-pressed, extra-virgin olive oil, or more if desired

1 tablespoon dried oregano, or 1 teaspoon chopped fresh

Sea salt and freshly ground black pepper

4 garlic cloves, sliced thinly

Salad

1 pint cherry tomatoes, halved

1 medium-size shallot, sliced thinly

2 to 3 pepperoncini, seeded and sliced thinly

2 to 3 ounces feta cheese, crumbled

¼ cup kalamata olives, quartered

2 tablespoons chopped, fresh flat-leaf parsley (fresh mint and dill are nice, too)

1 tablespoon red wine vinegar

Preheat the oven to 425°F and line a baking sheet with unbleached parchment paper.

Halve, stem, and seed the bell peppers and place on the prepared baking sheet. Coat inside and outside with 1 tablespoon of the olive oil.

Arrange the peppers cut side up and sprinkle with 1½ teaspoons of the dried oregano (or ½ teaspoon of fresh), plus salt and pepper to taste (½ teaspoon of salt is a good start). Place the sliced garlic in the cavities of the peppers.

↓

tips

EVEN QUICKER

Grill the pepper halves on both sides over medium heat until char marks appear and the peppers are softened, about 10 minutes.

MAKE IT VEGAN

Omit the cheese or use vegan feta.

recipe continues →

Arrange, cut side up, in a single layer and roast until softened, about 20 minutes. Remove from the oven and set aside.

Prepare the salad: Mix the cherry tomatoes, shallot, pepperoncini, feta, olives, parsley, vinegar, 1 tablespoon of the olive oil, the remaining 1½ teaspoons of dried oregano (or ½ teaspoon of fresh), plus a pinch of salt and pepper. Taste for seasoning.

Arrange the peppers on a platter and top with the tomato salad. Serve warm or room temperature.

ASK PAMELA

Do I have to wait for the oven to be preheated before putting food in?

If you're baking or if you're roasting something that needs the high heat, yes. Otherwise, you can place food in the oven before it reaches the set temperature.

TOMATO-ZUCCHINI BROIL

Ve **GF** **Vg-*a*** **DF-*a*** | SERVES 4

A cookbook about quicker cooking has to have at least one zucchini recipe, since it is one of the speediest veggies to cook. My mom used to halve small zucchini, top them with Parmesan cheese, and broil them. This recipe reminds me of her method, but here the zucchini get cooked a little more evenly and the tomatoes create a nice juiciness and add really good flavor. It's the perfect summer side dish because you also don't need the oven on for more than a few minutes. I often serve this with grilled shrimp or steak and sautéed corn.

↓

tip
—

MAKE IT VEGAN

Omit the Parmesan (or use vegan cheese).

- 2 tablespoons plus 1 teaspoon unrefined, cold-pressed, extra-virgin olive oil
- 1 pound zucchini, cut into ½-inch cubes
- 1 pound Roma tomatoes, cut into ¼- to ½-inch cubes
- 8 whole small to medium-size garlic cloves, peeled

- ½ teaspoon sea salt
- ¼ teaspoon freshly ground black pepper
- ½ cup plus 1 tablespoon grated Parmesan or pecorino (optional, but you'll likely need to add a bit more salt)
- 6 fresh basil leaves, julienned

Position an oven rack 6 to 7 inches from the broiler and preheat the broiler on HIGH. Oil a small sheet pan with 1 teaspoon of the olive oil.

In a large bowl, toss together the zucchini, tomatoes, and garlic with the remaining 2 tablespoons of oil, salt, pepper, and ½ cup of the Parmesan.

Transfer the mixture to the prepared sheet pan and spread out the mixture evenly. Broil for 5 minutes, then rotate the sheet pan in the oven and broil for another 5 minutes or until evenly browned.

Remove from the oven and mix in half of the julienned basil leaves.

When ready to serve, sprinkle with the remaining fresh basil and 1 tablespoon of Parmesan.

CHILI-SESAME KELP NOODLES with VEGGIES

| Vg | Ve | GF-*a* | | SERVES 6 |

Kelp is a highly nutritious, mineral-rich sea vegetable and kelp noodles are absolutely amazing. When prepared properly, these seaweed noodles resemble silky glass noodles but without all the starch. My best advice is to ignore the package directions that instruct you to rinse the squeaky noodles and serve. The real secret lies in soaking them in a warm water/lemon juice/baking soda solution that softens them up perfectly. You can serve them according to my recipe here or any way you serve pasta. They're also great in Anytime Summer Rolls (page 121).

tips

No need to grate the ginger and garlic if using a high-powered blender.

MAKE IT GLUTEN-FREE

Use gluten-free tamari or coconut aminos.

2 (12-ounce) packages kelp noodles

Juice of ½ lemon

1 tablespoon baking soda

2 medium-size carrots, grated or julienned, or 1 sweet bell pepper, julienned

2 celery stalks, or 1 cucumber, sliced thinly on the diagonal

1 cup frozen, shelled edamame, defrosted (boiled for a couple of minutes, if desired)

Handful of shredded purple cabbage, or 2 radishes, julienned

½ cup loosely packed fresh cilantro, roughly chopped (optional)

Dressing

3 tablespoons unrefined, cold-pressed, extra-virgin olive oil or avocado oil

3 tablespoons shoyu, tamari, or coconut aminos

3 tablespoons unseasoned rice vinegar

1 tablespoon pure maple syrup

1 tablespoon toasted sesame oil

1 tablespoon peeled and grated fresh ginger (see tip)

1 teaspoon hot sauce (I like sriracha), or more to taste

1 garlic clove, grated (see tip)

3 tablespoons toasted sesame seeds, or 1½ tablespoons tahini plus additional sesame seeds for garnish, if desired

In a medium-size bowl, soak the kelp noodles in hot water to cover, lemon juice, and baking soda until softened, about 20 minutes. Rinse and drain very well and pat dry with paper towels. Place all the dressing ingredients in a blender and process until smooth. Add the carrots, celery, edamame, cabbage, and cilantro to the noodles. Pour the dressing on top and toss to combine. Add the sesame seeds, if desired.

CHINESE-STYLE SAUTÉED GREEN BEANS

| Ve | Vg-*a* | GF-*a* | DF-*a* | | SERVES 3 OR 4 AS A SIDE DISH |

This is my favorite Chinese restaurant side dish and I could easily eat this entire recipe myself. In fact, I have, standing up over the stove, picking away at every salty, sticky, spicy green bean with my fingers. Luckily, this recipe is superfast to make, so I can make one skillet for me and another for the rest of the family. My favorite dinner is to serve these superflavorful green beans with rice and plain shrimp to soak up all the delicious sauce.

1½ tablespoons shoyu, tamari, or coconut aminos

2 teaspoons pure maple syrup or honey

1 tablespoon unsalted butter or vegan butter

2 tablespoons unrefined, cold-pressed, extra-virgin olive oil or avocado oil

1 pound green beans, trimmed

½ teaspoon sea salt

2 large garlic cloves, minced

1 teaspoon chili-garlic paste, or ¼ teaspoon of crushed red pepper flakes

In a small bowl, combine the shoyu, maple syrup, and 1½ tablespoons of water. Set aside.

In a large skillet, melt the butter with the olive oil over medium-high heat. Add the green beans and salt and sauté until the beans are browned and have shriveled a bit, 6 to 7 minutes.

Lower the heat to medium-low, add the garlic and chili-garlic paste, and sauté until fragrant, about 30 seconds. Pour the shoyu mixture into the pan and stir. Cook until the liquid thickens, 30 to 60 seconds. Serve immediately.

tips

MAKE IT GLUTEN-FREE

Use gluten-free tamari or coconut aminos.

MAKE IT VEGAN

Use maple syrup; vegan butter or all olive oil.

Starchy Sides

Although the word *starchy* may not be very appetizing on the face of it, starches are an important part of our diet. Carbohydrates are our primary source of energy—and there is definitely a difference among them. We want to focus on high-quality, slow-burning carbs, ones that have fiber and/or protein built in. My favorites are winter squashes, sweet potatoes, and legumes. Less so, but still in my family meals, are whole grains and pastas. There are many interesting pastas these days that are made with brown rice, quinoa, lentils, even an indigestible root called konjac. The goal is to keep low-fiber starches to a minimum to ensure stable blood sugar until the next meal.

Ironically, some of the more high-fiber whole grains, such as brown rice, einkorn, and nutritious beans, are not cooked quickly and therefore are not prominent in this book. I do cook them often for my family and in my classes, however. In this book, I am highlighting the grains that cook in thirty minutes or less, canned beans, quicker-cooking lentils, and methods for preparing dense starchy vegetables in less time. The key is having a well-stocked pantry or freezer with cooked legumes and quick-cooking grains.

Many of the recipes in this chapter have enough substance to be the center of a vegetarian or even vegan meal. Even though starches do not contain all the essential amino acids, we no longer feel obliged to combine them with other food groups to create a "complete protein." As long as our diet is varied over the course of a few days, we should be able to get what we need. I always pair a starchy side with at least a salad and/or nonstarchy vegetable, such as broccoli, spinach, green beans, or cauliflower. The pasta dishes in this chapter can be served as a side dish with animal protein or additional vegetables, or served on their own as a main dish. But something like the pureed beans (page 189) would be a wonderful meal with seared scallops or a mélange of sautéed vegetables.

COUSCOUS PILAF

DF · **Vg-***a* · **Ve-***a* · **GF-***a* | SERVES 6

Let's be clear—couscous is basically just really small pasta, not a whole grain. But it "cooks" (more like steams) so fast without any attention, it's a busy cook's best friend. A pilaf is merely dressed-up rice cooked with a little stock and some seasonings, for a little extra effort. I like to use organic, gluten-free or durum wheat couscous made from imported grains, so I can avoid glyphosate.

2 tablespoons unrefined, cold-pressed, extra-virgin olive oil or ghee

¾ cup diced onion or shallot

2 cups chicken stock, vegetable stock, or water

1 tablespoon red wine vinegar

¾ teaspoon sea salt (use more if your stock is unsalted or if you use water)

Freshly ground black pepper

1 (10-ounce) box couscous (1½ cups couscous)

⅓ cup almonds or pistachios, toasted and chopped (optional)

⅓ cup fresh herbs, chopped: flat-leaf parsley, cilantro, mint, dill, or a combo (optional)

½ cup pomegranate seeds or dried currants (optional)

In a medium-size saucepan, heat the oil over medium heat. Add the onion and sauté until tender and translucent, 3 to 6 minutes (shallots take less time).

Add the stock, vinegar, salt, and pepper to taste and bring to a boil over high heat. Turn off the heat and stir in the couscous. Cover and allow to sit for 10 minutes, or until the liquid is absorbed by the couscous.

Stir in the nuts, herbs, and pomegranate seeds (if using).

---

tips

Cauliflower rice can be added to the dish without adjusting the amount of couscous; add after the onion becomes tender. If the cauliflower is raw, sauté for a few minutes until tender. If the cauliflower rice is frozen, no need to sauté before adding the stock.

Use the Seed Out brand 60 Second Pomegranate Deseeder to remove pomegranate seeds fast and easy.

MAKE IT GLUTEN-FREE

Simmer 1 cup of quinoa with 1¾ cups of water instead of the couscous.

MAKE IT VEGAN

Use unrefined olive oil; vegetable stock or water.

SALSA RICE

Vg　Ve　GF　|　SERVES 4

One of my OCD pleasures is finishing a container of something or efficiently using up leftovers. Salsa never gets wasted in my house because we'll use it on eggs and tortillas, with chips and crudités, in my slow cooker chicken tacos, or cooked with rice. Salsa Rice tastes similar to a Spanish-style version but it requires less work, since you don't have to chop anything. I serve this with refried beans and an easy vegetable, such as sautéed kale or grilled zucchini for a quick, plant-based dinner or as the base for a burrito.

1 cup long-grain white or basmati rice

½ cup prepared salsa, red or green

¼ teaspoon sea salt

2 teaspoons unrefined avocado oil or extra-virgin olive oil

Place all the ingredients plus 1½ cups of water in a medium-size saucepan and bring to a boil over high heat. Lower the heat to low and simmer the rice, covered, for 18 minutes, or until the water is fully absorbed and the rice is tender. Do not lift the lid or stir the rice while it is cooking.

After the rice is cooked, it can continue to sit in the saucepan, covered, off the heat until ready to serve, up to 1 hour.

↓

tip

You can use brown rice in this recipe, but you will need to cook it for 45 to 55 minutes.

CAULI-RICE and QUINOA PESTO BOWL

Ve GF Vg-*a* DF-*a* | SERVES 4

This is actually a take on my most favorite quick meal of all, Not-Fried Rice, in Kitchen Matters. I love this combo so much that I always have the components on hand: I precook quinoa and freeze it, make pesto and freeze it in ice cube trays, and always have frozen cauliflower rice stashed in the freezer. Although I especially like quinoa for its high protein content, any cooked grain or lentils work well here.

1 tablespoon ghee (ghee with garlic is delicious here) or unrefined, cold-pressed, extra-virgin olive oil

4 cups raw cauliflower rice, fresh or frozen (see page 142)

4 cups cooked quinoa (see page 323)

Sea salt and freshly ground black pepper

6 to 8 tablespoons of your favorite pesto (pages 321–322)

2 handfuls of fresh baby spinach (optional)

In a large skillet, heat the ghee over medium heat. Add the cauliflower rice and sauté until tender, about 5 minutes, stirring often.

Add the cooked quinoa plus a pinch each of salt and pepper and sauté until warmed through, about 4 minutes.

Stir in the pesto and combine well. Add spinach, if using, and toss until just wilted. Serve warm or at room temperature.

↓

tips

This is also delicious with a fried or poached egg on top.

EVEN QUICKER

Buy cooked quinoa in the freezer section or from the supermarket salad bar.

MAKE IT VEGAN

Use olive oil; dairy-free pesto; do not add egg.

WARM POTATO SALAD with MUSTARD SEED DRESSING

Vg GF | SERVES 6

Potatoes may not be my favorite starchy vegetable, but give me some warm boiled spuds with a drizzle of olive oil, salt, and pepper, and I am in heaven. Potatoes are more nutritious than they get credit for because they are often ruined by peeling (most of the nutrition is in the skin and just underneath,) deep-frying, and overwhelming them with cream and fat. I like my potatoes light and fresh with a little crunch and zing—which is where this salad comes in. Take the time to prepare the rest of the ingredients for this dish while the potatoes are cooking and it will be ready in a flash. Although I love this warm, it holds up well at room temperature and is the perfect potluck dish all year long.

↓

tips

The potatoes may be flattened gently after being cooked, if desired.

To ensure the potatoes cook evenly, always start raw potatoes in room-temperature or cold water rather than adding them to already boiling water to cook.

2 pounds tiny baby potatoes, left whole, or Yukon Gold or red potatoes cut into 2-inch pieces

¼ cup whole-grain mustard

2 tablespoons unrefined, cold-pressed, extra-virgin olive oil

½ teaspoon sea salt

Freshly ground black pepper

½ cup chopped scallion

¼ cup capers, drained from brine

2 celery stalks with leaves left on, sliced

¼ cup pitted green olives, chopped

Place the potatoes in a large saucepan and cover with room-temperature water. Bring to a boil, lower the heat to a simmer, and cook until fork-tender, about 20 minutes. Drain.

In a serving bowl, whisk together the mustard, olive oil, salt, and pepper to taste.

Add the warm potatoes and toss to coat.

Add the scallion, capers, celery and celery leaves, and olives. Toss and serve warm, room temperature, or cold.

CHIPOTLE SWEET POTATO PANCAKES

| Ve | GF | DF-*a* | SERVES 4; MAKES ABOUT 9 PANCAKES |

Sweet potatoes are such a nutrient-dense, versatile vegetable. I love how they can go savory or sweet, but I don't love that it takes an hour (or more) to roast a whole sweet potato. Ricing the sweet potato into small, rice-size pieces allows me to create a patty from a raw state and ensure that it will cook through. I love serving these with something creamy, such as mashed avocado or cream cheese, to balance out the heat from the chipotle. But I've also eaten leftovers for breakfast the next day with sautéed spinach and a fried egg on top. My son suggests topping the patties with pulled barbecued chicken and ranch dressing!

tip

MAKE IT DAIRY-FREE

Use avocado, olive, or coconut oil; vegan cream cheese.

3 large eggs

1 medium-size sweet potato (8 ounces), cut into 2-inch chunks (I leave the peel on)

¾ cup blanched almond flour

1 teaspoon pure maple syrup

1 teaspoon cider vinegar

1½ teaspoons garlic powder or granulated garlic

1½ teaspoons paprika

1 teaspoon chipotle powder (or sub half smoked paprika for less heat)

1 teaspoon sea salt

½ cup finely chopped scallion (use a food processor if you like, but it will turn out better if you chop by hand)

2 tablespoons unrefined avocado oil, extra-virgin olive oil, coconut oil, or ghee

SERVING SUGGESTIONS: herb cream cheese (I like Kite Hill vegan chive), sliced avocado, sprouts, any kind, although I favor broccoli sprouts

Beat the eggs in a large bowl.

Put the sweet potato chunks in a food processor fitted with the metal S blade and pulse until it has the consistency finer than rice; you should have 2 cups of "rice." Transfer the sweet potato rice to the bowl with the beaten eggs. Add the almond flour, maple syrup, vinegar, spices, salt, and scallion to the sweet potato mixture and combine well.

recipe continues →

Heat 1 tablespoon of the avocado oil in a large skillet over medium heat. Scoop ¼ cup of the mixture onto the hot pan and press down lightly to flatten. Cook until golden brown, 2 to 3 minutes; flip, and cook for 2 to 3 minutes on the other side. Repeat until you've used up the entire mixture, adding additional oil as needed.

Serve with herb cream cheese or mashed avocado on top, garnished with sprouts if you like. Or freeze in between sheets of waxed or parchment paper.

SWEET POTATO COINS

Vg **Ve** **GF** | SERVES 4 AS A SIDE DISH

This is one of my default side dishes when I have little time for prep or cooking. I use the same preparation for regular potatoes, as well. I always keep the skin—it's less work, more fiber, and holds the shape of the sweet potatoes. My kids love these "coins" to dip into dressings, mustard, or dips, such as the Loaded Black Bean Dip (page 115). They're especially good with the Instant Pot Creamy Dijon Chicken (page 203).

2 medium-size sweet potatoes, any variety, sliced into ⅛-inch-thick rounds with the skin on

2 tablespoons unrefined, cold-pressed, extra-virgin olive oil, coconut oil, or avocado oil

1 teaspoon sea salt

¼ teaspoon freshly ground black pepper

Preheat the oven to 425°F and line a baking sheet with unbleached parchment paper.

In a large bowl, toss the sweet potato slices with the oil. Arrange them in one layer on the baking sheet and sprinkle with the salt and pepper.

Bake for 10 to 12 minutes, or until crispy on the outside and soft in the inside.

NOODLE and VEGGIE CURRY BOWL

`DF` `Vg-a` `Ve-a` `GF-a` | SERVES 4

Every January, I challenge myself to a pantry/freezer cleanout. But that doesn't mean I toss out food; instead, I use up as much as possible without grocery shopping. I become a little obsessed with finishing bags and containers of whatnot and making space in my freezer again. It is such a satisfying feeling knowing that I am saving money, being efficient, and not contributing to the huge problem of food waste. This recipe came about one January weeknight when I wanted to use up a few bags of frozen vegetables and a couple of packets of ramen noodles. It's a brothier, soupy version of the Quick Thai Curry recipe in my first cookbook, Kitchen Matters. Thai curries are a really fast, healthful meal if you have a good premade curry paste, a staple in my fridge at all times. Read your labels to make sure you are getting all-natural ingredients.

8 to 12 ounces noodles of choice (see tip)

1 tablespoon unrefined, virgin coconut oil

½ large onion, diced

3 to 4 tablespoons curry paste, such as Mae Ploy or Mae Anong brand (I prefer yellow)

½ teaspoon ground turmeric

1 (14-ounce) can full-fat coconut milk

2 tablespoons coconut palm sugar

4 cups vegetable stock or water (or use more coconut milk and less stock for a thicker soup)

3 tablespoons shoyu, tamari, or coconut aminos (or use Asian fish sauce for traditional flavor, although not vegan)

4 cups mixed chopped fresh and/or frozen vegetables (see tip)

Fresh cilantro, for garnish

1 lime, quartered

Bring a pot of water with kosher salt to a boil. Add the noodles and, following the package directions, cook until al dente. Drain and divide among individual bowls.

Meanwhile, in a large saucepan, heat the oil over medium heat. Add the onion and sauté until translucent, about 4 minutes.

recipe continues →

tips

Almost anything goes here: carrots, cauliflower, snap peas, shelled peas, eggplant, green beans, broccoli, cabbage, kale, bell peppers, potatoes, butternut squash, sweet potatoes are all favorites. Try to add denser, fresh vegetables (e.g., sweet potatoes) earlier than quick-cooking (e.g., snap peas) or frozen vegetables, so that everything is cooked and tender at the same time.

There are so many ways you can adapt this recipe I don't have the space to write them all out! You can use any noodle that you want, from spaghetti to glass noodles to kelp noodles to spiralized vegetables. For nonvegetable noodles, it's best to cook them separately to avoid making the broth too starchy. For spiralized vegetable noodles, feel free to drop them into the broth at the last minute and cook until you achieve the desired tenderness.

Add the curry paste and turmeric and sauté for 1 minute, breaking up the curry paste. Whisk in the coconut milk and sugar and bring to a simmer.

Add the stock, shoyu, and vegetables and bring to a boil. Lower the heat to a simmer and cook until the vegetables are tender. The amount of time will depend on which vegetables you use, but figure 5 to 15 minutes. Pour the vegetables and broth on top of the noodles in each bowl. Top with fresh cilantro and a squeeze of fresh lime juice.

↓

tips

This can be either a side or a main: If you use all veg and spiralized veg, it's great as a side. If you use rice noodles and peas and winter squash, it's a wonderful main.

MAKE IT GLUTEN-FREE

Use vegetable or gluten-free noodles; gluten-free tamari or coconut aminos.

MAKE IT VEGAN

Do not use Asian fish sauce.

PASTA with VEGAN EGGPLANT BOLOGNESE

Vg Ve GF-a | SERVES 6 AS A SIDE DISH

I adapted this recipe from the website of Jovial Foods. Jovial has a range of products, from pastas, tomatoes, and flours, which are all made with clean, organic ingredients. I use its brown rice caserecce here, but you can use your favorite. It's all about the sauce, anyway: This sauce tastes as though it has been simmering all day on the stove, but in reality it is superquick to come together. Eggplants and mushrooms have a hearty, earthy heft to them, making them a great stand-in for the traditional beef, especially in the summer when eggplants are in season and you're looking for a lighter dish. This is also fabulous on pasta alternatives, such as spaghetti squash.

↓

tips

—

EVEN QUICKER

Use precleaned and presliced mushrooms.

MAKE IT GLUTEN-FREE

Use certified gluten-free pasta.

1 medium-size eggplant, peeled and cubed

8 ounces fresh cremini mushrooms, caps wiped clean with a paper towel

½ medium-size onion, cut into 4 pieces

1 garlic clove

3 tablespoons unrefined, cold-pressed, extra-virgin olive oil

1 tablespoon finely chopped fresh parsley

1 (18-ounce) jar crushed tomatoes

1½ teaspoons sea salt

Pinch of dried oregano

Pinch of dried thyme

Pinch of dried basil, or a few small leaves fresh basil

Pinch of freshly ground black pepper

12 ounces of your favorite pasta, such as penne or orecchiette, or a pasta substitute (see page 182)

Place the eggplant, mushrooms, onion, and garlic in a food processor and pulse to a coarse chop.

Heat the oil in a large skillet over medium heat. Add the parsley and chopped vegetables. Cover and cook over low heat for 5 minutes.

Add the tomatoes, salt, oregano, thyme, basil, and pepper. Cook, covered, over medium heat, for 20 minutes, or until the sauce thickens.

Cook the pasta according to the package instructions.

Toss the pasta with the sauce and serve.

STAND-INS FOR PASTA

I grew up eating *a lot* of pasta, but nowadays, I make it very occasionally and in much smaller portions (no more than 1 cup of cooked pasta at one meal for me). It is very easy to overeat! I also try to incorporate a lot of vegetables with the pasta so it's not just a bowl of processed flour that will spike your blood sugar.

I know how easy it is to boil a pot of pasta and add almost anything to it for a superquick meal, so I've included several recipes in this book. Since gluten can be hard to digest and inflammatory, and since a lot of wheat is now being sprayed with toxic glyphosate (see page 34), I like to change it up with pasta alternatives. Here are some of my favorites that can be substituted in any recipe that calls for traditional pasta.

GLUTEN-FREE PASTA

Choosing your product: The flours used to make gluten-free pasta can vary from brown rice, corn, and quinoa to soy and potato starch. Be careful of brown rice pastas if you don't know the origin of the rice, as some rice may be contaminated with arsenic. Although most gluten-free pastas aren't contaminated with glyphosate, they tend to be quite starchy and lacking fiber, which is detrimental to blood sugar stability. So, just because it's gluten-free, doesn't mean you can eat as much as you want.

Cooking GF pasta: I have a special method for cooking gluten-free pasta so that it doesn't clump, lose its shape, or cook unevenly. Keep in mind that different brands and especially different flour blends will take different amounts of time, but the technique is the same.

○ Boil plenty of water and add 1 tablespoon of kosher salt. (This is to flavor the pasta. No need to waste expensive sea salt here.)

○ Add the pasta and stir often. (This is so that the pasta doesn't stick together.) You do not need to add oil to any pasta while it cooks, gluten-free or otherwise.

○ When you add the pasta, set your timer for the least amount of time that the package directions indicate. For example, if the box says to cook for 7 to 10 minutes, I set my timer for 7 minutes.

○ Lower the heat so that the water simmers and is not at a raging boil. This is important. Rapid boiling is what causes GF pasta to lose its shape.

○ *Most important step*: When the timer goes off, turn off the heat and let the pasta remain in the hot water. Taste the pasta. It should still be a little hard. Scoop out a cup or two of pasta water and reserve.

○ Allow the pasta to sit in the hot water with the heat off until it reaches your desired tenderness, which means you may need to taste it every 30 seconds.

○ Drain and immediately toss with your sauce, pesto, or whatever. *Do not rinse pasta*, unless you want to use it in a cold dish. The starches on the outside of the pasta will help sauces, and so on, stick. Use the reserved pasta water to add extra moisture to the pasta as needed. Keep in mind, gluten-free pasta does not sit as well as regular pasta, so try to serve it immediately or at the least, keep that reserved pasta water on hand in case.

LEGUME PASTA

If the legume pasta contains no gluten-grain flour, it is also a gluten-free pasta, since legumes do not contain gluten. Pastas made from lentils, chickpeas, black beans, and edamame are very popular because the fiber and protein content is much higher than regular pasta. The taste can be stronger, which you will notice if you're eating the pasta plain with butter. Cook legume pasta in the same method outlined for gluten-free pasta.

SHIRATAKI NOODLES

Shirataki noodles, a.k.a. Miracle Noodles, are a Japanese noodle made from the konjac plant. They have no calories and no carbs, making them ideal for pretty much any diet out there. Traditional shirataki noodles consist of mostly water and a soluble fiber called glucomannan, which has been shown to improve gut health because it contains prebiotics to nourish the good bacteria, reduce your risk of heart disease, and can help you lose weight by keeping you feeling fuller for longer. There are otherwise no nutrients in shirataki noodles. The texture is slightly rubbery, but they have no flavor if prepared properly. Some varieties of shirataki noodles contain soy or oats, so read your labels.

Here's how to prepare traditional shirataki noodles:

- Remove the noodles from the package, place in a colander, and rinse under cold water. They have a fishy smell—that's normal.

- Boil the noodles for 3 minutes and drain.

- Place the drained noodles back into the pot with nothing else, over medium heat, and dry-fry them until you remove the excess moisture. Now you can add your sauce, or other additions.

KELP NOODLES

Kelp noodles are normally made from a seaweed called kelp, plus water and sodium alginate, also derived from seaweed. They are translucent and low in carbohydrates and calories. Kelp noodles contain a lot of iodine, which we need but too much can affect thyroid function, so I wouldn't eat these every day. To me, the flavor is totally neutral, but if not prepared properly, the texture is squeaky and crunchy. Here's how I prepare them:

- In a medium-size bowl, soak the kelp noodles with hot water to cover, the juice of ½ lemon, and 1 tablespoon of baking soda until softened, about 20 minutes. Rinse and drain very well and pat dry with paper towels. If necessary, cut up the noodles with scissors to make smaller noodles. They are now ready to serve.

SPAGHETTI SQUASH

Spaghetti squash is a low-calorie, low-carbohydrate winter squash whose flesh, when cooked, can be raked into strands that resemble spaghetti. It is high in fiber and contains vitamins C and B$_6$ and manganese. Spaghetti squash is a little bland and slightly sweet. I like serving it with big flavors, such as lots of garlic, crushed red pepper flakes, veggies, and herbs.

My favorite method to prepare spaghetti squash is not the quickest, ironically. It can be microwaved, cooked in a pressure cooker, boiled, and steamed. But I prefer the flavor and texture after it has been roasted.

- Cut the squash in half lengthwise through the stem end. Scoop out the seeds.

- Rub the inside of the squash with olive oil and sprinkle with salt and pepper. Roast, cut side down, in a 375°F oven until a fork inserted

continues →

between the skin and flesh goes in easily and can pull the squash away from the skin. Depending on the size of the squash, this can take 30 to 45 minutes. Flip cut side up once it comes out of the oven. Rake the strands with a fork.

SPIRALIZED VEGETABLES

I think spiralizing vegetables started with zucchini (a.k.a. "zoodles"), but now you can spiralize so many veggies: sweet potatoes, beets, parsnips, butternut squash, and more. You can purchase a spiralizer (or even a Y-shaped peeler will do the trick) to make your own at home, or find already spiralized vegetables in the produce or freezer section of the grocery store. Vegetables in the shape of noodles won't fool anyone, but they are a much more nutritious, whole food option if you're looking for something beyond traditional pasta. And like traditional pastas, they lend themselves well to a variety of sauces and toppings.

○ To cook spiralized vegetables, sauté in oil for 2 to 7 minutes, depending on the water content of the vegetable (zucchini takes a couple of minutes; butternut squash can take 5 to 7 minutes.) The harder vegetables can be roasted at 400°F for about 10 minutes. Some people enjoy zucchini noodles raw with sauce, such as pesto.

CREAMY VEGAN MUSHROOM PASTA

Vg   Ve   **GF-a** | SERVES 6 AS A SIDE DISH

This pasta dish tastes decadent, but it is relatively light. I opt to use a wonderful, clean vegan cream cheese in place of a heavier dairy ingredient like the standard mascarpone or crème fraîche. The mushrooms and stock also add a richness here. Truffle oil is an indulgence but really adds an extra flavor note.

Kosher salt, for seasoning pasta water

1 pound pasta, such as tagliatelle, pappardelle, or orecchiette (really, whatever you like)

2 tablespoons unrefined, cold-pressed, extra-virgin olive oil

4 garlic cloves, chopped

10 ounces hen of the woods mushrooms, a.k.a. maitake, chopped or broken apart with your hands, or oyster mushrooms, sliced

7 ounces (more or less) shiitake mushrooms, stemmed, caps wiped clean with a damp paper towel, and cut into thin slices

1 sprig thyme

¾ teaspoon sea salt, plus more to taste

½ teaspoon freshly ground pepper, or to taste

¼ cup dry white wine, or 1 tablespoon freshly squeezed lemon juice + 3 tablespoons pasta water

1¾ cups mushroom or vegetable stock (or chicken stock, if not necessary to be vegan)

6 tablespoons Kite Hill almond milk cream cheese or soft vegan cheese, plain or chive

Truffle oil, for drizzling (optional)

Chopped fresh chives or flat-leaf parsley, for garnish (optional)

Bring a large pot of water to a boil, season generously with kosher salt, and cook the pasta according to the package directions.

Meanwhile, in a large sauté pan, heat the olive oil over medium heat. Add the garlic and sauté for 30 seconds, or until fragrant. Add the mushrooms, thyme, salt, and pepper and sauté until softened, about 6 minutes.

Add the wine and cook until the liquid is almost completely absorbed.

recipe continues →

↓

tips

———

Always remember the importance of saving some pasta water before you drain the pasta, so you can use it to supplement the sauce. Pasta water is richer and more flavorful than stock, for example. And you don't need extra oil.

You can also add the zest of a small lemon when you add the stock.

If you're not vegan, you can serve with grated Parmigiano-Reggiano on the side.

EVEN QUICKER

Buy cleaned, presliced mushrooms of any variety.

MAKE IT GLUTEN-FREE

Use gluten-free pasta.

MAKE IT VEGAN

Use mushroom or vegetable stock; vegan cheese.

Stir in the mushroom stock and cook until reduced by half, about 10 minutes. Whisk in the cream cheese and cook until slightly thickened but still saucy. Taste for seasoning.

When the pasta is al dente, remove a cup or two of pasta water and reserve. Drain the pasta and place directly in the pan with the mushroom sauce (it's okay if the pasta is very wet; the water will help keep things from drying out). Toss gently to coat and add some pasta water if the sauce starts to lose its moisture.

Remove the thyme sprig. Drizzle with truffle oil and a sprinkle of chopped fresh chives, if desired, and serve immediately.

WHITE BEAN PUREE
with GARLIC and SAGE

`Vg` `Ve` `GF` | **SERVES 4 TO 6**

This dish is what I make when I am too tired to think about what to make. I can come home from a long day of work (which for me is cooking) and create a fiber- and protein-rich meal in minutes if I have precooked beans in the pantry, which I always do! If we're eating a meatless meal, this bean puree is our entrée with some veggies and a salad on the side. But I'll also serve this comforting puree as a bed for Perfect Seared Scallops (page 258) or a simple sliced steak. Some advice: the garlic cloves and sage leaves are what everyone fights over, so you may want to make lots more.

↓

tip
—

These beans can also be made without pureeing. Simply add to the saucepan with the can liquid and heat through. Can be mashed with a potato masher, as well.

---

2 (15-ounce) cans white beans, such as cannellini or great northern, with ½ cup liquid from the can

2 tablespoons unrefined, cold-pressed, extra-virgin olive oil, plus more for finishing, if desired

6 large garlic cloves, sliced

12 fresh sage leaves, or a 3-inch sprig rosemary

Sea salt and freshly ground black pepper

Pour the beans and reserved liquid into a food processor fitted with the metal S blade. Process until smooth, or leave a little texture, if desired.

In a medium-size saucepan, heat the olive oil over medium heat. Add the garlic and sage to the oil and sauté until everything is fragrant, 1 to 2 minutes. Remove the garlic and sage from the oil with a slotted spoon and set aside in a small bowl or plate.

Pour the pureed beans into the same saucepan and stir, cooking over medium heat until warmed through, about 5 minutes. Do not heat over high heat because the beans will scorch. Season to taste with salt and pepper. Transfer to a shallow serving bowl and sprinkle with the reserved garlic and sage. Drizzle with additional oil, if desired.

WHEN IN DOUBT, SAUTÉ IT OUT

When I am starving and I need something fast, or when I am trying to clean out the fridge so the odds and ends don't go to waste, I make what I call Not-Fried Rice and it probably happens more than once a week. It's a fifteen-minute meal for which no recipe is required and the results are utterly satisfying and delicious. In *Kitchen Matters*, I included different variations on Not-Fried Rice, my favorite being an Italian version with tomatoes, mushrooms, and basil. Since then, I have taken many twists and turns on the basic premise of leftover rice sautéed with vegetables and/or protein, and now I will sauté *almost* anything and everything together, rice or no rice. As long as you know the basic formula for what can and cannot go into the pan and the order in which you add things to the pan, and that you need some seasoning, you'll get the hang of it in no time. Here are some basic tips to get you started:

o You can sauté just about anything together, but this sauté works best with leftover cooked grains or lentils, cooked animal protein, and fresh, frozen, or leftover cooked vegetables.

o You don't need to use any grains nor do you need to use animal protein.

o Try to avoid using overly wet, soupy ingredients; otherwise, the mixture can get goopy.

o Use the largest skillet you have, or use a wok.

o Have all your ingredients prepped and ready to go, because this is going to be quick!

o Add any kind of fat that works with your ingredients—olive oil, avocado oil, coconut oil, ghee, duck fat. Use enough to coat the bottom of the skillet, 1 to 2 tablespoons, depending on the size of your skillet.

o I usually start every sauté with chopped garlic and crushed red pepper flakes. You can add ginger and/or scallions or curry paste at the beginning, too. Sauté until just fragrant, about 1 minute.

o Add your denser, raw vegetables first, such as carrots and small cauliflower florets, and sauté for a couple of minutes, until no longer raw but still crisp. Then, keep adding vegetables in the order of how long they need to cook. Things like asparagus, mushrooms and kale could go next. Spinach, snow peas, diced zucchini might go after. Then, frozen vegetables, including frozen riced vegetables. Again, cook each vegetable until no longer raw, but not totally tender yet. Next, leftover cooked vegetables. Season with salt and freshly ground black pepper.

o Next, add cooked animal protein (if using) and sauté until warmed through.

o Next, add cooked grains (if using) or legumes and sauté until warmed through.

o Lastly, stir in fresh herbs and other seasonings, such as soy sauce (omit for gluten-free), hot sauce, leftover tahini sauce, or vinegar. Taste as you go and keep playing around with the seasonings. Top with gomasio or sesame seeds, Parmesan cheese or feta (omit for vegan), chopped nuts or seeds, avocado, or your favorite sauce or dressing. You can't really mess this up. Repeat tomorrow.

Instant Pot

The Instant Pot multicooker has become a very popular appliance, specifically for its pressure cooker feature. It allows you to cook things like tougher cuts of meats, dried legumes, and bone broth in much less time.

I created these recipes because of the constant demand from my students and readers. And naturally, a cookbook with a theme of cooking more quickly lends itself to pressure cooker recipes. That said, you can adapt almost any recipe to an Instant Pot, but sometimes it doesn't cut the overall cook time by much, if at all. I like to make the most of the Instant Pot by focusing on recipes that take an hour or more (such as basic roasted sweet potatoes) in the oven or on the stove.

A FEW TIPS FOR INSTANT POT SUCCESS

Keep in mind, many Instant Pot/pressure cooker recipes can be a bit misleading. A recipe's cook time is not its total time. Pressure cookers take quite a bit of time to achieve pressure, especially when they are full of liquid. One hack to help your machine achieve pressure more quickly is to bring any liquid, such as stock, to a boil before adding it to the machine.

Another tip is that unlike slow cookers, when you double or triple a recipe for a pressure cooker, the cook time will need to be adjusted. There is no formula for how much time to add, unfortunately. But I usually tack on another couple of minutes.

If the food isn't cooked to perfection after you open the machine, no need to bring it to pressure again. Usually, a few minutes, covered, on the sauté program will cook everything to doneness.

Finally, while there are many multicooker brands out there, note that these recipes have only been tested with the Instant Pot. Please note, different models of the Instant Pot have different interfaces. If the directions in these recipes don't match the features of your model, please refer to your Instant Pot manual.

INSTANT POT LENTIL and BROWN RICE SOUP

GF DF Vg-*a* Ve-*a* | SERVES 4

This is probably the soup I make the most often and one that I learned from my mother, so I have been eating it for a loooong time. I usually make a big pot on Sunday for lunch or dinner and then leftovers go into thermoses the next day for school lunches. Sometimes I add tomatoes and sometimes not; brown rice is optional and cauliflower rice is a newer addition. The lentils provide plenty of protein and fiber, so you really don't need to add any grains if you don't want.

3 tablespoons unrefined, cold-pressed, extra-virgin olive oil or avocado oil

3 large carrots, diced

3 celery stalks, diced

1 large onion, diced

3 garlic cloves, minced

1 pound fresh tomatoes, peeled, seeded, and chopped, or 1 (18-ounce) jar, drained

8 cups vegetable or chicken stock

2 cups French lentils, picked over and rinsed (see tip)

2 sprigs thyme, or 1 teaspoon dried

2 teaspoons sea salt

Freshly ground black pepper

2 big handfuls fresh spinach, kale, or chard (ribs removed), chopped coarsely into large pieces

½ cup cooked brown rice, or add raw with lentils and increase liquid by an additional 1 cup

↓

tips

QUICK TIP

Bring your stock to a boil before adding it to the pot. This will reduce the time it takes for the machine to achieve pressure.

You can use whatever lentils you can find, such as black or Puy, but note that cook times may vary.

MAKE IT VEGAN

Use vegetable stock.

Press the SAUTÉ button and wait a couple of minutes for the insert to heat up. Add the oil, carrots, celery, onion, and garlic into the insert and sauté until tender, about 5 minutes.

Add the tomatoes and cook for 1 minute.

Add the stock, lentils, raw brown rice if not using cooked, thyme, salt, and pepper to taste. Press the KEEP WARM/CANCEL button to turn the machine off. Secure the lid on top of the insert and lock it closed. Make sure the vent is closed. Press MANUAL and make sure it's on HIGH PRESSURE. Set the time for 12 minutes.

Once the machine has stopped cooking, release the vent for a quick release. Open the lid and taste the rice and lentils for doneness. If both are tender, stir in the greens. Serve with the precooked rice (if using).

INSTANT POT LEMONY BARLEY and VEGETABLE SOUP

| Vg-*a* | Ve-*a* | GF-*a* | DF-*a* | | SERVES 6 |

Barley is one of the more fiber-rich grains, which makes it a good blood sugar stabilizer. It releases a nice starchiness in soup, which helps thicken it up a bit. Soups like this used to be reserved for the weekends when I had more time. But using the pressure cooker program on the Instant Pot has allowed me to include this in my weeknight dinner rotation.

2 tablespoons unrefined, cold-pressed, extra-virgin olive oil

1 onion, chopped

3 large carrots, sliced

3 celery stalks, chopped

4 garlic cloves, chopped finely

1 tablespoon herbes de Provence (see tip)

8 cups vegetable, chicken, or turkey stock

¾ cup uncooked barley (see tip) or brown rice

2 teaspoons sea salt

Freshly ground black pepper

2 to 4 tablespoons freshly squeezed lemon juice (I like more lemon)

5 ounces fresh baby spinach leaves (about 5 cups, packed)

Grated pecorino or Parmesan cheese (optional)

Press the SAUTÉ button and wait a couple of minutes for the insert to heat up. Add the oil, onion, carrots, celery, and garlic into the insert and sauté until tender, about 5 minutes. Add the herbes de Provence and stir.

Add the stock, barley, salt, and pepper to taste. Press the KEEP WARM/CANCEL button to turn the machine off. Secure the lid on top of the insert and lock closed. Make sure the vent is closed. Press MANUAL and make sure it's on HIGH PRESSURE. Set the time for 12 minutes.

Once the machine has stopped cooking, release the vent for a quick release. Open the lid and taste the barley for doneness, as well as salt. If tender, stir in the lemon juice and greens and serve. Garnish with grated pecorino or Parmesan cheese, if desired.

↓

tips

Herbes de Provence is a mixture of dried herbs common in the Provence region of France. This blend may contain any variation of rosemary, thyme, oregano, savory, and/or marjoram. If you don't have herbes de Provence, feel free to use any combination of these dried herbs to equal 1 tablespoon.

Uncooked barley: I like brands labeled "pearled" but that actually have a light brown color to the grains instead of a white color.

MAKE IT GLUTEN-FREE

Use brown rice instead of barley.

MAKE IT VEGAN

Use vegetable stock; do not add cheese.

INSTANT POT CHICKEN CHILI VERDE

GF **DF-a** | SERVES 6

We absolutely love all types of chili—vegan, meat, poultry, red, green, white, you name it. It's a great meal for game day with a topping bar, and leftovers can be stretched the next day over baked potatoes or tortilla chips for a nacho platter. This version is a little lighter than the classic beef with tomatoes, but still hearty and superflavorful. You can use boneless chicken if you want, but the bones add a nice richness and some collagen to the stew.

1 tablespoon unrefined, cold-pressed, extra-virgin olive oil or avocado oil

1 large onion, chopped

2 poblano chiles, stemmed, seeded, and chopped coarsely (see tip)

6 garlic cloves, chopped

1 to 2 jalapeño peppers, stemmed, seeded, and diced

1 tablespoon ground cumin

2 teaspoons dried oregano

1 teaspoon chili powder, or to taste

2 pounds bone-in, skinless chicken parts (breasts, thighs, and/or drumsticks)

12 ounces dried white or pinto beans (soaked if you have time), or 3 (15-ounce) cans cooked beans, drained and rinsed

12 ounces fresh tomatillos, husks removed, chopped coarsely, or 1 (16-ounce) jar good-quality salsa verde

2½ cups chicken or vegetable stock, preferably homemade

2 teaspoons sea salt, or more if stock is unsalted

½ cup chopped fresh cilantro

SUGGESTED TOPPINGS: shredded cabbage, sour cream, lime wedges, tortilla chips

↓

tips

Poblano chiles may also be labeled as pasilla peppers at the supermarket.

Soaking the beans for 6 to 8 hours will help make them more digestible and can shave 5 minutes off the cook time.

MAKE IT DAIRY-FREE

Do not serve with the sour cream (or use dairy-free sour cream); use vegan chips.

Preheat the Instant Pot using the SAUTÉ setting. Add the oil, onion, poblano, garlic, and jalapeño and sauté until just starting to soften, about 3 minutes.

Stir in the spices and add the chicken pieces.

Add the beans, tomatillos, stock, and salt. Turn the machine off. Secure the lid on and turn the vent knob to SEALED. Press MANUAL and make sure it's on HIGH PRESSURE, SET TIME for 30 minutes if using dried beans or 15 minutes if using canned beans.

recipe continues →

When the chili has finished cooking, turn the vent to VENTING to quickly release the pressure.

Open the lid and transfer the chicken to a cutting board or bowl. Remove and discard the bones. Break up the chicken into bite-size pieces.

Puree a little of the chili with an immersion blender or remove 1 cup and blend in a regular blender. Taste the chili for seasoning and add the chicken back to the pot. Serve with your desired accompaniments.

INSTANT POT CHICKEN TINGA

DF **GF-a** | SERVES 6

Tinga is a classic Mexican taco recipe where chicken is simmered in a rich chipotle tomato sauce. You can eat it in tortillas as you would any taco, but because the sauce is so good, I love it in a bowl over rice, quinoa, or cauliflower rice with seasonal vegetables. Tinga is also superdelicious on top of Baked Pinto Bean Tostadas (page 277), as the base for enchiladas, and even in the Taco Salad (page 80).

↓

tip

MAKE IT GLUTEN-FREE

Serve with gluten-free tortillas.

½ medium-size onion, peeled

2 large garlic cloves

1½ cups tomato puree, crushed tomatoes, or diced tomatoes

½ cup vegetable, chicken stock, or water

1¼ teaspoons sea salt, plus more to taste

1 teaspoon dried oregano

1 teaspoon ground cumin

⅛ teaspoon ground allspice

2 tablespoons cider vinegar

2 teaspoons unrefined avocado oil or extra-virgin olive oil

1 dried bay leaf

2 dried chipotle peppers (do not use canned)

2 pounds boneless, skinless chicken pieces (thighs work best)

FOR SERVING: warmed tortillas, avocado, fresh cilantro, diced onion

With the lid off, set the Instant Pot to SAUTÉ to preheat.

In a blender, combine the onion, garlic, tomato puree, stock, salt, oregano, cumin, allspice, and vinegar. Blend until smooth.

Heat the oil in the Instant Pot. Add the mixture from the blender as well as the bay leaf and dried chipotle. Bring to a simmer and turn the machine off.

Place the chicken pieces in the sauce and cover with the lid, locking it into place. Set the valve to SEALED and press MANUAL. Make sure it is set on HIGH PRESSURE and set timer for 9 minutes. When the machine has finished cooking, you can opt for a quick release (turn the valve to VENTING).

recipe continues →

Open the lid and turn off the machine. Then, set the machine to SAUTÉ. Transfer the chicken to a plate. Remove the bay leaf and smash the chipotle peppers a bit. Allow the sauce to simmer while you shred the meat with two forks. Taste the sauce for salt. (If you want the sauce to be spicy, blend the chipotle peppers and sauce with an immersion blender.) Transfer the chicken back into the sauce and serve.

INSTANT POT CREAMY DIJON CHICKEN

`GF` `DF-a` | **SERVES 4 TO 6**

Oh my stars, is this so good. The first time I made this, my kids were practically licking their plates. Who am I kidding? I was, too! This creamy, tangy sauce is everything. Great on chicken, fish, roasted vegetables, potatoes, and grains, did I leave anything out? This is elegant enough to serve to company, but with the speed of the Instant Pot, quick enough to make for a weeknight.

↓

tip

—

MAKE IT DAIRY-FREE

Use cashew butter and water or coconut milk.

8 (5- to 7-ounce) bone-in, skin-on, chicken thighs, or 4 (8- to 12-ounce) bone-in, skin-on chicken breasts

Kosher salt (use about 1¼ teaspoons)

Freshly ground black pepper

2 teaspoons unrefined, cold-pressed, extra-virgin olive oil

2 large shallots, diced

¼ cup dry white wine

1½ cups chicken or vegetable stock

3 tablespoons whole- or coarse-grain Dijon mustard

3 tablespoons smooth Dijon mustard

2 tablespoons raw cashew butter + 2 tablespoons water, or ¼ cup heavy cream or coconut milk

Coarsely chopped fresh parsley, for garnish (optional)

Preheat the Instant Pot on the SAUTÉ setting. Meanwhile, pat the chicken dry with paper towels and season both sides with salt and pepper.

Add the oil to the insert and add as much chicken, skin side down, as will fit in the bottom of the insert. Cook until browned, 5 to 7 minutes. Transfer the chicken to a plate and repeat with any remaining chicken that didn't fit into the pot, also transferring that to the plate.

Add the shallots to the pot and cook until softened, about 2 to 3 minutes. Add the wine, scrape up any browned bits at the bottom of the pot with a wooden spoon, and cook until evaporated, about 3 minutes.

recipe continues →

Stir in the stock and whole-grain Dijon and bring to a simmer. Return the chicken, skin side up, and add to the pan any juices that accumulated on the plate.

Turn the machine off. Lock the lid into place and set the valve to SEALED. Press MANUAL and make sure it's on HIGH PRESSURE for 10 minutes. The machine will take about 8 minutes to come up to pressure. After the timer goes off, switch the valve from SEALED to VENTING (i.e., do a quick release).

Transfer the chicken to a plate or platter. Turn the machine off and switch to SAUTÉ. Whisk the smooth Dijon mustard into the sauce and simmer until reduced slightly, about 3 minutes.

Whisk in the raw cashew butter mixture or cream. Taste and season the sauce with salt and pepper as needed. Serve the sauce with the chicken and garnish with parsley, if desired.

INSTANT POT WHOLE SWEET POTATOES

Vg Ve GF | MAKES 2 TO 4 SWEET POTATOES

There are certain favorite foods that I would make more often, such as whole roasted sweet potatoes, if they didn't take so long. Depending on the size, whole sweet potatoes can take over an hour in the oven. They're one of the most nutrient-dense foods out there and one I could eat at any meal, so cooking them in the Instant Pot has been a game changer for me. The key is adjusting the time according to the diameter of the sweet potato. Skinnier sweet potatoes take less time than wider.

1 cup cold water

2 to 4 (8-inch-circumference) sweet potatoes, scrubbed clean

Place the steamer rack inside the Instant Pot. Add the cold water and place the whole sweet potatoes on the rack.

Lock the lid into place. Set the valve to SEALED and cook on high pressure for 27 minutes. After the timer goes off, perform a natural release of 10 minutes.

↓

tips

To cut time in half, cut the potatoes in half, lengthwise.

Use a piece of kitchen twine to measure the circumference of the potatoes and then measure the twine on a ruler.

PRESSURE COOKING GUIDELINES
———

6 inches:
15–20 minutes

8 inches:
25–30 minutes

10 inches:
35–40 minutes

12 inches:
45–50 minutes

Natural release:
10–11 minutes

INSTANT POT BEEF BOLOGNESE (RAGU)

GF	DF-*a*		MAKES ENOUGH FOR 1 POUND OF PASTA

Although I prefer a veggie "Bolognese" like the eggplant and mushroom version on page 181, my kids like this one the best. The Instant Pot tenderizes the meat much better than a quick simmer on the stovetop and the flavor is more developed. You can create an Instant Soup (page 86) with leftovers and a few added veggies and cooked pasta for a Lasagne Soup.

1 tablespoon unrefined, cold-pressed, extra-virgin olive oil

½ red onion, diced finely

1 carrot, diced finely

1 celery stalk, diced finely

1 garlic clove, minced

Pinch of crushed red pepper flakes

1 pound grass-fed ground beef, preferably not the leanest percentage

½ cup dry red or white wine

2 tablespoons tomato paste

28 ounces crushed tomatoes, preferably jarred in glass

2 teaspoons sea salt

Freshly ground black pepper

Chopped fresh parsley or basil, to finish (optional)

Preheat the Instant Pot on the SAUTÉ setting until hot. Add the oil to the insert and let heat, then add the onion, carrot, and celery and sauté until tender, about 5 minutes.

Add the garlic and red pepper flakes and sauté until fragrant, about 1 minute.

Add the beef, and sauté, breaking the meat up into small pieces with a wooden spoon or spatula. Cook until browned and sizzling, 6 to 7 minutes.

Add the wine and scrape any bits stuck on the bottom of the insert. Add the tomato paste, tomatoes, salt, and pepper to taste and bring to a simmer. Lock the lid in place, set valve to SEALED, and turn the machine off. Press MANUAL and make sure the machine is set to HIGH PRESSURE and set for 15 minutes.

After 15 minutes, release the pressure by turning the valve to VENTING. Once the machine has finished venting, open the lid and stir in the parsley, if desired. Taste for seasoning and serve.

tips

If you like a traditional Bolognese with heavy cream, stir ¼ cup of heavy cream or ¼ cup plain vegan cream cheese into the pot after the pressure has been released.

I don't use chipotle peppers in aluminum cans for the same reason I don't use canned tomatoes. The acidity of the peppers and vinegary sauce promote leaching of BPA and aluminum.

MAKE IT DAIRY-FREE

Do not use the cream or use vegan cream cheese for the above version.

INSTANT POT BEEF STEW

DF **Vg-a** **Ve-a** **GF-a** | SERVES 6 TO 8

Beef stew is nothing new, but whenever I make it and post it on my social media, so many people ask me for the recipe. It's a fall and winter staple in my kitchen and I hardly ever make it the same way twice, since I use whatever vegetables I have on hand. Even though I don't love beef, I really enjoy the vegetables in the sauce, which I will pair with some polenta or a cauliflower mash. Cozy food at its best in a fraction of the time!

2 pounds boneless stew meat, such as chuck or bottom round, cubed into 2-inch pieces, patted dry with paper towels

2 teaspoons dried thyme, or 1 big sprig fresh

1 teaspoon dried marjoram

1 teaspoon sea salt

Freshly ground black pepper

2 tablespoons unrefined, cold-pressed, extra-virgin olive oil

1 onion, chopped

1 carrot, chopped

1 celery stalk, chopped

2 large garlic cloves, chopped

¼ cup flour (all-purpose, einkorn, gluten-free blend, or tapioca flour)

2 tablespoons tomato paste

2 tablespoons shoyu, tamari, or coconut aminos

2½ cups beef or chicken stock (can substitute red wine for part of the stock)

4 to 5 cups of any combination of the following vegetables:

Cremini mushrooms, wiped clean and halved

Parsnips, cut into 2-inch pieces

Rutabagas, cut into 2-inch chunks

Yukon Gold or red potatoes, cut into 2-inch chunks

Carrots, cut into 2-inch pieces

Turnips, cut into 2-inch pieces

1 cup frozen green peas, thawed

Finely chopped fresh flat-leaf parsley, for garnish

tips

Peas can thaw while stew cooks.

MAKE IT GLUTEN-FREE

Use gluten-free flour blend or tapioca flour; gluten-free tamari or coconut aminos.

MAKE IT VEGAN

Swap in 2 pounds of veg for the meat and use vegetable stock instead of beef stock.

Season the beef with half of the thyme, half of the marjoram, and the salt and a few grinds of pepper. Using the SAUTÉ setting, preheat the Instant Pot.

Arrange the meat in one layer in the insert without crowding and cook until browned on all sides, 8 to 12 minutes. Transfer to a plate and repeat with the remaining meat.

Add the oil, then onion, carrot, celery, and garlic, and sauté until they just start to soften, about 5 minutes. Stir in the flour, tomato paste, and remaining thyme and marjoram, and cook until fragrant, about 2 minutes.

Add the shoyu, stock, meat, and all the vegetables except peas. Turn the machine off. Cover and set the vent to SEALED. Press MANUAL and make sure it's on HIGH PRESSURE to cook for 25 minutes. When the machine has finished cooking, switch the vent to VENTING. Open the lid and stir the peas into the stew. Serve garnished with parsley.

Mains

Ironically, I keep my proteins pretty straightforward and I would be perfectly content with a simple piece of fish or basic legumes most nights. But when I asked my students and blog readers where they found themselves to be the most challenged, the answer was unequivocally in the entrée department. Proteins, in general, can take longer to cook, and it can be difficult to find a wide variety of nutritious, family-friendly entrée recipes that are fast and easy.

My goal is for you to have most of these recipes on the table within thirty minutes. If you have less practice in the kitchen, such tasks as chopping and measuring may take you longer than for someone who has a higher comfort level. However, the recipes are still doable for any level, even if you are just stepping into your kitchen. Like any skill in life, the more you practice, the more fluid you will be. In fact, once you make any of these recipes enough times, you may be able to cook them from memory.

Another skill that comes with familiarity is the ability to eyeball measurements (with nonbaking recipes; baking needs to be exact). One day, take a few minutes to measure into the palm of your hand different measurements of salt and allow the visual of the amounts to make an impression on you. You'd be surprised how much more quickly you will cook without measuring every ingredient. Of course, the first time you make any recipe, it is always a good idea to read through it entirely and make it the way it is written. But once you're off and running, you will be eyeballing ingredients quicker than quick!

QUICKER CHICKEN MARBELLA

GF **DF** | SERVES 6

One of my first and favorite cookbooks is The Silver Palate Cookbook *from the well-known former New York City catering company by the same name. To date myself, I've owned the book since 1987! The recipe that I have made the most is Chicken Marbella, a delightful combination of sweet, tangy, and salty. Unfortunately, it's not always in the cards for me to marinate something overnight and cook it for an entire hour the next day. Plus, the original recipe called for an entire cup of brown sugar. Double yikes! So, I came up with a streamlined (and less sweet) version of the recipe with boneless, skinless chicken cooked on the stovetop, which can be ready in less than thirty minutes from start to finish.*

6 small boneless, skinless chicken breasts (thick end lightly pounded to make the breast even throughout), or up to 12 boneless, skinless thighs (the goal is to be able to fit everything in one pan)

2 teaspoons sea salt

Freshly ground black pepper

2 tablespoons unrefined, cold-pressed, extra-virgin olive oil or unrefined avocado oil

4 garlic cloves, minced

1 tablespoon dried oregano

¼ cup pitted Spanish green olives

¼ cup capers, drained from brine

8 prunes, halved

2 bay leaves

2 tablespoons white wine vinegar (see tip)

2 tablespoons pure maple syrup

1 cup chicken or vegetable stock

Finely chopped, fresh flat-leaf parsley or cilantro, for garnish (optional)

Pat the chicken dry with paper towels. Season both sides with salt and pepper.

Heat the oil in a large (at least 12-inch) skillet over medium heat. Add the chicken (the oil should be sizzling) in one layer without crowding and cook until browned on the underside, about 2½ to 3 minutes. Turn over and brown the other side, about 2½ to 3 minutes. You don't need to cook the chicken through at this point.

recipe continues →

↓

tips

If you don't have white wine vinegar, use red, which is what the original recipe calls for.

Patting animal protein dry with paper towels before searing ensures you will achieve a nice brown color and good flavor. If protein is wet, you will end up poaching or steaming it.

If breasts are very large (more than 12 ounces each), split them lengthwise to make two thinner cutlets from each breast.

For searing animal protein, consider getting a "splatter screen" for your skillet to prevent oil from creating a huge mess all over your stovetop. Cooking and eating are fun. Cleaning grease off your stovetop is not!

Remove the chicken from the skillet and set aside. Finish cooking the remaining chicken and remove from the pan. Add the garlic, oregano, olives, capers, prunes, and bay leaves to the skillet and sauté for a minute. Pour in the vinegar, maple syrup, and stock and scrape the bottom of the skillet to deglaze the pan. Bring the liquid to a simmer. Add the chicken back to the skillet and cook over medium heat until cooked through, about 5 minutes, flipping over at about the 2½-minute point.

You can put a meat thermometer in the thickest part of the chicken sideways to check the temperature. If you want to eat it right away, wait for it to get to 165°F. If you are going to let the chicken rest for a few minutes, you can turn off the heat when the temperature is 155° to 160°F. Serve with the pan juices and garnish with parsley.

WEEKNIGHT ARROZ CON POLLO

`GF` `DF` `Vg-a` `Ve-a` | SERVES 6

My Puerto Rican mother-in-law gave me a cookbook when I was first married, titled Puerto Rican Cookery. *Hint, hint. The first recipe I made was the Latin American classic arroz con pollo, the ultimate one-pot chicken and rice dish. Over the years, I tweaked the recipe to use more accessible ingredients and the latest iteration is a quick version with boneless, skinless chicken instead of bone-in, which takes much longer. By no means is this an authentic recipe, but it is doable and delicious!*

1½ teaspoons garlic powder or granulated garlic

1½ teaspoons dried oregano

1 teaspoon paprika

2 teaspoons sea salt

Freshly ground black pepper

1½ pounds boneless, skinless chicken pieces (breasts and/or thighs), patted dry and cut into 2-inch pieces (thighs can be cut in half)

2 tablespoons unrefined, cold-pressed, extra-virgin, olive or avocado oil

1 green bell pepper, seeded and chopped

1 onion, chopped

3 garlic cloves, chopped

¾ cup crushed or diced tomatoes, or 1 large fresh tomato, diced

1½ cups uncooked long-grain white rice

2 cups chicken or vegetable stock, or water

1 tablespoon capers, drained from brine

⅓ cup small whole pimiento-stuffed olives

½ cup frozen peas

Chopped fresh cilantro (see tip; optional)

In a medium-size bowl, mix together the garlic powder, oregano, paprika, 1 teaspoon of the salt, and a few grinds of black pepper. Add the chicken and toss to coat well. (This can be done a day in advance, if desired.)

In a 10-inch straight-sided skillet, heat the oil. Add the chicken pieces in one layer and brown on two sides, 2 to 3 minutes each side. Do not cook through and do not brown too much. Transfer the chicken back to the bowl (it doesn't

tips

The cilantro can also be added with the tomatoes. But if you are serving anyone who dislikes cilantro, it's easier to add it at the end.

MAKE IT VEGAN

Omit the chicken; use vegetable stock or water.

recipe continues →

matter that this had raw chicken in it, since the chicken still has to be cooked again.)

Add the bell pepper and onion to the skillet and sauté until slightly tender, about 5 minutes. Add the garlic and remaining teaspoon of salt and cook until fragrant, about 1 minute.

Add the tomatoes to the pan and increase the heat, scraping the bottom of the pan to deglaze and remove the bits stuck to the bottom. Add the rice, stock, capers, and olives and bring the liquid to a boil. Arrange the chicken pieces on top. Lower the heat to a simmer, cover, and cook for 20 minutes. Most of the liquid should have been absorbed. Stir in the peas and the cilantro (if using), cover again, and cook for 5 more minutes. Serve immediately or allow the dish to sit off the heat, covered, for 10 minutes.

SPICY PEACH SKILLET CHICKEN

DF **GF-*a*** | SERVES 4 TO 6

Sweet and spicy could be my middle name. In fact, I prefer this recipe with a little more heat, but I adhere to the lowest common denominator in my house (my son) with respect to spiciness. No-sugar fruit preserves are a great flavor booster, even cocktails, so I keep at least one in the fridge at all times. The peach preserves can be replaced with fig, apricot, or orange.

6 to 8 boneless, skinless chicken thighs, trimmed of excess fat

1 teaspoon sea salt, plus additional for seasoning

Freshly ground black pepper

1½ tablespoons unrefined, cold-pressed, extra-virgin olive oil or avocado oil

½ red or yellow onion, sliced ¼ inch thick through the root end

½ teaspoon crushed red pepper flakes, or ¼ teaspoon for less spicy

½ cup dry white wine or chicken stock

2 tablespoons unseasoned rice vinegar or white wine vinegar

¾ cup no-sugar-added peach preserves

2 tablespoons shoyu, tamari, or coconut aminos

2 peaches, cut into fourths, or 1½ cups of frozen peaches (see tip)

Thinly sliced fresh basil or mint leaves (optional)

↓

tips

If using frozen peaches, add the peaches after you pour in the wine and vinegar, right before you deglaze.

Sriracha can be used to taste instead of red pepper flakes. Other fresh herbs that are delicious in this recipe are chives and tarragon.

MAKE IT GLUTEN-FREE

Use gluten-free tamari or coconut aminos.

Pat the chicken dry with paper towels and season both sides with salt and pepper. Preheat a large (12- to 13-inch) skillet over medium heat and add the oil. Arrange the chicken in one layer in the skillet and allow to sear until golden, about 3 minutes. Turn over and sear until golden on the other side, 3 to 4 minutes. Transfer to a large plate or other container.

Add the onion to the skillet and sprinkle with salt. Sauté until just barely tender, about 3 minutes. Add the red pepper flakes and sauté for 30 seconds. Pour in the wine and vinegar and deglaze the pan by scraping the bottom with a wooden spoon or spatula. Bring to a simmer.

Stir in the preserves and shoyu. Add the chicken back to the skillet along with the fresh peaches and bring to a simmer. Turn once to coat the top side of the chicken. Continue cooking the chicken if at this point it is not fully cooked through. Top with fresh basil leaves (if using).

MOROCCAN SHEET PAN CHICKEN

GF DF Vg-*a* Ve-*a* | SERVES 4 TO 6

Sheet pan dinners, whereby a protein and vegetables are combined on the same sheet pan for a complete dinner and roasted, are having a moment. And for good reason—they're easy and usually quick. The key to a successful sheet pan dinner is pairing protein and vegetables with the same cook time. Here, I use sliced boneless, skinless chicken and quick-cooking vegetables. You can also use harder, denser vegetables, such as sweet potatoes or big pieces of cauliflower; they just need to go in the oven for about fifteen minutes before adding the chicken. Once you get the hang of it, you can come up with all sorts of combinations of ingredients for an unlimited number of sheet pan dinners!

Chicken

1 teaspoon sea salt

⅛ teaspoon freshly ground black pepper

¼ teaspoon ground turmeric

¼ teaspoon ground ginger

¼ teaspoon ground cinnamon

1 teaspoon ground cumin

Small pinch of cayenne pepper

1½ pounds boneless, skinless chicken breasts and/or thighs, sliced into 1-inch strips

1½ teaspoons pure maple syrup

1 tablespoon unrefined, cold-pressed, extra-virgin olive oil, avocado oil, or melted virgin coconut oil

———

5 ounces frozen artichoke hearts, defrosted or packed in water with no added preservatives, patted dry

2 medium-size carrots, peeled if desired, cut lengthwise into ¼-inch pieces

½ red onion, sliced thinly through the root

2 tablespoons unrefined, cold-pressed, extra-virgin olive oil, avocado oil, or melted virgin coconut oil

———

Sea salt and freshly ground black pepper, for sprinkling

Pinch of flaky salt (optional)

In a small bowl, whisk together the salt, pepper, turmeric, ginger, cinnamon, cumin, and cayenne. Place the chicken in a large container and drizzle with the maple syrup and the tablespoon of oil, then sprinkle with the spice

recipe continues →

↓

tips

Use sharp kitchen shears to easily trim fat from chicken, especially thighs.

Run hot water over the frozen artichokes in a colander to defrost them quickly. Pat very well with paper towels before adding to the sheet pan.

Green olives or lemon slices can also be added with the vegetables.

Store any leftovers in a glass container (always my preference anyway) as opposed to plastic, to avoid turmeric stains.

MAKE IT WITH SEAFOOD

Omit the chicken and use seafood, such as shrimp; the vegetables should be given a head start in the oven before adding the shrimp.

MAKE IT VEGAN

Omit the chicken; use 2 cups of cooked chickpeas, drained, rinsed, and patted dry. Toss the veggies and chickpeas with the oil and the spices, using the same cooking method as for the chicken.

mixture. Mix together until well coated. Cover and allow to sit at room temperature while you prep the remaining ingredients. You can let the seasoned chicken sit at room temperature for 1 hour or refrigerated up to 24 hours. The further in advance you can do this, the more flavorful the chicken will be.

Preheat the oven to 425°F and line a rimmed three-quarter sheet pan with unbleached parchment paper, unless you are using a stainless-steel pan (no need to use parchment, but do oil the stainless pan). Or use two smaller half sheet pans. If you put more than one sheet pan in the oven, consider cooking on the CONVECTION setting at 400°F for the same amount of time, but do check it a few minutes early to be safe.

Arrange the vegetables on the prepared sheet pan(s) and toss with the 2 tablespoons of the oil.

Arrange the chicken among the vegetables in one layer, if possible. Sprinkle everything with sea salt (try ½ teaspoon) and black pepper.

Bake for 15 to 20 minutes, or until the chicken is cooked through (do less time if you plan to cover and not serve it immediately). If you're unsure, use a thermometer to check the chicken's internal temperature (should be 165°F) or cut a piece open to check the color inside.

When finished, sprinkle with flaky salt, if desired.

SHEET PAN CHICKEN with ARTICHOKES, CHERRY TOMATOES, and ZUCCHINI

GF DF | SERVES 6

This is probably one of my favorite sheet pan dinners of all time. The spice flavors are great and go with everything. And I love roasting tomatoes, which burst and give off a beautiful juiciness. Like other sheet pan dinners, the veggies can be swapped for different ones; just make sure they have a cook time of about eighteen minutes because that's all you'll need to cook the chicken through.

1 teaspoon sea salt, plus more for sprinkling vegetables

Freshly ground black pepper

1 teaspoon paprika

1 teaspoon garlic powder or granulated garlic

Pinch of crushed red pepper flakes

1½ pounds boneless, skinless chicken breasts and/or thighs, sliced into 1-inch strips

3 tablespoons unrefined, cold-pressed, extra-virgin olive oil or avocado oil

1 pint cherry tomatoes

5 ounces frozen artichoke hearts, defrosted, or packed in water with no added preservatives, and patted dry

2 medium-size zucchini, cut into ½-inch rounds

In a small bowl, whisk together the salt, black pepper to taste, paprika, garlic powder, and red pepper flakes. Place the chicken in a large container and drizzle with 1 tablespoon of the olive oil and the spice mixture. Mix together until well coated. Allow to sit at room temperature, up to 1 hour, while you prep the rest of the ingredients, or cover and refrigerate for up to 24 hours.

Preheat the oven to 425°F and line a rimmed three-quarter sheet pan with unbleached parchment paper, unless you are using a stainless-steel pan (no need to use parchment on stainless steel, but you should oil the stainless pan). Or use two smaller half sheet pans.

recipe continues →

Arrange the vegetables on the prepared sheet pan(s) and toss with the remaining 2 tablespoons of olive oil. Sprinkle with salt and black pepper.

Arrange the chicken among the vegetables in one layer.

Bake for 18 to 20 minutes, or until the chicken is cooked through (use less time if you plan to cover it and serve it later). If you put more than one sheet pan in the oven, consider cooking on the CONVECTION setting at 400°F.

RANCH CHICKEN FINGERS

GF-*a* **DF-*a*** | SERVES 6

There's always that one recipe that I think is not that exciting and then my kids tell me it's their favorite thing. Hello, Ranch Chicken Fingers. Of course, if I'm going to serve chicken tenders, it's going to be my way with higher-quality ingredients and not deep-fried. The herbs and spices here make these adult-friendly, as well.

tips

MAKE IT GLUTEN-FREE

Use gluten-free bread crumbs or their almond meal alternative.

MAKE IT DAIRY-FREE

Use eggs, egg whites, or soy-free Vegenaise; vegan bread crumbs.

Crumb Mixture

2 tablespoons dried parsley

1½ teaspoons dried dill

1 teaspoon dried chives

1 tablespoon garlic powder

1 tablespoon onion powder

1 teaspoon sea salt

Freshly ground black pepper

1 cup panko bread crumbs or dried bread crumbs, or ¾ cup almond flour or meal + ¼ cup tapioca flour or cassava flour

2 large eggs or 4 large egg whites, lightly beaten; or 1 cup buttermilk; or 1 cup soy-free Vegenaise

2 large boneless, skinless chicken breasts, cut into 1-inch-wide strips (or use 12 tenders)

¼ cup unrefined, cold-pressed, extra-virgin olive oil or avocado oil

SERVING SUGGESTION: Herbed Yogurt Dipping Sauce from *Kitchen Matters* or your favorite barbecue sauce

Prepare the crumb mixture: Mix together all the dry ingredients in a shallow dish, such as a pie plate or small baking dish.

Place the eggs (or your egg-free substitute) in a separate shallow dish. Dip the chicken into the eggs, then the crumb mixture. Set aside on a plate or sheet pan until all chicken pieces have been coated.

Heat the oil in a large skillet over medium heat. When the oil is hot but not smoking, add all the chicken. It should fit in one layer without crowding the pan, but do this in batches if necessary. Cook until the underside is golden brown, 5 to 6 minutes. Flip over and cook until browned underneath and the chicken feels firm, 4 to 5 minutes.

Serve with the yogurt sauce or barbecue sauce on the side.

CHICKEN SHAWARMA BURGERS

GF-*a*   DF-*a* | SERVES 6

One of the most popular main dish recipes from my first book, Kitchen Matters, *is Chicken Shawarma. I understand why. It's easy, light, superflavorful, and lends itself to a fun toppings bar. We can also enjoy it in different ways: my kids stuff their chicken into a pita and I prefer it in a salad or in a bowl. This recipe seasons ground chicken with the same (anti-inflammatory) spices for a phenomenal burger that can be eaten the same way as the shawarma.*

1½ teaspoons ground cumin

1½ teaspoons paprika

½ teaspoon garlic powder

½ teaspoon ground turmeric

⅛ teaspoon ground cinnamon

⅛ teaspoon cayenne pepper

1 teaspoon sea salt

Freshly ground black pepper

1½ pounds ground dark meat chicken

⅓ cup grated onion

Unrefined, cold-pressed, extra-virgin olive oil or avocado oil

SERVING SUGGESTIONS: pita, hamburger bun, salad, large lettuce leaves

OPTIONAL ACCOMPANIMENTS: tzatziki or white sauce (recipes follow), pickled vegetables, shredded lettuce, tomato

In a large bowl, whisk together spices, salt, and black pepper to taste. Add the ground chicken and onion and combine well by hand.

Form the mixture into six 4-inch-diameter, ½-inch-thick patties.

Heat a large skillet or griddle, preferably cast iron, over medium-high heat. Oil lightly with the oil. Cook each patty for 9 minutes, or until cooked through, flipping at the 4½-minute point. When done, the patty should spring back when lightly pressed in the center.

Serve in pita, on hamburger buns, in a lettuce wrap, or in a salad, with your desired accompaniments.

MAKE IT GLUTEN-FREE

Serve with gluten-free bread or salad.

MAKE IT DAIRY-FREE

Use nondairy yogurt and soy-free Vegenaise to make the tzatziki or white sauce.

recipe continues →

Tzatziki

1½ tablespoons freshly squeezed
lemon juice

1 garlic clove, minced

2 Persian cucumbers, grated or diced

1 cup whole unsweetened plain Greek
yogurt or nondairy yogurt

1½ teaspoons white wine vinegar

1 tablespoon finely chopped fresh
mint or dill (optional)

½ teaspoon sea salt

Combine all the ingredients in a small bowl and stir. Can be made ahead of
time and stored in the fridge.

White Sauce

⅔ cup whole unsweetened plain Greek
yogurt or nondairy yogurt

⅓ cup good-quality mayonnaise or
soy-free Vegenaise

3 garlic cloves, minced

1 tablespoon freshly squeezed
lemon juice

⅛ teaspoon sea salt

⅛ teaspoon paprika

Freshly ground black pepper

Combine all the ingredients in a small bowl and stir. Can be made ahead of
time and stored in the fridge.

GRAIN-FREE GREEK TURKEY MEATBALLS

GF-a **DF-a** | MAKES 24 MEATBALLS

Most meatballs are made with ground meat mixed with fresh and dried bread crumbs so that the meatballs remain tender and not tough. I'm not opposed to eating whole-grain bread every now and then, but if I'm going to eat bread, I want to have the pleasure of actually eating bread! The way around using the bread crumbs in this recipe is by adding moisture with the onions, tomato paste, and oil, and the tenderizing effects of shoyu, plus cooking them at a superhigh temperature for a short time (bonus—they're done quick!). My kids have never met a meatball they didn't like, and these are no exception. I have served these many different ways, even at the same meal. See my suggestions below.

2 pounds ground turkey, preferably dark meat

2 medium-size garlic cloves, grated finely (I use a medium-grate Microplane for this)

½ cup finely grated red onion (I do this in a mini food processor and process until it is like wet onion paste)

⅓ cup fresh flat-leaf parsley leaves, chopped finely

3 tablespoons finely chopped fresh mint, or 1½ tablespoons dried

4 teaspoons dried oregano

2 tablespoons tomato paste

1½ tablespoons unrefined, cold-pressed, extra-virgin olive oil

2 tablespoons shoyu, tamari, or coconut aminos

1¼ teaspoons sea salt

½ teaspoon freshly ground black pepper

SERVING SUGGESTION: crumbled feta or Tzatziki Sauce (page 230) plus lettuce wraps, pita, or cooked rice and vegetables

Preheat the oven to 500°F. If your oven doesn't go that high, set the temperature for as high as you can. Line a rimmed baking sheet with unbleached parchment paper or set a wire rack inside it.

Gently mix together all the meatball ingredients in a large bowl.

recipe continues →

↓

tips

Another option is to serve with doctored-up tomato sauce (add dried thyme and dried oregano, plus fresh parsley) and top with fresh mint leaves and crumbled feta.

If you want the meatballs extra crispy, you can fry them first in oil in a skillet and finish them in the oven for 8 to 10 minutes.

I use a 1¾-inch-diameter swing-arm ice-cream scoop to easily form all the meatballs. That way, each meatball is the same size and will cook at the same rate.

MAKE IT GLUTEN-FREE

Use gluten-free tamari or coconut aminos; serve in a lettuce wrap or with rice and vegetables.

MAKE IT DAIRY-FREE

Use nondairy yogurt to make the tzatziki sauce; do not use feta.

Form 2 tablespoons of the meat mixture into a ball (see tip) and place on the prepared baking sheet (or wire rack, if using). Repeat with the remaining mixture.

Bake for 14 to 16 minutes, or until cooked through. (If you're not sure, stick a meat thermometer in the center of a meatball and it should register 165°F. Otherwise, cut one open and make sure it is no longer pink in the center.)

Serve the meatballs with feta or tzatziki sauce in a lettuce wrap or with pita, or in a bowl with cooked rice and vegetables.

CURRIED TURKEY and VEGETABLE STIR-FRY

DF **Vg-a** **Ve-a** **GF-a** | SERVES 6

I am pretty obsessed with the ease and incredible flavor of premade curry paste and it's easy to find brands that are 100 percent natural. I use it in soups and stews, as well as this stir-fry. Ground meats are my go-to when I have limited time to cook. But this recipe can easily be made vegan (see tips). Feel free to get creative with your garnishes, too. It takes no time to sprinkle fresh herbs, chopped toasted cashews, and a squeeze of fresh lime juice on top.

2 tablespoons unrefined virgin coconut oil or cold-pressed, extra-virgin olive oil

½ onion, diced

2 pounds ground dark meat turkey or chicken

1½ tablespoons green or yellow curry paste, such as Mae Ploy

1 sweet bell pepper, any color, seeded and chopped

1 cup diagonally sliced sugar snap peas or asparagus

2 cups shredded green cabbage (any variety)

2 tablespoons shoyu, tamari, or coconut aminos

⅔ cup full-fat coconut milk (canned)

SERVING SUGGESTIONS: fresh mint leaves, fresh cilantro leaves and tender stems, lettuce cups, steamed rice

tips

MAKE IT GLUTEN-FREE

Use gluten-free tamari or coconut aminos.

MAKE IT VEGAN

Use crumbled tempeh in place of the ground turkey, or prepare with cooked grains and veggies, or all veggies.

Heat the oil in a large skillet over medium heat. Add the onion and sauté until almost tender, about 5 minutes.

Add the turkey and sauté, breaking up the meat with a spatula or a potato masher, until almost cooked through, about 5 minutes.

Add the curry paste and stir into the turkey mixture, about 1 minute.

Add the vegetables and sauté for 2 to 3 minutes, until crisp-tender.

Pour in the shoyu and coconut milk and stir until combined. Bring to a simmer and cook until almost all the coconut milk is absorbed, just a few minutes more.

Serve with fresh mint and/or cilantro leaves. Nice with steamed rice or lettuce cups.

SAUTÉED BEEF with MIDDLE EASTERN SPICES

DF **GF-*a*** | SERVES 4 TO 6

I don't make beef often, but when I do make it, I always use the best grass-fed beef I can find and I cook it either really quickly in a stir-fry like this, in a pressure cooker, or a slow cooker. Grass-fed beef can be tricky to cook properly because of its lower fat content. When steak is overcooked, it can be really tough. But this recipe is so easy and tasty, you'll get it right every time. Cumin, coriander, and paprika are one of my favorite spice combinations because together they pack such a balanced, warm, aromatic, and earthy punch. The cooked, seasoned beef is delicious stuffed inside a roasted bell pepper half or over roasted potato coins or cooked grains.

tip

MAKE IT GLUTEN-FREE

Use gluten-free tamari or coconut aminos.

1½ pounds grass-fed beef, such as rib eye, NY strip, or sirloin, cut into thin strips against the grain

¾ teaspoon ground cumin

¾ teaspoon ground coriander

¾ teaspoon paprika

1 teaspoon sea salt

Freshly ground black pepper

2 tablespoons unrefined, cold-pressed, extra-virgin olive oil or avocado oil

1 medium-size onion, halved and sliced ¼-inch thick

2 tablespoons shoyu, tamari, or coconut aminos

1 tablespoon red wine vinegar

In a medium-size bowl, combine the beef with the cumin, coriander, paprika, salt, and pepper.

Heat a wok or a large (12- to 13-inch) pan over medium heat and heat the oil. If you don't have a large skillet, cook the meat in two batches in a smaller skillet. You don't want the strips of meat to be on top of one another. Sauté for 2 to 3 minutes, just until cooked about medium. Transfer the meat to a fresh bowl or plate.

Add the onion to the skillet and sauté until just softened, 3 to 4 minutes. Add the shoyu and vinegar and scrape the bottom of the skillet with a wooden or silicone spatula or spoon, trying to dislodge any cooked on brown bits. Bring to a simmer and add back the meat. Toss to coat and heat through. Serve.

KOREAN BEEF FAJITAS

DF **GF-a** | SERVES 6

Traditional fajitas are an easy, family-friendly meal that I cook often accompanied by the regular cast of such characters as guacamole and salsa. Here, I've switched up tradition by using an Asian flavor profile for the marinade. Just a note about Thai sriracha and Korean gochujang, the hot sauces I suggest in the spicy sauce. Sriracha is one of my favorite hot sauces and has a sweet, vinegary, garlic flavor, while gochujang is a thick, fermented hot sauce with an earthy, sweet, spicy, umami flavor. Some may argue that gochujang is a little more complex than sriracha; I love both and I give you permission to use either one here. You can make these fajitas with different types of protein or all vegetables. I'm all about the condiments, anyway!

tips

If you have the time, you can make the marinade ahead and marinate the meat overnight.

MAKE IT GLUTEN-FREE

Use gluten-free tamari or coconut aminos; lettuce leaves or gluten-free tortillas.

2 tablespoons shoyu, tamari, or coconut aminos

1½ teaspoons coconut palm sugar

1 tablespoon unseasoned rice vinegar

1 large garlic clove, chopped very finely

1½ teaspoons toasted sesame oil

1½ teaspoons peeled and chopped fresh ginger

Pinch of crushed red pepper flakes

1¼ to 1½ pounds (or whatever you can get) grass-fed beef flank steak, cut across the grain on a diagonal into 1-inch-thick slices or left whole (marinating can be longer if the steak is whole)

1½ tablespoons unrefined, cold-pressed, extra-virgin olive oil or avocado oil

1 red onion, sliced thinly

1 sweet bell pepper, any color, seeded and sliced thinly

¼ teaspoon sea salt

Sriracha Mayo

½ cup soy-free Vegenaise or your favorite mayonnaise

2 tablespoons sriracha or gochujang

Pinch of sea salt

To Serve

8 tortillas of your choice or large lettuce leaves

2 cups shredded cabbage, any kind, and/or prepared kimchi

Cilantro sprigs, for garnish (optional)

recipe continues →

In a large, shallow dish, combine the soy sauce with the sugar, vinegar, garlic, toasted sesame oil, ginger, and red pepper flakes, stirring to dissolve the sugar. Add the sliced flank steak and coat thoroughly in the marinade. Marinate the steak at room temperature for as long as you have time for, up to 1 hour. Otherwise, to make ahead, marinate for up to 8 hours in the refrigerator.

In a large skillet, heat the oil over medium heat. Add the onion and pepper along with the salt and sauté until just tender, about 6 minutes.

Heat a grill or a griddle over medium-high heat. Working in batches, grill the steak until the slices are browned and medium-rare, 1 to 2 minutes per side. Alternatively, grill the whole steak for 2½ to 3 minutes on each side for medium-rare, 4 minutes on each side for medium-well. Transfer the meat to a cutting board and cover. Allow to rest for 5 to 10 minutes before slicing *against* the grain.

Mix all the sauce ingredients together and refrigerate until ready to serve.

Warm the tortillas on a skillet heated over medium heat, 30 to 60 seconds per side. I like to keep the tortillas warm in a thin, clean kitchen towel.

Serve the steak and vegetables with the warm tortillas, sauce, and cilantro (if using).

SAUSAGE and RICED VEGETABLE SKILLET

DF **Vg-a** **Ve-a** **GF-a** | SERVES 4

Imagine a dish like paella, but without the rice. That's a good, basic description for this. One of the key ingredients here is the meat. Precooked, processed sausages are a whole other thing with nitrates and nitrites and other preservatives and I don't suggest buying them. You can actually make sausage meat yourself, just purchase ground poultry or pork and season it with such spices as fennel seed, garlic, and paprika or a premade Italian sausage seasoning blend. You can also sub many different types of a vegan meat substitute, such as tempeh, if desired. This is delicious over a roasted sweet potato, in a bowl with avocado, or over rice, of course.

2 teaspoons unrefined, cold-pressed, extra-virgin olive oil, plus more as needed

1 pound fresh (not precooked) bulk sausage meat (out of the casing; see tip)

1 small bunch kale, stemmed and chopped

Sea salt and freshly ground black pepper

12 ounces fresh or frozen cauliflower rice and/or another riced vegetable, such as broccoli rice or sweet potato rice

½ teaspoon garlic powder

1 teaspoon smoked paprika

1 teaspoon ground turmeric

1 cup fresh diced tomatoes, or jarred with a little juice

2 tablespoons tomato paste

1 cup roasted red peppers, chopped

½ cup fresh flat-leaf parsley leaves and tender stems, chopped

1 tablespoon shoyu, tamari, or coconut aminos

↓

tips
———

If you can't find bulk sausage, buy fresh sausage links and squeeze the meat from the casings. I prefer mild Italian chicken or turkey sausage.

Add some heat with a pinch or more of crushed red pepper flakes along with the garlic powder.

MAKE IT GLUTEN-FREE
———

Use gluten-free tamari, or coconut aminos.

MAKE IT VEGAN
———

Use crumbled tempeh or vegan sausage crumbles.

Heat a large skillet over medium heat, then add the oil. Place the sausage meat in the skillet and sauté, breaking up the meat into pieces. You can use a potato masher to really get it into small, uniform pieces. Sauté until cooked through and browned slightly, 5 to 6 minutes. Transfer the sausage meat with a slotted spoon to a clean bowl and set aside.

recipe continues →

Add the kale and a big pinch of salt and a little pepper to the same skillet and sauté until softened, 3 to 4 minutes, adding more oil to the pan if needed.

Add the cauliflower rice to the skillet and sauté until softened, about 5 minutes. Frozen cauliflower will soften in less time than fresh, but fresh cauliflower may need a little extra moisture to prevent it from sticking. You can add a splash of water, tomato juice, or white wine, if needed.

Stir in the garlic powder, paprika, and turmeric and cook for a minute. Add the tomatoes and tomato paste and sauté, scraping any brown bits stuck on the bottom of the pan. You can add a little tomato juice from the jar if you have it and need it.

Add the remaining ingredients plus the cooked sausage meat to the skillet and combine well. Cook until everything is warmed through. Taste for salt and pepper and season accordingly.

WILD SALMON CALIFORNIA BOWLS

GF **DF-*a*** | SERVES 4

I love California cuisine and its emphasis on fresh, seasonal produce and vibrant food. Whenever I am shopping at one of the many farmers markets in LA, I feel instant gratitude for such bounty and inspiration. "Bowls" have been a phenomenon in So Cal that is still going strong, including in my kitchen. This recipe is something I came up with when I was envisioning my perfect California-inspired meal. I could eat this for breakfast, lunch, or dinner, and you could even make a huge platter of this and serve it at a party. It would be so perfect for a bridal shower or baby shower—it really is that versatile!

↓

tips

EVEN QUICKER

Use canned wild salmon, drained, in place of the fresh salmon.

MAKE IT DAIRY-FREE

Use olive or avocado oil to cook the salmon.

1½ cups uncooked quinoa, rinsed if desired

2 large, firm but ripe avocados, pitted and peeled: ½ avocado reserved for dressing, 1½ avocados sliced or cubed

1½ tablespoons chopped shallot (about 1 small shallot)

½ cup fresh cilantro leaves and tender stems, or mint leaves

3 tablespoons unseasoned rice vinegar or freshly squeezed lemon juice

½ teaspoon sea salt, plus more for seasoning salmon

Freshly ground black pepper

1 pound wild skin-on salmon, cut into 4 equal-size fillets

1 tablespoon unrefined, cold-pressed, extra-virgin olive oil, avocado oil, or ghee

1 (4-ounce) container sprouts, such as radish or broccoli (use whatever you can find)

2 small watermelon radishes, trimmed, halved, and julienned

2 oranges (navel or Cara Cara are both great), peeled and chopped

Combine the quinoa and 2¼ cups of water in a medium-size saucepan. Bring to a boil over high heat. Lower the heat to a simmer, cover, and cook for 15 minutes, or until all the water has been absorbed. Remove from the heat, but keep covered while you prepare the rest of the recipe.

Prepare the dressing: In a food processor or blender, combine the pitted and skinned avocado half, shallot, cilantro, vinegar, salt, pepper to taste, and

recipe continues →

3 tablespoons of water. Blend until smooth and creamy. If the dressing is too thick, add a little water, a teaspoon at a time. This makes about ¾ cup of dressing.

Season the salmon with a sprinkle of salt and pepper on the fleshy side. In a sauté pan over medium-high heat, heat the oil. Add the salmon, skin side up. Cook for 2 minutes. Flip the salmon over and cook for another 2 to 3 minutes, or until medium rare in the center. Cook longer if desired.

Scoop the quinoa into individual bowls and top each with one piece of salmon, plus sprouts, watermelon radish, avocado, and orange chunks. Drizzle with the avocado dressing.

HERBED SWEET and SPICY GLAZED WILD SALMON

GF **DF** | SERVES 4 TO 6

We all have our "company dish," the one we can rely on when we have people over and are entertaining. This is the recipe that never fails me and that always gets rave reviews. I can make it for one or for fifty (which I have!) with ease. Inevitably, everyone asks what is in "that sauce," which is nothing more than fig preserves, sriracha, salt, and pepper. Sweet and spicy wins every time!

1 (24-ounce) wild salmon fillet (skin-on or skinless)

About 2 teaspoons unrefined, cold-pressed, extra-virgin olive oil, for drizzling

¾ teaspoon sea salt

Freshly ground black pepper

3 tablespoons no-sugar-added fig preserves or other similar fruit preserves, such as apricot

¼ teaspoon sriracha or hot sauce

1 cup mixed fresh tender green herbs (flat-leaf parsley, mint, dill, or any combination), chopped finely

Preheat the oven to 425°F. Line a rimmed baking sheet with unbleached parchment paper.

Place the salmon on the prepared baking sheet. Drizzle the salmon with olive oil and rub to coat evenly. Sprinkle with salt and pepper.

In a small bowl, combine the preserves and sriracha. Spread a thin layer on the salmon.

Press the herb mixture on top of the salmon to cover evenly.

Roast the salmon for 10 to 12 minutes, or until the fish flakes evenly when poked with the tip of a paring knife. You want the fish to be slightly rare in the center. Cut crosswise into serving pieces.

SHEET PAN CITRUS-CHILI COD with FENNEL

GF **DF** | SERVES 4 TO 6

This is another favorite sheet pan dinner, but with seafood. Remember if the vegetables and protein have different cook times, whatever needs to cook longer needs to get started in the oven first. In this case, while the vegetables roast, you have time to make the "marinade" and bring the cod closer to room temperature. You can sub salmon or halibut for the cod, but give cod a try. It's easy to find wild, and it's a wonderfully flaky, mild white fish that even most kids like. Serve this as is or with the Couscous Pilaf (page 168).

tip

You can finish roasting the vegetables and leave them out at room temperature for an hour before adding the fish.

1 red onion, cut into ½-inch wedges

2 large fennel bulbs, trimmed, each cut through the core into 6 wedges, fronds reserved for garnish

1 red chile pepper (such as Fresno), sliced thinly

1 small orange, any variety, sliced into ¼-inch-thick slices

2½ tablespoons unrefined, cold-pressed, extra-virgin olive oil

1 teaspoon sea salt, plus more for sprinkling

Freshly ground black pepper

3 tablespoons freshly squeezed Meyer lemon or regular lemon juice

2 garlic cloves, minced

1 teaspoon sriracha, or more to taste

½ teaspoon ground coriander

1½ teaspoons pure maple syrup or honey

1 (24-ounce) wild cod fillet (skin-on or skinless)

Preheat the oven to 425°F. Line a large rimmed baking sheet with unbleached parchment paper.

Mound the onion, fennel wedges, chile pepper, and orange slices on the prepared baking sheet. Drizzle with 1½ tablespoons of the olive oil and a sprinkle of salt and black pepper. Spread out evenly over the prepared baking sheet. Roast in the oven for 20 minutes.

Make the marinade: In a medium-size bowl, whisk together 1 tablespoon of water, the remaining tablespoon of olive oil, and the lemon juice, garlic, sriracha, coriander, maple syrup, the teaspoon of salt, and a few grinds of black pepper.

Place the cod on the baking sheet. You can cook the fish on top of the vegetables or move them to the perimeter of the baking sheet. Drizzle the cod with the marinade.

Roast in the oven for 8 to 12 minutes (10 minutes per inch thickness), or until the fish flakes evenly when poked with the tip of a paring knife. You want the cod to be slightly rare in the center. Cut crosswise into serving pieces. Garnish with reserved fennel fronds, if desired.

PARMESAN BAKED ROCKFISH with CHERRY TOMATOES

GF-*a* | SERVES 6

Italians don't usually mix dairy and seafood, but I like to go against tradition sometimes. I think butter and fish are terrific together, but Parmesan cheese adds a nutty saltiness to this mild fish that is divine, especially when it mingles with the tomato juices. It's such a simple recipe, but I believe fish shouldn't be complicated. Rockfish is similar to cod, but a little thinner. Any fillet of a mild white fish will be perfect in this recipe (see tip). I love this fish dish with sautéed greens and grilled eggplant.

6 rockfish fillets (about 2 pounds total), patted dry with a paper towel

Sea salt (see tip)

Freshly ground black pepper

2 tablespoons unsalted butter, melted

2 tablespoons plus 1 to 2 teaspoons unrefined, cold-pressed extra-virgin olive oil

½ cup fresh bread crumbs (see tip), panko bread crumbs, or almond flour/meal

¾ cup finely grated Parmesan or pecorino cheese

Grated zest of 1 lemon (cut the rest of the lemon into wedges to serve with the fish, if desired)

2 cups cherry or grape tomatoes

Preheat the oven to 425°F and line a large rimmed baking sheet with unbleached parchment paper. Season the fish lightly with salt and pepper.

In a medium-size bowl, combine the melted butter, 2 tablespoons of the olive oil, and the bread crumbs, cheese, and lemon zest. Press the mixture evenly over the fish.

Toss the cherry tomatoes with the remaining 1 to 2 teaspoons of oil and a sprinkle of salt and arrange around the fish.

Bake until cooked through and the fish flakes easily with a fork, 6 to 8 minutes, depending on the thickness of the fish. If the crumb topping hasn't browned, you can put the fish under the broiler (6 inches away) for 30 to 60 seconds, or until golden brown. Serve immediately with lemon wedges.

↓

tips

Other fish you can use include flounder, cod fillets, or Petrale or Dover sole. The thinner the fish, the shorter the cook time.

To make fresh bread crumbs, take fresh bread and process in a blender or food processor.

MAKE IT GLUTEN-FREE

Use fresh gluten-free bread crumbs or almond flour/meal.

BRANZINO FILLETS with FRESH TOMATOES and BASIL

GF **DF** **Vg-*a*** **Ve-*a*** | SERVES 6

I think roasting a whole fish is one of the simplest preparations possible with the most delicious results. The bones keep everything very moist and it's almost impossible to mess up. A whole roasted branzino with flaky sea salt, good olive oil, and a squeeze of lemon juice is my perfect meal. But deboning many whole fish at dinner is a little time-consuming. So, I often ask the fishmonger for branzino fillets, which I can broil in minutes. Yes, minutes! Add this fresh tomato-basil topping or Salsa Verde (page 320) or the 5-Minute Cherry Tomato Sauce from my blog, for a superlight, easy meal.

2 pounds fresh tomatoes, chopped, or cherry tomatoes, halved

3 large garlic cloves, smashed lightly with a knife

¼ cup fresh basil leaves, torn by hand, small leaves left whole

¼ teaspoon sea salt

Unrefined, cold-pressed, extra-virgin olive oil

Freshly ground black pepper

6 branzino or black sea bass fillets, skin on, scaled, pin bones removed, rinsed, and patted dry

Prepare the tomato mixture: In a medium-size serving bowl, combine the tomatoes, garlic, basil, salt, and enough olive oil to coat, 3 to 4 tablespoons. Taste for seasoning and set aside.

Preheat the broiler and arrange the rack about 6 inches from the heat source. Lightly oil a large, rimmed baking sheet with olive oil. Try not to overdo it or have puddles of oil on the pan, as that will cause smoking when it's under the broiler.

↓

tip
—

Choose the largest fillets you can find since they are pretty small.

MAKE IT VEGAN

Sear cauliflower steaks (see page 326) instead of fish.

Season the fleshy side of the fish with salt and pepper and place, flesh side down, on the prepared baking sheet. Drizzle the skin with a little olive oil, about 1½ teaspoons per fillet. Sprinkle with a little more salt and pepper.

Place the pan under the broiler and cook until the fish skin is golden and crisp and the fish is opaque and cooked through, 4 to 7 minutes depending on the size of the fillet. Remove from the oven.

Discard the garlic from the tomato mixture. Taste the tomatoes for salt.

If you want the skin to stay crispy, serve skin side up with the tomato mixture on the side. If it doesn't matter, arrange the fillets on a platter with the tomato mixture spooned on top.

TUNA "CEVICHE" with AVOCADO

GF **DF-a** | **SERVES 4**

Trust me when I tell you this "poor man's ceviche" is shockingly fabulous. Light, fresh, and zingy, this recipe takes canned tuna to a whole new level. Just promise me you'll seek out wild tuna that has been tested and confirmed to have minimal or no mercury. You can easily make a lunch out of this with avocado and lettuce leaves, or eat it as a light snack with plantain chips or your favorite tortilla chips.

¼ cup very thinly sliced red onion

Juice of 2 limes

Sea salt

2 (7-ounce) cans good-quality albacore tuna packed in water, drained (see tip)

½ jalapeño pepper, stemmed and seeded, or fresh chile pepper of choice, minced

1 avocado, pitted, peeled, and cubed or sliced (see directions)

¼ cup chopped fresh cilantro

SERVING SUGGESTIONS: lettuce leaves, plantain chips, tortilla chips, sweet potato chips, hollowed-out avocado peels

Place the red onion in a small bowl and toss with the juice of 1 lime and a pinch of salt. Allow the onion to soak in the juice.

Place the tuna in big chunks in a serving bowl. Add the jalapeño, the juice of the other lime, and the red onion with its soaking juice and stir gently to combine. Either fold in the avocado cubes or top with avocado slices. Garnish with the cilantro. Serve with your desired accompaniments.

↓

tips

If you are using unsalted tuna, you'll need to add a pinch or two of salt to the mixture.

MAKE IT DAIRY-FREE

Use vegan tortilla chips.

POMEGRANATE GLAZED SALMON

GF **DF** | SERVES 4

Pomegranate molasses is one of those wonder condiments that you don't know what in the world you would use it for until you taste it. Tart and sweet and tangy, it is reduced pomegranate juice with the consistency of a thick, aged balsamic vinegar. I had it first in Turkey, where I noticed it was used in the same way balsamic vinegar would be—drizzled over raw tomatoes, on grilled meats, and over fresh fruit. I love it on yogurt or pancakes and blended into dips. Salmon and pomegranate molasses are particularly good together, with one balancing the richness of the other. This recipe couldn't be simpler but looks very impressive with a few garnishes. It's lovely with Couscous Pilaf (page 168) or Cauliflower Rice (page 142) and a green vegetable.

Olive oil, for pan (optional)

1 (1¼-pound) piece wild salmon, or 4 (5-ounce) pieces

¼ cup no-sugar-added pomegranate molasses, such as Sadaf brand

1 tablespoon pure maple syrup or honey

1 teaspoon sea salt

½ teaspoon freshly ground black pepper

OPTIONAL GARNISHES: fresh pomegranate seeds, minced fresh flat-leaf parsley

Preheat the oven to 425°F. Line a sheet pan with a piece of unbleached parchment paper that fits underneath the salmon and is no larger; otherwise it will burn. Alternatively, omit the paper and oil the sheet pan with olive oil. Place the salmon on the prepared pan.

In a small bowl, combine the pomegranate molasses and maple syrup. Brush the salmon with the glaze. Sprinkle with the salt and pepper.

Roast in the oven for 5 minutes, then switch the oven to the BROIL setting and broil 6 inches from the heat for 1 to 2 minutes. Garnish with fresh pomegranate seeds and parsley, if desired.

PERFECT SEARED SCALLOPS

GF **DF-*a*** | MAKES 16 LARGE SCALLOPS; SERVES 3 OR 4 PEOPLE

Scallops look intimidating, but they're a cinch to make—if you follow a few basic tips. Browning any protein is all about fighting off that moisture—moisture on the scallops and in the scallops. How to keep the moisture to a minimum? First, seek out wild, dry-pack scallops as opposed to wet-pack scallops (the latter means they have been treated with a preservative to hold onto moisture). Once you are ready to make the recipe, patting the scallops dry and not overcrowding the pan are also key steps. I prefer scallops really simply prepared, but if you like, you can add a couple of teaspoons of butter and some lemon zest at the end to dress these scallops up.

16 large wild scallops, defrosted if frozen, rinsed under cold water (see headnote)

Unrefined, cold-pressed, extra-virgin olive oil or unsalted butter, or a mixture of the two (about 1 tablespoon)

Sea salt

Freshly ground black pepper

Freshly squeezed lemon juice, if desired

↓

tips

Use a silicone pastry brush to evenly coat your pan with butter or oil.

See page 7 for how to clean your pan afterward.

MAKE IT DAIRY-FREE

Use olive oil.

Place the scallops on a layer of paper towel and place another paper towel on top. Allow the scallops to sit on the paper towels for 10 minutes. You want the paper to absorb as much excess moisture as possible.

Heat the largest skillet you own, or two skillets, over medium heat until hot but not smoking. Cast iron, stainless steel, and nonstick all work. Add enough oil to lightly coat the bottom of the skillet(s). The key to a nice golden crust on the scallops is to not use too much oil. You should not have any oil pooling anywhere in the skillet(s).

Place one scallop in the skillet and if it starts to sizzle, add the remaining scallops, leaving 1 inch between each of them so they don't steam one another.

Cook for 2 to 3 minutes, or until beautifully golden and caramelized on the underside. Turn them over and repeat. The scallops should be slightly translucent in the center. Remove from heat and serve with a squeeze of lemon.

SHEET PAN SHRIMP with BROCCOLI

DF **GF-*a*** | SERVES 4

When I am thinking of a really quick dinner, shrimp comes to mind. This recipe is the best of both worlds: a stir-fry–meets–sheet pan supper. Supereasy and fast, and healthier than your average Chinese takeout. My kids crave this dinner on the regular with basic steamed rice or rice noodles. I've also made this with snow peas and superthinly sliced carrots. Sprinkle with sesame seeds for a restaurant-worthy dish.

tip

MAKE IT GLUTEN-FREE

Use gluten-free tamari or coconut aminos.

5 cups small broccoli florets

2 tablespoons avocado oil

Sea salt (I use about ¼ teaspoon)

2 large garlic cloves, minced

1 teaspoon peeled and grated fresh ginger

½ teaspoon crushed red pepper flakes

1 tablespoon honey

¼ cup shoyu, tamari, or coconut aminos

1 pound wild large shrimp, peeled, deveined, rinsed, and patted dry

Preheat the oven to 425°F. Line a rimmed half sheet pan with unbleached parchment paper, if desired.

Place the broccoli on the sheet pan, drizzle with the oil, and sprinkle with salt. Toss to coat, spread out on the pan, and roast in the oven for 10 minutes.

Make the sauce: Whisk together the garlic, ginger, red pepper flakes, honey, and shoyu in a large bowl. Toss the shrimp with the sauce in the bowl and pour everything onto the sheet pan of roasted broccoli. Spread out in one layer. Roast for another 6 minutes, or until the shrimp are pink throughout. (Smaller shrimp will take a minute less.) Serve immediately.

SPANISH GARLIC SHRIMP

GF **DF** | SERVES 4

In Spain, this recipe, called gambas al ajillo, *is a popular tapas or small plate item. You can absolutely serve this with drinks as an hors d'oeuvre, but it works really well as a main dish. Normally, this dish is as much about the garlicky, shrimp-infused olive oil as it is about the shrimp, but I cut way back on the oil because it's just not really necessary. I love these shrimp over rice or cauliflower rice, which takes on the garlic oil very well. But they're equally good in a nontraditional way over zucchini noodles or spaghetti squash. My son let me know, though, that this recipe couldn't serve four people because he could eat the whole pan himself!*

¼ cup unrefined, cold-pressed, extra-virgin olive oil

6 garlic cloves, chopped coarsely

1 bay leaf

½ teaspoon paprika

Pinch of crushed red pepper flakes

1¼ pounds large wild shrimp, deveined and peeled but with the tails on, defrosted if previously frozen, and tossed in a bowl with 1 teaspoon sea salt

¼ cup dry white wine, dry Marsala, or sherry

2 tablespoons minced, fresh flat-leaf parsley

Heat the oil in a medium-large skillet over medium-low heat. Add the garlic, bay leaf, smoked paprika, and red pepper flakes. The mixture should barely sizzle so that you infuse the oil with flavor but don't burn the garlic, which would make it bitter. Sauté until the garlic is just starting to turn a pale golden color, about 2 minutes.

Add the shrimp and increase the heat to medium-high. Cook for 3 minutes, turn the shrimp over, and add the wine. Cover and remove from the heat. Allow to sit until the shrimp are cooked through, 3 to 4 minutes. Garnish with the parsley and serve.

tip

If you have time, you can dissolve a pinch of saffron in hot wine and add it to the dish. It's a traditional ingredient in many Spanish dishes and adds a unique flavor and beautiful yellow color. It's really expensive, though, and not an essential pantry ingredient.

MEXI-VEGGIE RICE STUFFED PEPPERS

Vg Ve GF | SERVES 5

Sure, you can stuff a pepper and then roast it. But why not roast the pepper while you're making the filling and then stuff it and serve it? There's no advantage to cooking the pepper with the filling, so I'll choose the faster option, thank you. This recipe takes a very veggie route with all riced vegetables rather than traditional rice stuffing. If you're worried this won't be hearty enough for a main, this stuffing really resembles rice in its texture and appearance, and the vegetables are really filling.

5 medium-size bell peppers, any color

2 tablespoons unrefined, cold-pressed, extra-virgin olive oil, plus more for peppers

½ onion, minced (can be done in a food processor with the pulse button)

1 garlic clove, minced

1 cup fresh or frozen peas or corn kernels

1 tablespoon chopped fresh cilantro, plus more for garnish (optional)

1 jalapeño pepper, seeded and diced, or a pinch of cayenne pepper

1½ teaspoons sea salt

¼ teaspoon freshly ground black pepper

¼ cup tomato paste + ¼ to ½ cup water (see tip), or ¾ cup tomato-based salsa

4 cups fresh or frozen riced vegetables, such as broccoli rice, cauliflower rice, and/or zucchini rice, or cooked, white or brown rice or gluten-free grain of choice

Preheat the oven to 400°F. While it heats, trim the tops off the bell peppers, just enough to remove the stem. If you want, dice up any pepper that you removed with the stem. Scoop out and discard the seeds. Rub the outside of the peppers with a little olive oil. Place, cut side up, in a baking dish and place in the oven, even if not fully heated to 400°F. Bake for 15 to 20 minutes, or until just softened.

Meanwhile, heat the olive oil in a large skillet over medium heat. Add the onion to the pan. You can also add any pepper bits you may have diced. Sauté until the onion is softened, about 2 minutes, then add the garlic, peas, cilantro, jalapeño, salt, and pepper and sauté for 1 minute.

recipe continues →

↓

tips
———

Use ¼ cup of water if using frozen riced vegetables and ½ cup of water if using fresh. Omit the water if using prepared salsa.

If you want to add cheese, you can sprinkle a little shredded cheese on top of each stuffed pepper (I recommend Monterey Jack, Cojita, or Parmesan) and broil until melted.

If you want to add meat, you can brown some ground meat in the skillet before adding the onion. Remove from the pan and then proceed with the recipe by sautéing the onion. Add the cooked meat to the skillet once all the vegetables are cooked.

If you can't get your peppers to stand up, slice the smallest bit off the bottom to flatten the surface.

For a smaller serving (for a side dish), slice the peppers halfway through the stem and serve ½ pepper per person.

Stir in the tomato paste and water (see tip) and bring to a simmer.

Add the riced vegetables to the skillet and combine well. Taste for seasoning.

Remove the peppers from the oven. Spoon the riced vegetable mixture into each pepper and fill to the top. Garnish with cilantro, if desired.

MAKE IT VEGAN

Do not add meat or cheese (or add vegan cheese).

INSIDE-OUT VEGETARIAN SPRING ROLL BOWL

Vg **GF-*a*** | SERVES 3 OR 4

You know those deep-fried spring rolls, a.k.a. egg rolls, with the healthy cabbage filling? Wellll, there's about a teaspoon of cabbage in those rolls. This recipe takes the greasy, oily, deep-fried roll, turns it inside out, and makes a meal out of the good stuff—that delicious cabbage filling. I'll throw in a sweet-and-sour sauce to be a fun mom, but I eat this bowl without anything because it's really flavorful enough.

2 tablespoons shoyu, tamari, or coconut aminos

1½ teaspoons mirin or unseasoned rice vinegar

1 teaspoon toasted sesame oil

2 tablespoons avocado oil

2 garlic cloves, minced

4 scallions, white and green parts sliced thinly

½ head cabbage, shredded (about 5 cups)

1 cup julienned or shredded carrot (about 1 large carrot)

2 cups sliced shiitake mushrooms, caps wiped clean with a damp paper towel, tough stems discarded

1 cup bean sprouts (omit if you can't find them)

SERVING SUGGESTION: 2 cups cooked white, black, or brown rice

Sweet-and-sour sauce (recipe follows)

tips

EVEN QUICKER

Use a bag of preshredded coleslaw mix and add the green onions and mushrooms.

MAKE IT GLUTEN-FREE

Use gluten-free tamari or coconut aminos.

In a medium-size bowl, combine the shoyu, mirin, and sesame oil and set aside.

Heat a large skillet or wok over medium heat, then add the avocado oil. When the oil is hot, add the garlic and green onion. Sauté for about 30 seconds, or until fragrant.

Add the cabbage, carrots, and mushrooms. Sauté until the vegetables have softened slightly, about 5 minutes.

Add the bean sprouts and sauté for about 1 minute. The bean sprouts should still be crisp. Pour in the shoyu mixture and toss to coat the vegetables.

recipe continues →

To serve, scoop the rice into individual bowls and top with the vegetable mixture. Drizzle with sweet-and-sour sauce (if using).

Sweet-and-Sour Sauce

2 teaspoons arrowroot powder

⅓ cup cider vinegar

⅓ cup light brown sugar or coconut palm sugar

2 tablespoons ketchup (Primal Kitchen makes a sugar-free ketchup)

2 teaspoons shoyu, tamari, or coconut aminos

Whisk together all the sauce ingredients plus 2 tablespoons of water in a small saucepan and cook for 3 to 4 minutes, or until thickened. Store in the fridge for 5 to 7 days.

BLACK BEAN AND MUSHROOM BURGERS

Ve **Vg-a** **GF-a** **DF-a** | SERVES 6

I have craved a veggie burger many times, only to be disappointed that the recipe called for ingredients to have been already roasted, such as a sweet potato, or cooked, such as brown rice; and then you need to let the patty sit in the fridge for half a day. So much for instant gratification! This veggie burger is meaty and hearty and can use ingredients right now from your pantry. And, it will be on your plate in less than thirty minutes. The burger sauce is ridiculously good and can be mixed together while the burgers are cooking.

¼ cup ground flaxseeds

3 tablespoons room-temperature water

1½ tablespoons Worcestershire sauce or any color miso

1 tablespoon cider vinegar or ketchup

1 cup toasted walnuts

½ teaspoon garlic powder

½ teaspoon ground cumin

¼ teaspoon ground coriander

¾ teaspoon sea salt

½ teaspoon freshly ground black pepper

4 ounces cremini mushrooms, caps wiped clean

⅔ cup old-fashioned rolled oats

3 cups cooked black beans, or 2 (15-ounce) cans, drained and rinsed

Unrefined, cold-pressed, extra-virgin olive oil or avocado oil, for cooking

6 whole wheat hamburger buns or butter lettuce leaves, for serving

IDEAS FOR CONDIMENTS: pickled or grilled onions, tomato, avocado, sautéed mushrooms, cheese, burger sauce (recipe follows)

↓

tips

If you'd like to use a regular egg instead of flax, you can swap in one egg for the flaxseed and water and skip straight to the second step.

Make sure the beans aren't saturated with water before adding to the bowl.

MAKE IT GLUTEN-FREE

Use gluten-free buns or lettuce leaves; gluten-free miso.

MAKE IT VEGAN

Use certified gluten-free oats; vegan Worcestershire sauce or miso; vegan buns or lettuce leaves; do not add cheese (or use vegan cheese).

Mix the ground flaxseeds, water, Worcestershire, and vinegar in a small bowl and let sit on the countertop for 15 minutes. Do this while you prep the rest of the ingredients.

In a food processor fitted with the metal S blade, combine the walnuts, garlic powder, cumin, coriander, salt, and pepper and process until fine and crumbly. Add the flax mixture, mushrooms, and oats. Pulse (do *not* puree) until a coarse mixture forms.

recipe continues →

Place the beans in a large bowl and mash coarsely with a potato masher. Do not mash to a puree. The mixture should be coarse and lumpy with some whole beans. Add the walnut mixture and stir to combine.

Fill a ½-cup measuring cup with the bean mixture and form a patty, then transfer to a plate. Repeat the procedure until you have six patties. The patties can be cooked now or refrigerated overnight, if you wish. Pour enough oil into a skillet or onto a griddle to coat the bottom lightly and heat over medium-high heat. Cook the patties for 2 to 3 minutes on each side, or until browned.

Serve with buns or lettuce leaves and your desired accompaniments.

Burger Sauce

6 tablespoons soy-free Vegenaise

1½ tablespoons ketchup

1 tablespoon dill relish

1½ teaspoons prepared yellow mustard

1 small garlic clove, minced

Whisk together all the sauce ingredients in a small bowl.

CHICKPEA TACO LETTUCE CUPS

Ve **GF** **Vg-*a*** **DF-*a*** | SERVES 4 TO 6

Eating less meat is good for the planet, good for your health, and good for your wallet. Yes, I do have many meat recipes in this book because I know it can be part of a healthful diet for many people. But I get much more excited about creating and eating amazing plant-based recipes, such as these chickpea tacos. If you've never had a vegan taco before, you're in for a pleasant surprise. My students all commented how they didn't expect to like these as much as they did. Tacos are all about the seasoning and the toppings, so why can't the humble chickpea make as good a taco filling as meat? It can!

2 tablespoons unrefined avocado oil or cold-pressed, extra-virgin olive oil

3 cups cooked chickpeas, or 2 (15-ounce) cans, drained and rinsed

2 teaspoons chili powder

2 teaspoons ground cumin

¾ teaspoon smoked paprika

½ teaspoon garlic powder

½ teaspoon onion powder

½ teaspoon dried oregano

¼ teaspoon chipotle powder, or to taste

½ to ¾ teaspoon sea salt, depending on whether the chickpeas are salted

1 head romaine lettuce, leaves separated

ACCOMPANIMENTS: guacamole or sliced avocado, pico de gallo, shredded cheese, pickled onions or jalapeño peppers, sliced radishes

Heat a large skillet over medium heat. Heat the oil, add the chickpeas, and stir to coat with the oil. Add the chili powder, cumin, paprika, garlic powder, onion powder, oregano, chipotle powder, and salt and sauté until fragrant, 2 to 3 minutes.

Serve the chickpeas in lettuce leaves with your desired accompaniments.

↓

tips

Sometimes I like to add a few spoonfuls of salsa to the skillet after the chickpeas have cooked with the spices.

MAKE IT VEGAN

Do not add cheese.

BROCCOLI and ROASTED TOMATO STROMBOLI WREATH

Ve **Vg-*a*** **DF-*a*** | SERVES 4 OR 5

Don't be intimidated by this recipe. It sounds harder than it looks, but you'll be able to assemble the wreath in the time it takes the oven to preheat. I started making this stromboli for Christmas gatherings, but it soon became such a favorite that my kids (and friends) begged me to make it all year for weekend lunches and game days. You can use whatever vegetables you want, as long as they have been cooked first. Last night's leftover roasted or grilled vegetables, as well as frozen/defrosted vegetables are perfect here. It's a really fun thing to make with your kids and even more fun to eat.

tip

MAKE IT VEGAN

Use almond-based ricotta; add vegan cheeses (if using).

---

2 tablespoons unrefined, cold-pressed, extra-virgin olive oil

6 garlic cloves, sliced thinly

2 cups frozen broccoli florets, defrosted and patted dry if superwet, chopped

¼ teaspoon sea salt

Freshly ground black pepper

Pinch of crushed red pepper flakes (optional)

Unbleached all-purpose flour or spelt flour, for dusting countertop

1 pound fresh prepared whole wheat or white pizza dough, at room temperature for 15 to 30 minutes

1 cup ricotta, either whole milk—or almond milk–based

½ cup jarred roasted tomatoes or homemade roasted cherry tomatoes

OPTIONAL ADD-INS: 1 cup shredded mozzarella or vegan cheese, a handful of grated Parmesan or vegan alternative, sautéed mushrooms or spinach, pesto

Marinara sauce, warmed, for serving (optional)

Preheat the oven to 450°F. Place a piece of unbleached parchment paper on the countertop, cut to a size that would fit a half sheet pan.

Heat the olive oil in a small skillet over medium-low heat and add the garlic. Cook until the garlic is fragrant and the edges just start to turn golden, about 2 minutes.

recipe continues →

Place the chopped broccoli in a medium-size bowl. Remove the garlic with a spoon and add it to the broccoli along with the salt, pepper, and red pepper flakes. Pour about half of the oil on top and mix to combine. Set aside the skillet with its remaining olive oil.

Lightly dust the countertop with flour. Roll the dough into a 20 x 6-inch rectangle. Transfer to the bottom edge of the parchment paper.

Spread the ricotta down the center of the dough to cover a 20 x 3-inch strip. Top evenly with broccoli and tomatoes. Sprinkle with your desired add-ins, if you wish.

With kitchen shears, cut 1½-inch-long diagonal slits (½ to ¾ inch apart) on both sides of filling. Fold the tabs over filling and pinch the tabs together to seal. Carefully pull both ends together at the top of the paper to form a circle and pinch ends together to seal.

Brush the dough with the reserved garlic oil. Bake until the dough is browned, 18 to 20 minutes. Serve as is or with a bowl of warmed marinara sauce placed in the center.

BAKED PINTO BEAN TOSTADAS

Ve **Vg-*a*** **GF-*a*** **DF-*a*** | MAKES 8 TOSTADAS

Tostadas are merely a crispy, flat corn tortilla piled high with meat or beans and other fresh toppings, such as lettuce, tomatoes, cheese, and guacamole. It's a total mess to eat, but that's part of the fun. You can skip those bags of deep-fried tostada shells at the market and make your own really fast at home. And when I say really fast, I mean, don't step away from the oven while you're broiling them, because you could end up setting them all on fire while you're filming a how-to video for your online class. (Ask me how I know this.) If you don't eat corn tortillas, try your hand at making these with grain-free tortillas.

2 tablespoons unrefined avocado oil or cold-pressed, extra-virgin olive oil

½ large onion, chopped finely

1 jalapeño, seeded and diced finely

3 (14-ounce) cans cooked pinto or black beans—do *not* drain

½ teaspoon sea salt, plus more for sprinkling

Fresh cilantro, minced (optional)

8 (6-inch) soft corn tortillas

Unrefined, cold-pressed, extra-virgin olive oil or avocado oil, for brushing

OPTIONAL TOPPINGS: chopped tomato, shredded cabbage, diced onion, fresh cilantro, shredded Cheddar or Monterey Jack cheese

Heat the oil in a large saucepan over medium heat. Stir in the onion, lower the heat to medium-low, and cover. Stirring occasionally, cook until softened, but not browned, about 10 minutes. Add the jalapeño and cook until tender, about 1 minute.

Pour all the bean liquid into a large measuring cup. Add the beans (no need to rinse) and salt to the saucepan. Add 1½ cups of bean liquid to the pot (save the rest in case you need it) and bring the liquid to a simmer. Cook over medium heat until warmed through, about 8 minutes. Puree the beans with an immersion blender or in a food processor until your desired consistency is reached.

recipe continues →

tips

MAKE IT GLUTEN-FREE

Use gluten-free tortillas.

MAKE IT VEGAN

Do not add cheese (or use a good vegan cheese).

You can also use a potato masher in the pot. Transfer back to the pot if a food processor was used and cook (here's where you can add some minced cilantro, if you like) over medium-low heat until thickened, about 10 minutes. The beans will thicken as they sit. If you need to thin out the beans, add a little of the reserved can liquid.

Position an oven rack about 6 inches from heat. Preheat the oven to BROIL.

While you're cooking the beans, arrange the tortillas, without overlapping, on a baking sheet. Brush both sides of each tortilla with oil. Sprinkle the top with salt.

Broil the tortillas for about 2 minutes on one side. Be sure to watch them so they don't burn. Flip over and broil for 1 to 2 minutes on the opposite side. They will crisp up as they cool. These can be made the day before and kept in a covered container at room temperature.

To serve, spread a dollop of beans on each tortilla and top with your desired toppings. Eat like a pizza. Kind of messy, but fun!

CHIPOTLE TOFU TACOS

Ve **Vg-***a* **GF-***a* **DF-***a* | SERVES 4

This is my husband's favorite vegan dinner. Tofu cubes are coated in a delicious chipotle seasoning and baked, not fried, until lightly crisp. In a perfect world, we'd take time to press the moisture out of the tofu and then a few more hours to marinate it. But even if you press the tofu for five minutes and marinate while the oven is preheating, these will still be amazing. Use these delicious nuggets in lettuce cups, tortillas, or a bowl.

1 (12- to 15-ounce) block extra-firm tofu, preferably organic/non-GMO and sprouted

Marinade

1 tablespoon unrefined, cold-pressed, extra-virgin olive oil

1 tablespoon shoyu, tamari, or coconut aminos

1 tablespoon fresh orange juice or apple juice

2 teaspoons pure maple syrup

1 tablespoon arrowroot powder or non-GMO cornstarch

½ teaspoon chipotle powder

½ teaspoon chili powder

½ teaspoon garlic powder

½ teaspoon smoked paprika or regular paprika

Avocado-Lime Crema (**optional**)

1 large ripe but firm avocado, pitted and peeled

½ cup soy-free Vegenaise, whole unsweetened Greek or regular yogurt, or sour cream

½ cup fresh cilantro leaves and tender stems

Juice of 1 lime (about 2 tablespoons)

¼ teaspoon of salt, plus more to taste

———

Warm corn tortillas or whole lettuce leaves, for serving

IDEAS FOR ACCOMPANIMENTS: pickled onions, shredded cabbage, radishes, salsa

tips

A tofu press is a great tool to have if you make tofu regularly.

MAKE IT GLUTEN-FREE

Use gluten-free tamari or coconut aminos.

MAKE IT VEGAN

Use soy-free Vegenaise for the crema.

Preheat the oven to 400°F and line a large rimmed baking sheet with unbleached parchment paper.

Squeeze the moisture out of the tofu: Slice in half lengthwise, wrap the blocks with paper towels, and place on a cutting board. Place something heavy, such as a skillet filled with cans, on top and allow to sit for 15 minutes

recipe continues →

or longer, if possible. Cut into 1-inch cubes. Don't worry if they can only sit for a couple of minutes.

In a medium-size bowl or a container that can hold the tofu in one layer, mix together all the marinade ingredients until well combined. Add the tofu and gently coat each piece, trying not to break the cubes. If you have time, allow to marinate for 30 minutes, up to 4 hours. Otherwise, proceed to the baking step below.

Meanwhile, make the crema: In a food processor fitted with the metal S blade or in a blender, combine all the crema ingredients and process until smooth, adding a tablespoon or two of water to thin it out, if necessary.

Arrange the tofu in one layer on the prepared baking sheet and bake for 20 to 25 minutes, tossing the tofu halfway, until the tofu is golden on the edges. Serve with tortillas or lettuce leaves as a taco with the avocado crema or on a salad.

VEGETARIAN LARB

DF **Vg-***a* **GF-***a* **Ve-***a* | SERVES 4

If you're not familiar with this dish, the name might throw you off. Larb is a classic Thai salad, usually made with meat. I decided to make a tofu version of it, with all the same flavors and loaded up with lots of fresh herbs. This is a really pretty dish and quick as can be if you have a food processor to do some chopping for you. It's superdelicious in a bowl over black rice or eaten in lettuce cups.

↓

tips

———

MAKE IT GLUTEN-FREE

Use gluten-free tamari or coconut aminos.

MAKE IT VEGAN

Do not use Asian fish sauce.

2 large shallots, peeled and roughly chopped

2 large garlic cloves

8 ounces shiitake mushrooms, wiped clean with a damp paper towel

2 tablespoons unrefined avocado oil, coconut oil, or cold-pressed, extra-virgin olive oil

Sea salt

1 teaspoon coconut palm sugar, maple sugar, or light brown sugar

¼ teaspoon crushed red pepper flakes, or more to taste

14 ounces extra-firm tofu, preferably organic and sprouted, crumbled (by hand)

1 tablespoon shoyu, tamari, coconut aminos, or Asian fish sauce (not vegan)

Juice of ½ lime

FOR SERVING: lettuce leaves; fresh mint, Thai basil, and cilantro leaves; thinly sliced scallions

Place the shallots and garlic in a food processor fitted with the metal S blade. Pulse until finely chopped. Transfer to a bowl and set aside. Place the mushrooms in the food processor and pulse until finely chopped.

Heat the oil in a large skillet or wok over medium heat. Add the shallot mixture and sauté until fragrant, about 3 minutes.

Sprinkle with salt and add the sugar and red pepper flakes and sauté for 1 minute. Add the mushrooms and tofu and increase the temperature to medium-high. Smash the tofu with a potato masher until the pieces are very small. Sauté, stirring frequently, until the mushrooms are tender, about 5 minutes.

Add the shoyu and lime juice and stir to combine.

Serve the larb in lettuce leaves with the fresh herb leaves and scallions.

VEGGIE-STUFFED GRILLED PORTOBELLO MUSHROOMS

Vg **Ve** **GF** | SERVES 4

These portobello mushrooms make such a beautiful and impressive presentation. But it's not just looks. The flavor is amped with a little secret trick: brushing the insides with balsamic vinegar and oil. Once you've done that, you can really fill it as you like. Do seek out deep mushrooms with a good lip as opposed to flat ones that won't hold the filling intact.

4 large portobello mushrooms

4 tablespoons unrefined, cold-pressed, extra-virgin olive oil

2 tablespoons balsamic vinegar, not aged

Sea salt and freshly ground black pepper

1 small yellow onion, sliced (or use leeks, shallot, or green onions)

½ sweet bell pepper, any color, seeded and sliced

½ bunch kale, stemmed and chopped

4 garlic cloves, chopped finely

¼ teaspoon crushed red pepper flakes, or to taste

¼ cup jarred roasted tomatoes or sun-dried tomatoes in oil, chopped

½ (15-ounce) can white beans, such as great northern or cannellini, drained and rinsed (about ¾ to 1 cup)

Preheat a grill to medium-high heat.

Prepare the mushrooms: Remove, dice, and reserve the stems. Scrape out the gills with a spoon and discard. Wipe the caps clean with a damp paper towel.

Use 1½ teaspoons of olive oil to rub the outside of the mushrooms. Mix together 1½ tablespoons of the olive oil and all the balsamic vinegar in a small bowl. Brush on the inside of the mushrooms. Sprinkle with salt and pepper to taste and set aside while you prepare the filling.

recipe continues →

In a large skillet, heat 2 tablespoons of oil over medium heat. Add the reserved diced mushroom stems, onion, bell pepper, and kale. Season with a pinch of salt and pepper and sauté until tender, about 5 minutes.

Add the garlic and red pepper flakes. Sauté until fragrant, about 60 seconds.

Stir in the jarred tomatoes and white beans. Taste for seasoning.

Divide the vegetable mixture equally among the mushroom caps.

Grill the mushrooms, filling side up, for about 7 minutes, or until tender. Serve immediately or at room temperature.

Desserts

There is no shortage of big, sweet dessert recipes in the world, but I don't crave over-the-top, sugar-loaded, insulin-spiking sweets. I can't imagine a life without the occasional dessert, but I prefer to make them with much less of the concentrated sweeteners that standard desserts have; with more natural sweeteners; and in reasonable portions.

The recipes in this chapter taste like legitimate desserts without sacrificing flavor or texture. You'll find brownies, blondies, cookies, and more—but with a fraction of the sweetness. You may even be able to reduce the sweeteners further if you are used to barely sweet desserts. But keeping consistent with the rest of the book, you should be able to make most of these recipes in less than thirty minutes. So, invite your friends over at the last minute, and skip the trip to the bakery.

CRISPY NUT BUTTER CHOCOLATE BALLS

| Ve | GF | Vg-*a* | DF-*a* | | MAKES 16 BALLS |

What is better than nut butter and chocolate? For me, not much. I made these once to satisfy a craving for chocolate (I was trying to avoid my son's stash of Halloween candy that he hides underneath his bathroom sink). I randomly added a few of my favorite crunchy bits, such as chopped peanuts, hemp seeds, and granola to nut butter and made little balls, which I then dipped in dark chocolate. So far, I've never had a combination I didn't like!

1 cup all-natural creamy or crunchy nut or seed butter

4 teaspoons pure maple syrup

4 teaspoons arrowroot powder

¾ cup puffed cereal, such as millet, rice, or quinoa

6 ounces dark chocolate, chopped

Flaky sea salt, if desired

Line a baking sheet (or whatever your freezer can accommodate) with unbleached parchment paper and set aside.

In a medium-size bowl, mix together the nut butter, maple syrup, and arrowroot powder until blended.

Add the puffed cereal and mix until evenly distributed.

Shape into 1-inch balls and place on the prepared baking sheet. Place in the freezer for 20 minutes, or until firm.

Melt the chocolate in a heatproof bowl set over a pot of simmering water (or use a double boiler, if you have it).

Once melted, remove the bowl of chocolate from the heat and dip the balls into the chocolate mixture. Remove with a fork, letting the excess chocolate fall back into the bowl. Place the balls back on the baking sheet. Before the chocolate coating has set, sprinkle the chocolate-covered balls with a pinch of flaky salt, if desired.

Let the balls air dry for 3 to 5 minutes, or until hardened. Store in the fridge in a container lined with parchment.

tip

You can sub hemp seeds, gluten-free granola, and/or raw cacao nibs for some of the cereal.

MAKE IT VEGAN

Use vegan chocolate, vegan granola.

NO-BAKE BROWNIES

Vg **Ve** **GF** | MAKES SIXTEEN 2-INCH-SQUARE BROWNIES

A confession: These aren't quite like a traditional cake brownie, but they are pretty remarkable. The texture is quite fudgy, and they are sweetened only with dates and fortified with walnuts. These are not just fast, but I could argue, good for you, too. Store in the fridge or freezer for a chocolate fix anytime the craving strikes.

Unrefined, virgin coconut oil, for pan

2 cups raw walnut halves or pieces

2½ cups Medjool dates, pitted (about 25 dates or 1 pound)

1 cup raw cacao powder or unsweetened cocoa powder

½ teaspoon sea salt

Coconut palm sugar (optional)

⅔ cup chopped pecans

2 tablespoons raw cacao nibs (optional)

Oil an 8-inch square baking dish with coconut oil and line with unbleached parchment paper.

In a food processor fitted with the metal S blade, process the walnuts to a fine crumb.

Add the dates, cacao powder, and salt and process until the mixture forms a smooth mass. Taste for sweetness and add coconut palm sugar to taste, if necessary. I have never found it necessary.

Stir in the pecans and cacao nibs and transfer the mixture to the prepared baking dish. Press the dough evenly in the dish and refrigerate, covered, for a few hours to set, or in the freezer for 15 to 20 minutes to set more quickly. Store in the refrigerator.

↓

tips

———

Greasing a baking pan or dish helps parchment paper stick and makes it easier to press in batter.

SALTY SNACKS BLONDIES

Ve **Vg-*a*** **GF-*a*** **DF-*a*** | MAKES SIXTEEN 2-INCH-SQUARE BLONDIES

We host a lot of game days at our house, and for a Super Bowl many years back, I wanted to come up with an easy dessert that was fun and in the spirit. I decided to make a blondie batter with crunchy, salty snacks folded in. I've seen potato chips used in chocolate chip cookies, but I wanted to use ingredients that were cleaner than that. If you can find dye-free chocolate candies, those would be fun in the team colors for a big game.

4 tablespoons unsalted butter or vegan butter, at room temperature, plus more for pan

¾ cup creamy or crunchy almond butter or other all-natural nut butter

2 large eggs or flax eggs (see page 16)

1 large egg yolk, or omit for egg-free/vegan

¾ cup coconut palm sugar, maple sugar, or light brown sugar

1 teaspoon pure vanilla extract

¾ cup millet flour, all-purpose flour, or any grain flour

1 teaspoon aluminum-free baking powder

¼ teaspoon sea salt

½ cup semisweet chocolate chips

¼ cup shelled, roasted peanuts, preferably salted

¾ cup plain air-popped popcorn, plus a few pieces for sprinkling on top

½ cup chopped pretzels

¼ cup whole pretzels

Preheat the oven to 350°F. Butter an 8-inch square baking pan with the butter and line the bottom with unbleached parchment paper so that the bars are easy to remove.

Beat together the butter and almond butter in a bowl, using an electric mixer, until creamy. Beat in the eggs, egg yolk, coconut sugar, and vanilla until smooth.

In a small bowl, whisk together the millet flour, baking powder, and salt. Mix the flour mixture into the egg mixture until just combined. Stir in the chocolate chips, peanuts, popcorn, and chopped pretzels. Spread the batter evenly in the prepared pan. Press onto the top the whole pretzels and a few popcorn pieces.

tips

EVEN QUICKER

To soften the butter quickly, before you do anything else, cut the butter into teaspoon-size slices and lay them out on the wrapping paper or a plate.

Look for millet flour in the baking section or near gluten-free flours. Or, to make your own, grind whole grains of millet into a powder in a clean coffee or spice grinder.

MAKE IT GLUTEN-FREE

Use millet or other gluten-free flour; gluten-free pretzels.

MAKE IT VEGAN

Use vegan butter; flax eggs; vegan chocolate chips; vegan pretzels.

Bake until a toothpick inserted into the center comes out with a few moist crumbs on it, about 25 minutes. Do not overbake! Remove from the oven and let cool in the pan for at least 45 minutes before cutting into sixteen squares. You can eat these sooner, but they won't slice as cleanly. Leftovers can be stored in the refrigerator for up to a week. These also freeze beautifully.

PEANUT BUTTER OATMEAL CHOCOLATE CHIP COOKIES

| Vg | Ve | GF-a | | MAKES TWENTY 2½-INCH COOKIES |

These cookies are beyond fabulous, chewy, sweet enough with the perfect touch of saltiness—and they happen to be vegan. Don't let that turn you off. One advantage of a vegan cookie dough is that it is edible raw, too! You can have some fun with this recipe and swap chopped peanuts, dried blueberries, and/or candied ginger for the chocolate chips.

1 cup oat flour (see tip)

1 teaspoon baking soda

1 teaspoon sea salt

1 cup unsweetened, unsalted all-natural peanut butter

3 tablespoons melted unrefined virgin coconut oil

1 cup pure maple syrup

2 teaspoons pure vanilla extract

1½ cups old-fashioned rolled oats

1 cup vegan dark chocolate chips or chunks (nonvegan can be used if not necessary to be vegan)

½ teaspoon flaky sea salt, such as Maldon, for sprinkling (optional)

Preheat the oven to 350°F. Line two baking sheets with parchment paper.

Whisk together the oat flour, baking soda, and salt in a medium-size bowl.

In a large bowl, stir together the peanut butter, coconut oil, maple syrup, and vanilla until well combined.

Stir the flour mixture into the peanut butter mixture.

Fold in the rolled oats and chocolate chips.

Use a 1¾-inch ice-cream scoop to form dough into balls, and place on the prepared baking sheets. You can fit one dozen on a sheet. Flatten cookies slightly with the tines of a fork (you won't actually see the crisscross pattern, but the surface of the cookies will look better than if you flattened them with the palm of your hand). Sprinkle each with flaky sea salt, if desired. Bake for 13 to 15 minutes, or until cookies begin to brown and the tops look dry.

↓

tips

If you need to make oat flour, place 1¼ cups rolled oats in a food processor or high-speed blender and process until powdery.

MAKE IT GLUTEN-FREE

Use gluten-free oat flour and gluten-free rolled oats.

Remove from the oven, let cool a few minutes, then transfer to a wire rack to cool completely.

ASK PAMELA

If I want to freeze cookies, should I freeze them raw or cooked?

I suggest freezing the raw dough, either in dollops or as a log, which you can defrost, slice, and bake.

WATERMELON CAKE

Ve **GF** **Vg-***a* **DF-***a* | SERVES 4; EASILY MULTIPLIED TO SERVE MANY

This isn't exactly a cake made from watermelon (yikes!), in as much as a slab of watermelon dressed up and cut like a dessert pizza. Whatever you call it, it's always light and refreshing in the summer as a last-minute afternoon snack or as a dessert after a barbecue. Since the base of the "cake" is watermelon, I'm pretty generous with the whipped cream and chocolate!

1 round crosswise slice, about 1 inch thick, cut from a whole watermelon

1 cup whipped cream (recipe follows), whipped coconut cream (recipe follows), lightly sweetened Greek yogurt, or prepared vanilla pudding

Any combination of the following toppings:

2 cups fresh seasonal fruit (e.g., peaches, blackberries, blueberries, kiwis, mango), cut into bite-size pieces, if necessary

Sliced almonds

Melted dark or semisweet chocolate

Unsweetened coconut flakes, untoasted or toasted

tips

I like leaving the rind on so people can eat this easily with their hands.

To melt chocolate: Use a double boiler, or place a heatproof bowl atop a pot of simmering water, add the chocolate to the bowl, and stir frequently until smooth.

Mini watermelons work well here, as does freeze-dried fruit if you have it.

MAKE IT VEGAN

Use whipped coconut cream; vegan chocolate.

Quarter the watermelon round into four equal pizza slice–shaped wedges. Transfer to a serving plate and place back together into a circle.

Spread the whipped cream on the center, leaving the rind uncovered. Top as desired and serve.

Whipped Cream (makes 1 cup)

1 cup heavy cream

1 tablespoon unbleached cane sugar

1 teaspoon pure vanilla extract (optional)

Whip the heavy cream with the sugar and vanilla (if using) on high speed in a large bowl (preferably chilled) of an electric mixer fitted with the whisk attachment until soft peaks form, 3 to 4 minutes.

recipe continues →

Whipped Coconut Cream (makes 1 cup)

1 (14-ounce) can coconut cream,
    chilled in refrigerator overnight

1 teaspoon unbleached cane sugar

⅛ teaspoon pure vanilla extract

Whip the coconut cream with the sugar and vanilla on high speed in a large bowl (preferably chilled) of an electric mixer fitted with the whisk attachment until soft peaks form, 3 to 4 minutes.

MEYER LEMON–OLIVE OIL ALMOND CAKE

Ve **GF** **DF-a** | MAKES ONE 9-INCH CAKE OR 8 TO 12 CUPCAKES

I've been holding on to this recipe for so long and could hardly wait to share it with you. This cake is just perfect: The texture is tender; the flavor is bright and lemony; and because the base is almond flour, this cake lasts for a week in the fridge with no loss in moisture or texture. It is at once earthy and elegant, and it's also the easiest cake you'll ever put together. Just blend all the ingredients together in a food processor or blender and bake. If you need an under-thirty-minute recipe, then make cupcakes. If you have a few extra minutes, you can have this beautiful cake.

2 cups fine blanched almond flour (not almond meal)

½ cup organic cornmeal (see tip)

2 teaspoons aluminum-free baking powder

½ teaspoon baking soda

¾ teaspoon sea salt

¼ cup unrefined, cold-pressed extra-virgin olive oil, plus more for pan

3 large eggs

1 cup plain, unsweetened whole milk yogurt or nondairy yogurt

½ cup pure maple syrup or honey

Grated zest of 3 large Meyer lemons, or 1 tablespoon zest from a regular lemon

¼ cup Meyer lemon juice (about 1 large Meyer lemon), or 2 tablespoons regular lemon juice + 2 tablespoons orange juice

2 tablespoons limoncello (optional)

1 tablespoon powdered sugar (optional)

Fresh berries (optional)

Preheat the oven to 350°F. Oil the bottom and sides of a 9-inch springform pan with olive oil and line the bottom with unbleached parchment paper. If using a muffin tin, line the bottoms of eight to twelve wells with unbleached parchment liners.

In a food processor fitted with the metal S blade, combine all the ingredients, except powdered sugar and fresh berries. Process until well blended, scraping down the sides of the bowl once to make sure all ingredients are well incorporated.

recipe continues →

↓

tips
___

Fine cornmeal will have less texture than medium grind/coarse or use an equal amount of arrowroot powder for a grain-free cake. You will need to use grain-free baking powder, as well.

You can add 2 tablespoons of poppy seeds to the food processor after blending, if desired.

To make a small cake, halve all the ingredients and bake in a parchment paper–lined 6-inch round cake pan.

MAKE IT DAIRY-FREE

Use nondairy yogurt.

Pour the batter into the prepared cake pan or muffin tin, filling the wells almost to the top.

Bake in the middle of the oven for 30 to 40 minutes for the cake or 20 to 25 minutes for cupcakes, until the tops are lightly browned and springy to the touch and a toothpick comes out clean. The baking time will depend on your oven. Remove from the oven and allow the cake or cupcakes to cool in the pan for 5 minutes before transferring to a wire rack to cool completely. Serve with a dusting of powdered sugar and fresh berries, if desired.

MICROWAVE CHOCOLATE MUG CAKE

Ve GF-*a* DF-*a* | SERVES 1

The idea of a one-minute chocolate cake is so seductive. In one minute, I can satisfy my chocolate cravings without a box mix? Well, not all is what it seems. The problem I encountered with every recipe I tried was in using a whole egg for one mug cake. Most grain-based cakes call for two eggs for an entire cake, so using one whole egg with so little flour made the texture not really cakelike. One egg yolk, however, made the cake the perfect consistency. I wish I had known about this miracle when I was in college!

4 teaspoons unsalted butter or vegan butter

1 tablespoon milk, any kind

¼ teaspoon pure vanilla extract

1 large egg yolk

2 tablespoons maple sugar or cane sugar

4 teaspoons unsweetened cocoa powder

⅛ teaspoon aluminum-free baking powder

Pinch of sea salt

2½ tablespoons whole wheat pastry flour or your favorite GF flour blend (I prefer gluten-free flour in this recipe)

Big pinch of semisweet chocolate chips (optional)

Place the butter in a 12-ounce microwaveable mug. Microwave on HIGH for 30 seconds to melt.

With a fork, stir in the milk, vanilla, and egg yolk.

Add the sugar, cocoa powder, baking powder, and salt and stir until smooth.

Stir in the flour until just combined. Drop in the chocolate chips (if using).

Microwave on 50 percent power for 1 minute 30 seconds, or until set and no longer wet. (This was the perfect time for my microwave.) Allow to sit for 1 minute before eating. Best eaten right after microwaved.

↓

tips

If you need ideas for what to do with the leftover egg white, add it to a batch of pancakes or waffle batter, or a frittata or scrambled eggs.

MAKE IT GLUTEN-FREE

Use a gluten-free flour blend.

MAKE IT DAIRY-FREE

Use vegan butter; nondairy milk; vegan chocolate chips (if using).

STOVETOP APPLE CRISP

Ve **Vg-***a* **GF-***a* **DF-***a* | SERVES 6 TO 8

If there is one dessert that I have made consistently with rave reviews for the last thirty years, it is a seasonal fruit crisp. What's not to love about warm, tender fruit with a sweet, crunchy topping? Arguably, only a scoop of ice cream could make it better. Well, I think cooking a fruit crisp faster would make it better for me! This is a two-step process, but each step takes under ten minutes, which sure beats the normal one-hour cook time. A little bonus is that you can prepare both the fruit and the topping the day before, if you need to.

Topping

⅔ cup whole-grain flour, such as oat flour, whole wheat pastry, white whole wheat, or a good GF flour blend

⅓ cup old-fashioned rolled oats (optional, but I prefer them in here)

½ cup maple sugar, packed light brown sugar, cane sugar, muscovado sugar, or coconut palm sugar (or a combo)

¼ teaspoon ground cinnamon

¼ teaspoon sea salt

¾ cup chopped pecans

½ teaspoon pure vanilla extract

6 tablespoons unsalted butter, unrefined virgin coconut oil (see tip), or vegan butter, such as Miyoko's Creamery, melted

Filling

1 cup unsweetened apple cider or juice

1 tablespoon arrowroot powder

1½ pounds organic apples, peeled or unpeeled (my preference), cored, and sliced ¼ inch thick (about 3 large or 6 to 7 small apples)

¾ teaspoon ground cinnamon

⅛ teaspoon ground nutmeg

⅛ teaspoon ground allspice

⅛ teaspoon sea salt

↓

tips

The coconut oil topping doesn't cluster quite as much as the other two fat options.

The apple filling can be made a day in advance. Cover and refrigerate. Reheat in the same pan when ready to serve. If you're tight on time, make the filling and top with your favorite granola.

Use a 13-inch pan to make a double batch.

MAKE IT GLUTEN-FREE

Use certified gluten-free oat flour or a gluten-free flour blend; gluten-free rolled oats.

MAKE IT VEGAN

Use coconut oil or vegan butter; if serving with ice cream, make sure it is vegan.

Prepare the topping: Combine the flour, oats, maple sugar, cinnamon, salt, and all the pecans in a bowl.

Stir in the vanilla and melted butter until the mixture resembles wet sand and no dry flour remains.

Transfer the flour mixture to a 10-inch skillet. Cook over medium-low heat, stirring constantly, until lightly browned, 6 to 8 minutes; transfer to a flat

recipe continues →

plate to cool. It will crisp up as it cools. Wipe out the skillet with a paper towel. You'll use the skillet again to cook the apples.

Prepare the filling: In a small bowl, whisk together 2 tablespoons of the apple cider and the arrowroot powder. Set aside.

In a medium-size bowl, combine the apples, remaining ¾ cup plus 2 tablespoons of apple cider, cinnamon, nutmeg, allspice, and salt.

Transfer the apple mixture to the skillet and bring to a simmer over medium heat. Cover, lower the heat to medium-low, and cook for 6 to 8 minutes, or until tender, stirring apples at about the 6-minute point.

Once the apples are tender, lower the heat to low and immediately stir in the arrowroot mixture. Mix until the arrowroot mixture is evenly distributed and the juices have thickened, about 1 minute.

Top the warm apple filling with the crisp topping and serve immediately. Or scoop the fruit into individual bowls and spoon the topping on top.

MIXED BERRY FRUIT COOKIE PIZZA

Ve **GF** **Vg-a** **DF-a** | SERVES 6

This is basically a huge cookie cut like a pizza. It's a recipe I turn to when I want to make a fast, healthy-ish treat. The first time I made it, my kids and I broke it up at the kitchen table and started eating it all different ways. I loved it plain with a cup of tea. My husband smeared it with chocolate nut butter and added a couple of raspberries. My daughter topped hers with Greek yogurt and chia jam. The point is there are so many ways to enjoy this. The recipe multiplies easily so you can make several very quickly and top them different ways, which is a fun idea for feeding a crowd of mixed palates and mixed ages.

Crust

2 cups blanched fine almond flour (not almond meal)

¼ teaspoon sea salt

¼ teaspoon baking soda

2 teaspoons pure vanilla extract

1½ tablespoons unrefined coconut oil, melted

3 tablespoons pure maple syrup

Topping

8 ounces cream cheese, vegan (such as Kite Hill) or regular, at room temperature, or strained Greek yogurt (see tip)

3 tablespoons pure maple syrup

½ teaspoon pure vanilla extract

Fresh berries (all of one or a combination of blueberries, raspberries, sliced or diced strawberries, blackberries)

Your choice of toppings (see tip)

Prepare the crust: Preheat the oven to 350°F and line a baking sheet with unbleached parchment paper.

Combine all the crust ingredients in a medium-size bowl, using a wooden spoon, then use your hands to form a ball of dough.

Place the dough on the prepared baking sheet and flatten out with your hands or the bottom of a measuring cup to make a 9-inch circle or make two 6-inch

recipe continues →

↓

tips

The possibilities are endless when it comes to toppings. You can use any seasonal fruit and an array of other toppings, such as toasted seeds, chopped nuts, toasted coconut flakes, hemp seeds, edible flowers, or a drizzle of dark chocolate or nut butter. Instead of sweetened cream cheese, you can use melted dark chocolate, nut butters, mascarpone or ricotta cheese, or Whipped Coconut Cream (page 298). For a more grown-up version, try using savory ingredients with the fruit, such as basil, lemon zest, balsamic vinegar, or ginger.

To strain Greek yogurt, line a colander with a clean, thin kitchen towel, such as a flour sack towel. Spoon the yogurt into the towel, cover, and refrigerate at least 3 to 4 hours. The yogurt will be the consistency of cream cheese. You can even replace the towel after 4 hours and strain a second time, for an even thicker consistency. Not quick, but worth knowing how to do!

cookies. I like a rustic edge, but you can push the edge in to make it more smooth and perfect.

Bake for 15 to 20 minutes, or until lightly golden brown and slightly puffed. Remove from the oven and allow to cool either on the pan or by transferring the cookie and parchment to a wire rack (it will cool faster this way).

Prepare the topping: In the bowl of a mixer, beat together the cream cheese, maple syrup, and vanilla until light and fluffy, 1 to 2 minutes. Spread on the cooled crust.

Top with fresh berries, slice into wedges, and serve.

↓

tips

You can make this ahead and leave it covered at room temperature for a couple of days. Frost and top just before serving.

MAKE IT VEGAN

Use a vegan cream cheese; vegan chocolate; coconut whipped cream.

GRILLED MIXED BERRY PACKETS

Ve **Vg-*a*** **GF-*a*** **DF-*a*** | SERVES 1

Dessert was a special occasion food when I was a child. After dinner, my mother put out a bowl of whatever fruit was in season and some nuts with nutcrackers. When I became a mom, I never started a habit of dessert after dinner unless it was mostly fruit. These packets are a fun and quick way to serve berries that will feel more like a treat. The best part is that everyone can top their berries their own way. This is also a perfect dessert if you're camping or if you don't want anything to clean up afterward.

¾ cup fresh or frozen, defrosted berries

¼ teaspoon pure maple syrup or maple sugar

Toasted coconut, chocolate shavings, toasted nuts, granola for topping, or serve with frozen yogurt or ice cream

Preheat a grill to medium-high heat. Cut one 12-inch-square rectangle each of foil and unbleached parchment paper. Place the parchment on top of the foil.

Arrange the berries in the middle of the parchment and drizzle with the syrup, or sprinkle with the sugar. The fruit will cook more evenly if it's in one layer.

Crumple everything up in the foil and cook, covered on the grill grates or coals for 5 to 7 minutes, or until the berries begin to burst.

Open the packet carefully, top the fruit with your desired toppings, and eat.

↓

tips

Don't go smaller than 12 x 9 inches with the foil/paper packets.

EVEN QUICKER

No need to preheat the grill; put the packets on a gas burner over medium heat and cook for the same amount of time.

MAKE IT GLUTEN-FREE

Use gluten-free granola for topping.

MAKE IT VEGAN

Use vegan chocolate shavings and/or granola; serve with nondairy yogurt or vegan ice cream.

MAPLE ROASTED STONE FRUIT

Ve **GF** **Vg-*a*** **DF-*a*** | SERVES 4

Roasting fruit intensifies its flavor and sweetness and adding a creamy dollop just adds a little decadence. Almond extract is much stronger than vanilla extract, so a little goes a long way. Almonds are very complementary with stone fruit, since they are all a member of the Prunus genus. This recipe is the perfect healthful end to a late spring/summer meal or an indulgent brunch.

tip

MAKE IT VEGAN

Use vegan butter; serve with nondairy frozen yogurt or vegan ice cream.

4 teaspoons pure maple syrup

1 teaspoon pure vanilla extract

¼ teaspoon pure almond extract

8 apricots, halved and pitted

2 tablespoons unsalted butter or unrefined virgin coconut oil or vegan butter, divided into 8 equal dots

Chopped almonds, pecans, or pistachios

Sweetened Greek yogurt, vanilla frozen yogurt or ice cream, lightly sweetened crème fraîche

Preheat the broiler. Combine the maple syrup, vanilla, and almond extract in a small bowl.

Arrange the apricots, cut side up, on a rimmed baking sheet or in a baking dish. Brush the cut side with the maple mixture. Dot with the butter. Broil 6 inches from the heat for 2 to 5 minutes, or until softened and golden brown. Serve with chopped nuts and Greek yogurt.

NO-CHURN PEACH or MANGO GELATO

Ve **GF** **Vg-*a*** **DF-*a*** | SERVES 4

I included a luscious, no-churn strawberry gelato recipe in Kitchen Matters *and it is still a dessert I make all the time. You can't beat an almost all fruit "gelato" that uses a food processor over an ice-cream maker. But instead of washing, chopping, and freezing fresh fruit, I created a simplified, quicker version for this book, using already-frozen fruit that you probably have in the freezer for smoothies anyway. I was delighted to test this recipe with mango and peach to find out they puree into a silky, sorbetlike consistency just as well as strawberries.*

2 pounds frozen peach slices or frozen mango cubes

¼ cup unsweetened yogurt, any kind

½ cup pure maple syrup, or to taste, depending on sweetness of the fruit (see tip)

Place the fruit with the yogurt and maple syrup in the bowl of a food processor fitted with the metal S blade. Turn the machine on and puree the mixture, stopping a few times to scrape down the bowl with a spatula. Continue to puree until a smooth, creamy consistency is achieved. This could take a few minutes. Taste for sweetness. Serve immediately or store in the freezer. If the gelato freezes solid, allow it to sit at room temperature for about 10 minutes.

↓

tips

Swap in a little peach schnapps for some of the maple syrup. The alcohol will help to prevent the gelato from completely freezing solid.

You can use a high-powered blender, but it will take a little more effort to use the tamper to push the fruit down; you'll also need to scrape the sides occasionally.

MAKE IT VEGAN

Use nondairy yogurt.

MAGIC CHOCOLATE HARD SHELL

Vg | Ve | GF | SERVES 1 OR 2

I really thought the Magic Shell product from the 1970s was truly magic. Imagine pouring a thick chocolate sauce over ice cream that would harden on contact, resulting in a shell you could crack with your spoon. Such fun! There were a lot of very unnatural ingredients in that bottle, but coconut oil was the one that created all the "magic." It's pretty easy to duplicate this sauce with much healthier ingredients.

1 tablespoon cacao powder, or ¼ cup vegan dark chocolate disks or bar chocolate (see tip)

1 tablespoon unrefined virgin coconut oil, at room temperature

½ teaspoon pure maple or date syrup

In a small saucepan, melt together all the ingredients over low heat, stirring regularly.

Remove from the heat, let cool for about 1 minute, then drizzle over your desired frozen treat, allowing it to set before cracking it with a spoon.

tip

If using dark chocolate versus cacao powder, omit the syrup.

Basics

There are certain recipes that I use over and over again in my cooking. These are basic things, such as hard-boiled eggs, flavored nut butters—some that you can buy, but all are pretty easy to make at home to have on hand.

FLAVORED NUT BUTTERS

Vg | Ve | GF | MAKES 16 OUNCES FLAVORED NUT BUTTER

Making nut butter from scratch is actually not that hard, but it can burn out your food processor. Not worth it! So, I like to buy good organic almond butter or other nut butter (your local grocery store may have a machine in-house that makes it fresh) and drop it into my food processor with some fun flavors to make my own specialty blends. Transferred into cute glass canning jars, these nut butters also make a great gift. Here are some of my favorites that are mere ideas for you to do your own thing:

- 16 ounces almond butter + 2 tablespoons pure maple syrup + ½ teaspoon ground cinnamon + 2 tablespoons chia seeds
- 16 ounces peanut butter + 2 tablespoons honey + pinch of salt
- 16 ounces almond butter + 2 tablespoons raw cacao + 2 tablespoons pure maple syrup + pinch of cayenne pepper + pinch of salt
- 16 ounces raw cashew butter + 1 tablespoon coconut oil + 1 teaspoon pure vanilla extract + pinch of salt + 2 tablespoons cacao nibs

HARD-BOILED EGGS

GF | DF

I've done a 180 on my hard-boiled egg technique. The way to get your shells to come off easily, even with very fresh eggs, which are notoriously hard to peel, is to add the eggs to already boiling water.

Prepare a medium-size bowl with ice water.

Bring a pot of water to a boil. The water should be deep enough to cover the eggs well.

Slide the eggs in gently. I place an egg on a large spoon and place the spoon into the water on the bottom of the pot and allow the egg to slide off. Or you can do many eggs at once with a spider or a skimmer.

Set your timer accordingly:

- 6 minutes: liquidy yolk, but cooked whites
- 8 minutes: jammy yolk
- 10 minutes: mostly hard yolk, but the center still slightly soft
- 12 minutes: uniformly cooked, firm yolk

Submerge the eggs in the ice water bath and allow them to chill for at least 1 minute. Crack the egg on both ends and peel under running water. Or chill, unpeeled, in the refrigerator for up to 7 days.

QUICK PICKLED VEGETABLES

| Vg | Ve | GF | | MAKES 2 CUPS |

I love having these in the fridge for sandwiches, salads, wraps, tacos, chili, and bowls! Pick a vegetable. These are my favorites, but there are others you can use:

¼ cup vinegar (white, red wine, white wine, rice, or cider vinegar)

1 tablespoon granulated cane sugar

½ teaspoon kosher salt

4 medium-size shallots, or

1 red onion, sliced thinly, or

Bunch of radishes, cut into fourths or sixths or

2 carrots, peeled and sliced into rounds or long matchsticks

Combine 1 cup of water and the vinegar, sugar, and salt in a small saucepan and bring to a boil. Add the prepared vegetables and simmer for 15 minutes. Remove from the liquid and set aside in a bowl to cool. Store in a glass jar in the refrigerator for up to 1 month.

SALSA VERDE

Vg | Ve | GF | **MAKES ABOUT 1 CUP SALSA**

This is my go-to pesto alternative; it is both dairy-free and nut-free but still packed with flavor. Drizzle this on any protein, cooked vegetables, or eggs, or stir into beans or grains. Play around with different combinations of fresh herbs depending on what you have in the fridge or garden.

1 cup chopped, fresh flat-leaf parsley

2 tablespoons capers, drained and chopped

1 medium-size garlic clove, minced

Zest of 1 small lemon (about 1½ teaspoons)

Pinch of crushed red pepper flakes

Sea salt

⅔ cup good olive oil

1 tablespoon white wine vinegar

Mix all ingredients in a bowl or pulse in a food processor to achieve your desired texture. Store in the refrigerator for up to a week. Taste before serving and adjust the seasonings (vinegar and salt) accordingly.

MY FAVORITE EVERYDAY SALAD DRESSING

Vg | Ve | GF | **MAKES ABOUT 1 CUP DRESSING**

I've been making this vinaigrette once or twice a week for about fifteen years and it's still my #1 favorite. I know it so well, I don't even measure the ingredients anymore!

1 small shallot, minced

¾ to 1 teaspoon sea salt

Freshly ground black pepper

1 teaspoon Dijon mustard

2 teaspoons pure maple syrup

2 tablespoons raw cider vinegar or red wine vinegar

2 tablespoons unseasoned rice vinegar or fresh lemon juice

¾ cup unrefined olive oil or ½ cup olive oil + ¼ cup flax oil

Shake everything in a glass jar with a screw-top lid or whisk in a medium-size bowl. Store at room temperature for a few days or in the refrigerator for a week. If you're using real olive oil, it will solidify in the fridge after a few days. Allow the dressing to sit at room temperature for 20 minutes to come back to a liquid state.

BASIL-PARSLEY PESTO

Ve **GF** **Vg-a** **DF-a** | MAKES 2 CUPS PESTO

Pesto is the condiment I use more than any other, on pizza, quesadillas, pasta, spaghetti squash, and in salad dressings and stir-fries. I like lightening up a traditional all-basil pesto with a bit of parsley. If you like variety, I've included a recipe for anchovy pesto; also see page 119 for my recipe for roasted red pepper pesto.

¼ cup walnuts

¼ cup pine nuts or hemp seeds

1½ to 2 tablespoons chopped garlic

2½ cups lightly packed, fresh basil leaves

2½ cups lightly packed, fresh flat-leaf parsley leaves

¾ teaspoon sea salt

A couple of grinds of black pepper

1 cup unrefined, cold-pressed, extra-virgin olive oil

½ cup grated Pecorino Romano or Parmesan cheese

↓

tip

MAKE IT VEGAN

Omit the salt and cheese and sub in a dark miso paste.

Place the walnuts, pine nuts, and garlic in a food processor fitted with the metal S blade. Process until finely chopped.

Add the basil leaves, parsley, salt, and pepper. With the motor running, slowly pour the olive oil into the bowl through the feed tube and process until the pesto is finely pureed. Add the grated cheese and puree until well blended.

ANCHOVY PESTO

GF **DF** | MAKES ABOUT 1 CUP

I love the addition of anchovy paste to this pesto. You can't tell it's in there, but it's like an umami flavor bomb. Use it just as you would any traditional pesto.

⅓ cup blanched almonds or walnuts, toasted if desired

3 medium-size garlic cloves

1 cup packed, fresh flat-leaf parsley, mint, and/or cilantro leaves (I like ¾ cup parsley + ¼ cup mint)

1 tablespoon anchovy paste, or a few anchovy fillets (or more if desired)

2 teaspoons white wine vinegar

¼ teaspoon crushed red pepper flakes (or more to make it spicy)

¼ teaspoon sea salt

Freshly ground black pepper

½ cup unrefined, cold-pressed extra-virgin olive oil

Place the nuts and garlic in a food processor fitted with the metal S blade. Process until finely chopped. Add the herbs, anchovy paste, vinegar, red pepper flakes, salt, and pepper to taste. With the motor running, slowly pour the olive oil into the bowl through the feed tube and process until the pesto is finely pureed.

Store in the refrigerator for 5 to 7 days.

BASIC WHITE BASMATI RICE

Ve **GF** **Vg-a** **DF-a** | SERVES 4

This is my go-to rice method and has so much more flavor than just plain rice, but still just as easy. Use Countertop Foods golden butter and a pinch of kitchari spices (see tip, page 146) for a different flavor profile.

1 cup uncooked white basmati rice, rinsed under cold water if desired

1 medium-size garlic clove, smashed with the side of a knife

½ teaspoon sea salt

2 teaspoons olive oil, unsalted butter, avocado oil, or vegan butter

Combine the rice, 2 cups of water, and the garlic, salt, and oil in a medium-size saucepan. Bring to a boil over high heat. Lower the heat to a simmer, cover, and cook for 18 minutes, or until all liquid has evaporated. Do not stir or peek while cooking. If there's time, allow to sit off the heat, covered, for 10 minutes.

↓

tips

Add 1 cup of riced cauliflower or other riced vegetables with the other ingredients. No need to adjust the quantity of water.

Freeze the rice in a container with a tight lid in quantities that you are likely to use (don't freeze a huge amount).

MAKE IT VEGAN

Use olive or avocado oil, or vegan butter.

BASIC QUINOA

Vg | Ve | GF | MAKES ABOUT 4½ CUPS
COOKED QUINOA

Quinoa is a high-protein grain (although technically a seed) with a light, fluffy texture and nutty flavor. It is one of my favorite plant-based proteins, which I love in soups, salads, and stir-fries.

1½ cups uncooked quinoa, rinsed in a fine-mesh sieve
Pinch of sea salt

Place the quinoa, 2⅔ cups of water, and the salt in a medium-size saucepan and bring to a boil. Cover, lower the heat to a simmer, and cook, covered, for 15 minutes, or until all the water is absorbed. Turn off the heat and allow to sit, covered, for 5 to 10 minutes. Fluff with fork and serve.

Freeze for up to 3 months in a covered container, in quantities that you will use.

BASIC LENTILS

Vg | Ve | GF | MAKES 2½ TO 3 CUPS
COOKED LENTILS

Lentils are my favorite vegan protein source. They are so tasty, filling, and loaded with fiber and protein. If I have them cooked in the fridge or freezer, they're an easy protein in a salad, stir-fry, or bowl.

1 cup dried lentils—my favorite are Puy, picked through and rinsed
¾ teaspoon kosher salt

Place the lentils, 3 cups of water, and the salt in a medium-size saucepan and bring to a boil over high heat. Lower the heat to a simmer, cover, and cook until tender, 25 to 30 minutes. You can also cook them in your Instant Pot set to HIGH PRESSURE for 12 minutes. Different varieties of lentils cook in different amounts of time, so refer to the package directions, if applicable.

Drain and store in the refrigerator for up to 1 week. Lentils also freeze well.

BASIC BEANS with A QUICK-SOAK METHOD

Beans are a very economical source of plant-based protein and so versatile. I keep many varieties of both dried and canned beans in my pantry for salads, soups, purees, even blended into desserts. One pound of dried beans yields about the equivalent of four 15-ounce cans. Even though I keep canned beans on hand, I prefer cooking my own to save money. You just need to plan in advance since they take some time to cook. Presoaking can improve digestibility.

Place dried beans in a large pot and cover with water by 3 to 4 inches. Bring to a boil, cover, and remove from the heat. Allow to soak for 1 hour.

Drain the beans and boil in fresh water to cover by 3 to 4 inches for 1 to 2 hours, or until tender, depending on the type of bean.

Slow cooker method

My 6½-quart slow cooker can accommodate up to 2 pounds of dried beans. Cook the beans covered in fresh water in a slow cooker for 6 to 7 hours on LOW or 4 to 5 hours on HIGH.

(Although this method takes longer than 30 minutes, I wanted to include it here since having a base of beans available is one key to quicker cooking.)

Pressure cooker method

Pressure cook the beans covered with water (do not exceed the MAX line in the insert) on high pressure for 30 to 35 minutes. Use the quick-release method at the end of the cook time.

I like to add a big pinch of kosher salt to the beans right before they have achieved tenderness. In the case of pressure-cooked beans, salt after the lid is removed and allow the beans to sit with the cooking liquid and salt for 10 minutes.

BASIC PAN-SEARED TOFU

Vg **Ve** **GF** | SERVES 2 TO 4, DEPENDING ON USE

Tofu is an easy plant-based protein to add to salads, stir-fries, and bowls. Searing it gives it a desirable crispy texture. Tofu has virtually no flavor, so it goes with anything and takes on the flavors of any dressing or sauce.

1 (14-ounce) package extra-firm tofu, preferably organic and sprouted

1 cup gluten-free flour blend, arrowroot powder/flour, tapioca flour/starch, or cassava flour

2 tablespoons avocado or coconut oil, depending on what else you will serve with it

Cut the tofu into 1-inch thick slabs and lay on top of two layers of paper towels on a cutting board. Cover with another two layers of paper towels. Place a baking dish or baking sheet on top of the tofu and weigh it down with a heavy pot or canned goods. Allow the moisture to be absorbed from the tofu for at least 30 minutes, but you can cut this short if necessary. Alternatively, you can place the whole block of tofu in a tofu press and allow it to sit in there for 15 to 30 minutes. Cut into 1-inch thick slabs.

Remove the tofu from the paper towels and dredge in the flour. Shake off the excess.

Heat the oil in a large skillet over medium heat. Add one slice of tofu. If it starts to sizzle, add the remaining slices (or whatever will fit into the pan) in one layer. Do not allow the slices to touch. Cook until the underside is golden brown, 5 to 6 minutes. Flip over with a metal spatula and cook the other side until golden brown, 5 to 6 minutes. Repeat with the remaining slices.

SEARED CAULIFLOWER STEAKS

Vg Ve GF | MAKES 6 "STEAKS"

Cauliflower steaks are my favorite meat substitute. They can take on any sauce or seasoning that animal protein can and still feel substantial on their own. Cauliflower steaks are also a great option when you want a lighter meal.

2 large heads cauliflower or 3 medium-size heads, preferably ones with tight clusters of florets

Avocado oil

Sea salt

Freshly ground black pepper

Preheat the oven to 375°F.

Trim away the big outer leaves from the cauliflower and trim the bottom stem end. With the stem end facing up, cut straight through the middle of the core. Trim the rounded side on each half that isn't cut, keeping the core intact, giving you two "steaks" with flat sides. Reserve the florets that were cut off. A large head of cauliflower might yield three or four steaks.

Heat a large cast-iron pan over medium-high heat. Add the avocado oil and then arrange the cauliflower steaks in one layer in the skillet. Season with salt and pepper. Sear until the underside is golden, about 4 minutes. Carefully flip over and cook the other side until it is golden, 3 to 4 minutes.

Place the pan in the oven and roast the cauliflower for 8 to 10 minutes, or until tender (test it by piercing the core with a knife).

VEGETABLE STOCK

Vg Ve GF | MAKES ABOUT 3 QUARTS STOCK

Homemade vegetable stock is so much better than anything you can buy in the store and for a fraction of the price. This recipe calls for certain quantities of fresh vegetables, but I often use (washed) scraps that might otherwise be composted or discarded: tops of leeks, parsley stems, woody ends of asparagus, shiitake mushroom stems, carrot peels, ends from squashes, fennel tops, and so forth. You can freeze these scraps until you are ready to make stock. I usually avoid beets (the color bleeds); tomatoes (too acidic); and sulfur-containing vegetables, such as cabbage, broccoli, and cauliflower, since their flavors can be overpowering. To increase the nutrients in the stock, simmer with a strip of kombu (kelp).

3 large onions, cut into large chunks

2 large parsnips, unpeeled, cut into large chunks

2 large carrots, unpeeled, cut into large chunks

3 celery stalks, cut into large chunks

8 ounces white mushrooms, chopped

6 large garlic cloves, crushed

A few sprigs fresh parsley

2 sprigs thyme, or 2 bay leaves

Place all the ingredients plus 4 quarts of water in a large pot and bring to a boil over high heat. Lower the heat and simmer, uncovered, for 30 to 60 minutes.

Remove the pot from the heat and strain the stock into a large bowl, pushing against the vegetables to extract additional liquid. Discard the vegetables.

Store in the refrigerator for up to 5 days, or in the freezer for up to 3 months.

CHICKEN STOCK

GF **DF** | MAKES 4 TO 5 QUARTS STOCK

Homemade chicken stock makes a huge difference in the flavor of soups and stews. It does take some time to prepare, so I tend to make a lot at once and freeze it in different quantities. To make bone broth, simply simmer the broth for 18 to 72 hours.

4 pounds bony organic chicken parts, such as backs, necks, and wings (if you can get chicken feet, use them!)

6 quarts cold water (see tip)

1 tablespoon cider vinegar (see tip)

1 large onion, peeled and halved

2 carrots, peeled

2 celery stalks, cut if necessary

2 teaspoons sea salt

A few sprigs parsley

Place the chicken parts in a large stainless-steel stockpot. Add the cold water and vinegar. Bring to a boil over high heat.

Immediately lower the heat to low and skim off with a slotted spoon any foam that rises to the surface. Try not to skim off any of the fat, or you will lose a bit of flavor. At this point, it is important to keep the stock to a simmer and *not* a boil.

After skimming off all the foam, add the onion, carrots, and celery. Cook, uncovered, at a gentle simmer for 4 to 5 hours. About 10 minutes before finishing the stock, add the sea salt and parsley.

Strain the stock into a large glass or stainless-steel bowl. Allow to cool for 2 hours before covering and refrigerating.

Ladle into quart-size containers or whatever size is most useful and refrigerate overnight. The next day, skim off the congealed fat at the top of each container. Refrigerate the stock for up to 5 days or freeze for up to 3 months.

tips

Cold water draws the flavor out of the meat and bones.

Acidic wine or vinegar added during cooking helps to draw minerals, particularly calcium, magnesium, and potassium, into the broth.

KITCHEN CALCULATIONS

I did the math, so you don't have to!

   If you are increasing or decreasing the amount a recipe serves, it is important to know the volume of your cookware, especially with respect to baking. Sometimes, we don't have the size pan specified in the recipe and we need to know the closest substitutes. Getting as close as possible to the right size is the goal.

Area of Commonly Used Bakeware and Cookware

6-inch round	28 sq. inches
8-inch round	50 sq. inches
8-inch square	64 sq. inches
9-inch round	64 sq. inches
9-inch square	81 sq. inches
10-inch round	78.5 sq. inches
11-inch round	95 sq. inches
12-inch round	113 sq. inches
13-inch round	133 sq. inches
8½ x 4½-inch loaf pan	38 sq. inches
9 x 5-inch loaf pan	45 sq. inches
11 x 7-inch baking dish	77 sq. inches
13 x 9-inch baking dish	117 sq. inches

Acknowledgments

My goal has remained consistent over the last decade and a half—to help people support better health through food and cooking. Teaching cooking classes will always be my first love, but has its limits with how many people I can reach. So, the opportunity to have not just one cookbook published, but two, is a dream come true. Whereas teaching a cooking class can be accomplished single-handedly, giving birth to a cookbook cannot. And ironically, a cookbook about quick cooking does not come together any more quickly than any other cookbook! I have so many incredible people to thank for helping me make this book the best it could be.

To my three angels, Emma, Anna, and Andrew. You are my number one reason for constantly pushing myself to create the best-tasting, healthiest food possible. Thank you for sometimes eating the same dish multiple nights in a row, for trusting me when I put cauliflower in your oatmeal, for lending me your capable hands to make dinner prep go more quickly, and so much more. I am so proud that over the years you have learned enough about food, nutrition, and cooking that you can all independently make good choices and cook something wonderful on your own.

To my husband, Daniel. You were my original picky eater and my biggest cheerleader. I love you for more reasons than I can name here, but not the least of which is for your unwavering encouragement and providing me the freedom to do what I love every day. I am the luckiest girl in the world to have you by my side on this journey where anything is possible.

To my parents, Lois and Mario. You may not realize it, but this is all because of you. You instilled in me an education of what real food is and where it comes from, and why it's worth making an effort to cook for your family. Thank you for providing me with all the tools I needed to get to this point in my life. And an extra thank you to my dad, whose sudden passing while I was finishing this book made me even more grateful for him. Dad, thank you for teaching me that that family and health are more important than anything else.

To my assistants Erika Suarez and Devon Francis, and my intern, Catalina Odio, who made this an even more fun project than my first book. I could not have done this without you!

To my incredible photographer and team leader, Amy Neunsinger; you were once again a joy to work with and I appreciate your talent so much. To my talented food stylist, Frances Boswell; thank you for bringing these recipes to life with such grace and finesse. Andy Mitchell, you were again a trooper putting up with a kitchen of all women day in and day out. Thank you for being the best sounding board and making all the photos the best they could be.

Thank you to my agent, Brandi Bowles, to my publisher, Hachette Books, and my wonderful editor, Renée Sedliar, for believing in me once again. And to the whole team, including Mary Ann Naples, Michelle Aielli, Michael Barrs, Anna Hall, Amanda Kain, Cisca Schreefel, along with Toni Tajima, for helping me produce a book that I am so proud of.

Index

About Pamela Salzman

I have loved good food and enjoyed cooking for as long as I can remember. I bought my first cookbook in the second grade (I'll never forget the title, The Calling All Girls Party Cookbook!), and found my way into the kitchen as much as I could. As a child, while other kids were at the playground, I was helping my father in the garden, watering plants and vines and watching miracles happen. I come from a large Italian-American family with twenty-eight first cousins (on one side of the family!) where sit-down holiday dinners for eighty-five people are the norm. Some of my fondest memories are of simple family gatherings, both large and small, with long tables of bowls and platters piled high, the laughter of my cousins echoing, and the comfort of tradition warming my soul.

The food I grew up with was never fancy, but I knew where it came from and it was always real. It wasn't until I was an adult that I learned more about the nourishing and healing power of food. I wanted to help people grasp the importance of proper nutrition and eating real food (hint: not processed or full of chemicals), but I wasn't sure where to start. I was asked to teach a "healthful cooking class" for a group of young mothers; the business grew organically from that first class and I knew I had a message—and a new mission—in life.

pamelasalzman.com

@pamelasalzman